Huli Ramantswana's canonical-dialogic reading of Genesis 1–3 is a good example of how contemporary approaches to biblical studies can uncover novel and exciting perspectives on biblical narratives. The author demonstrates how these passages, beyond the concerns of prior historical-critical or other synchronic approaches, reveal several layers of dialogue, within various units of the text, between adjacent units of Gen 1–3 and between this passage and other passages in the Hebrew canon. The result of such dialogical reading shows a more complex scenario than a simple motion between a perfect creation in Gen 1:1–2:4 and a degenerate creation in Gen 2:5–3. Rather, the question of good and bad, as two sides of a coin, remain interwoven into the tapestry of the entire narrative, and for the good reason of propelling a non-ideal creation towards its full potential. I recommend this work to students, scholars, and pastors alike, both for its academic rigor and for its ease of language.

Michael K. Mensah, PhD
Lecturer,
Department for the Study of Religions, University of Ghana, Legon, Ghana

This is a fascinating book. Its canonical-dialogical reading goes beyond traditional methods and church dogmas, and tries to do justice to the multiple voices about creation found in the Old Testament. In Genesis 1–3, creation is portrayed as "very good" and inherently bad simultaneously. The book's canonical-dialogic approach interrogates the ongoing internal dialogue in Genesis 1–3 and within the wider Old Testament, including other creation traditions in the Psalter and the Prophets, and the building of the sanctuary in the second half of Exodus. This book will stimulate debate in the church and academia about our understanding of creation.

Esias E. Meyer, DTh
Professor of Old Testament and Hebrew Scriptures,
University of Pretoria, South Africa

In his exploration of the concept "God saw that it was good," Professor Ramantswana highlights the importance of intertextuality within the creation narrative, particularly in the passages of Genesis 1:1–2:4a and Genesis 2:4b–25. He emphasizes that a thorough understanding of this complex idea requires examining the internal dialogue among these texts. The book also delves into the conflicts presented within the creation story, focusing on different paradigms. This examination is designed to aid both scholars and everyday readers of the Bible, regardless of their religious background, in their spiritual growth and understanding. Professor Ramantswana argues that the creation narrative is multifaceted and becomes challenging to interpret when its various elements are viewed in isolation. By treating the creation story as a cohesive whole, the book enables readers to gain a more comprehensive understanding of its dynamics.

Tshokolo J. Makutoane, PhD
Academic Head of the Department of Hebrew,
University of the Free State, South Africa

God Saw That It Was Good, Not Perfect

A Canonical-Dialogic Reading of Genesis 1–3

Hulisani Ramantswana

ACADEMIC

© 2024 Hulisani Ramantswana

Published 2024 by Langham Academic
An imprint of Langham Publishing
www.langhampublishing.org

Langham Publishing and its imprints are a ministry of Langham Partnership

Langham Partnership
PO Box 296, Carlisle, Cumbria, CA3 9WZ, UK
www.langham.org

ISBNs:
978-1-83973-944-6 Print
978-1-78641-084-9 ePub
978-1-78641-085-6 PDF

Hulisani Ramantswana has asserted his right under the Copyright, Designs and Patents Act, 1988 to be identified as the Author of this work.

All rights reserved. No part of this publication may be reproduced, stored in a retrieval system or transmitted, in any form or by any means, electronic, mechanical, photocopying, recording or otherwise, without the prior written permission of the publisher or the Copyright Licensing Agency.

Requests to reuse content from Langham Publishing are processed through PLSclear. Please visit www.plsclear.com to complete your request.

Scripture quotations marked (RSV) are from Revised Standard Version of the Bible, copyright © 1946, 1952, and 1971 National Council of the Churches of Christ in the United States of America. Used by permission. All rights reserved.

Scripture quotations marked (NRSV) are from the New Revised Standard Version Bible, copyright © 1989 National Council of the Churches of Christ in the United States of America. Used by permission. All rights reserved.

Scripture quotations marked (NIV) are taken from the Holy Bible, New International Version®, NIV®. Copyright © 1973, 1978, 1984, 2011 by Biblica, Inc.™ Used by permission of Zondervan.

Scripture texts in this work marked (NAB) are taken from the *New American Bible, revised edition*© 2010, 1991, 1986, 1970 Confraternity of Christian Doctrine, Washington, D.C. and are used by permission of the copyright owner. All Rights Reserved. No part of the New American Bible may be reproduced in any form without permission in writing from the copyright owner.

Scripture quotations marked (NEB) are taken from the New English Bible, copyright © Cambridge University Press and Oxford University Press 1961, 1970. All rights reserved.

Scripture quotations marked (NKJV) are from the New King James Version (NKJV). Copyright © 1982 by Thomas Nelson, Inc. Used by permission. All rights reserved.

All Scripture quotations marked (NET), are from the New English Translation (NET). NET Bible® copyright ©1996-2006 by Biblical Studies Press, L.L.C. www.bible.org. Used by permission. All rights reserved worldwide.

Scripture quotations marked (ESV) The Holy Bible, English Standard Version® (ESV®), copyright © 2001 by Crossway, a publishing ministry of Good News Publishers. Used by permission. All rights reserved.

British Library Cataloguing-in-Publication Data
A catalogue record for this book is available from the British Library

ISBN: 978-1-83973-944-6

Cover & Book Design: projectluz.com

Langham Partnership actively supports theological dialogue and an author's right to publish but does not necessarily endorse the views and opinions set forth here or in works referenced within this publication, nor can we guarantee technical and grammatical correctness. Langham Partnership does not accept any responsibility or liability to persons or property as a consequence of the reading, use or interpretation of its published content.

Contents

List of Abbreviations ix

Acknowledgements xi

Chapter 1 1
   Introduction: Trends in the Study of Genesis 1–3 and Methodology
      Some Trends in the Study of Genesis 1–3 3
         Modern Critical Readings of Genesis 1–3..3
         Synchronic and Canonical Readings of Genesis 1–3 8
         Postmodern Interpretation 12
      Methodology: Canonical-Dialogic Reading 13
         Canonical Approach..13
         Dialogism 15

Chapter 2 37
   Internal Dialogue in Genesis 1:1–2:4a:
   God Saw That It Was Good, But Not All Was Good
      Introduction 37
      The Good Creation – "God Saw That It Was Good"............................38
      Genesis 1:1–2:4a – Good in Contrast to What? 40
         From an Unproductive and Uninhabited Earth to a
            Productive and Inhabited Earth..40
         Coexistence of the Good with the Bad 48
         Second Day – A Separator between Heaven and Earth...............54
      Conclusion 58

Chapter 3 59
   Genesis 1:1–2:4a in Dialogue with Genesis 2:4b–25:
   Paradisiacal Situation Not All That Good
      Introduction 59
      Dialogic Relationship Between Two Creation Narratives..................61
      Paradiasical Situation Not All That Good 65
         Limited Divine Presence in the Garden of Eden 65
         Adam, Image of God – Dust from the Ground 68
         The Good and the Bad in Paradise: The Tree of Life and
            the Tree of the Knowledge of Good and Bad 74
         Creation of Woman as a Correction of a "Not Good"
            Situation and the Separation from God 80
      Conclusion 83

Chapter 4 85
   Genesis 1:24–2:4a in Dialogue with Genesis 3:1–24
   (Fall Creation Story): The Fall of Humanity within the
   Scope of God's Very Good Creation
      Introduction 85
      Humanity Pronounced "Good" or Not 87
      Genesis 1:24–31 in Dialogue with Genesis 3 92
         The Presence of a Deceptive Serpent in the Garden, a
            Sacred Space 95
         Clean and Unclean Food 100
      Fallen but Functional Creation 103
      Conclusion...113

Chapter 5 115
   Conflicts at Creation
      Introduction 115
      Creation with or without Conflict, or Conflicts at Creation.............116
      Rebellion in the Sea..120
      Rebellion on Land 128
      Conclusion...137

Chapter 6 139
   Creatio in Extremis: First Creation as Paradigm for Eschatological
   Uncreation and Re-Creation
      Introduction 139
      Genesis 1–11: Creation – Uncreation – Re-creation Pattern............140
      Israel's Prophets: Eschatological Uncreation and New Creation......146
         The Day of Judgment as a Day of Uncreation............................147
         Eschatological New Creation 155
      Conclusion...170

Chapter 7 171
   Conclusion

Bibliography..177

List of Figures

Figure 1: Progressive Reading Models of Genesis 1–3 86

Figure 2: The Good Creation within the Seven-Day Framework 103

List of Abbreviations

Apocrypha and Pseudepigrapha

Apoc. Ab.	*Apocalypse of Abraham*
3 Bar.	3 Baruch
L.A.E.	Life of Adam and Eve
2 En.	2 Enoch (Slavonic Apocalypse)
4 Ezra	4 Ezra
Jub.	Jubilees
Odes Sol.	Odes of Solomon
T. Ash.	Testament of Asher

Secondary Sources

ABD	*The Anchor Bible Dictionary*. Edited by D. N. Freedman. 6 vols. Doubleday, 1992
CAT	M. Dietrich, O. Loretz, and J. Sanmartín, *The Cuneiform Alphabetic Texts from Ugarit, Ras Ibn Hani and Other Places (KTU: 2nd, enlarged edition)*. ALASPM 8. Munster: Ugarit-Verlag, 1995.
Crux	*Crux*
HKAT	Handkommentar zum Alten Testament
HSM	Harvard Semitic Monographs
JSOT	*Journal for the Study of the Old Testament*
NIDOTTE	New International Dictionary of Old Testament Theology and Exegesis
RSMS	The Religious Studies Monograph Series
SBL	Society of Biblical Literature

Miscellaneous

frg.	Fragment
LXX	Septuagint
MT	Masoretic Text

Acknowledgements

This book stems from my PhD dissertation, which I completed in 2010 at Westminster Theological Seminary, Philadelphia, under the guidance of Prof. Douglas J. Green. I am deeply grateful to Prof. Green for his unwavering mentorship and support. The book represents the foundational phase in my development as a biblical scholar. Methodologically, my interest then was in canonical-dialogic reading of the Bible as a metanarrative. My approach to reading the Bible has since evolved to embrace the lenses of African Biblical Hermeneutics and decoloniality.

My journey would not have been possible without the Reformed Churches in South Africa, Snyod Soutpansberg, granting me an extended leave of absence to pursue my studies. I am also indebted to the Light Reformed Community Church, where I currently serve as a pastor, for their support and encouragement in my continued scholarship pursuits.

Since 2011, I have had the privilege of collaborating with many of my colleagues at the University of South Africa and having insightful conversations. I extend my particular appreciation to Prof. Madipoane Masenya (Ngwan'a Mphahlele), Prof. Elelwani B. Farisani, Prof. Ndikho Mtshiselwa, and Prof. Gerrie Snyman for their contributions to my academic growth.

During my studies at Westminster Theological Seminary, I received financial support from the International Students' Scholarship, John Stott Ministries, and the National Research Foundation of South Africa. I am deeply grateful for their generosity, which enabled me to focus on my studies.

I cannot overstate how crucial my family's role has been in my academic journey. I appreciate all the support that I have received from my family members. I am grateful to my late mom, Nditsheni Johannah Ramantswana, and my dad, Nndwakhulu Jack Ramantswana, who offered me unwavering encouragement and prayers, and I am forever grateful for their love. I owe a special debt of gratitude to my wife, Thabelo, for all her sacrifices, support, and encouragement and for standing by me during the difficult times. I am grateful to my daughters, Mudanagundo, Mulindavhawe, and Muendananwi, who continually prayed for me.

Hulisani Ramantswana

CHAPTER 1

Introduction: Trends in the Study of Genesis 1–3 and Methodology

The Old Testament (Hebrew Bible) begins with two creation narratives, Genesis 1:1–2:4a and 2:4b–3:24; thus it can be said that the canonical story begins with creation. When the Old Testament is taken together with New Testament, the canonical story ends where it begins – creation. From a canonical perspective, Genesis 1–3 may even be described as a riddle that the rest of the canonical story intends to solve.

Genesis 1–3 is commonly regarded as the foundational narrative of the biblical story line of creation-fall-redemption-and-consummation.[1] In this reading, the narrative progression of Genesis 1–3 is from good to bad or from a state of perfection to imperfection.[2] The refrain "God saw all that he made and behold it was very good" (Gen 1:31, cf. 1:4, 10, 12, 18, 21) is

---

1. As Spykman points out, the adoption of the biblical story line methodologically implies "adopting the canonical order of Scripture, beginning with the Genesis narrative, which itself begins with the creation." Spykman, *Reformational Theology*, 144. In the Reformed tradition, Genesis 1–3 is often treated in the development of the doctrine of creation under which the following subjects are often treated: creation *ex nihilo*, the *imago Dei* (human origins, human nature, and human destiny), original sin, the fall, and covenant. See Hodge, *Systematic Theology*, 550–74; Reymond, *Systematic Theology*, 383; Erickson, *Christian Theology*, 365–86; Berkhof, *Systematic Theology*, 120–80; Bavinck, *In the Beginning*, 34–39, 95–225; Grudem, *Systematic Theology*, 439–528.

2. Bavinck, *Reformed Dogmatics*, 28.

generally interpreted as implying that, prior to the fall of humanity, creation was "perfect" – undistorted, with no imperfection.[3]

This reading is complicated by two factors among others: Firstly, there is the dual possibility of creation, the possibility that creation *could or could not* develop in accordance to God's will. This idea exists in germinal form in the presence and instruction regarding the tree of the knowledge of good and evil or as will be referred to throughout this study, the tree of the knowledge of good and bad. Second, there is the presence of a deceptive serpent in the garden of Eden or paradise, which is resolved by projecting back another fall in the spiritual realm prior to the fall of humanity – the fall of Satan. This reading, however, still necessitates the question: was creation prior to the fall of humanity good or bad, or perhaps a combination of both? Does "good" in Genesis 1 necessarily denote perfection?

In this book, I read the two creation narratives, Genesis 1:1–2:4a and Genesis 2:4b–3:24, in dialogue with each other as mutually enriching each other and therefore, in my view Genesis 1–3 in its final form presents the first creation in its original state of goodness as a nonideal beginning in anticipation of an ideal eschatological new creation. Stated differently, the first creation in its state of goodness is sub-eschatological, that is, short of entering Yahweh's Sabbath. I do not read Genesis 1–3 text in isolation, rather I read it taking Old Testament canon or the Hebrew Bible as a whole as providing the broader theological context within which to make sense of this text.

---

3. As Bavinck argues, "the good has priority, not only in an ideal sense but in reality. The fallen world in which we live rests on the foundations of a creation that was very good inasmuch as it came forth from the hands of God." Bavinck, *Reformed Dogmatics*, 28. Wolters explains this view as follows: "The expression 'formless and empty' in verse 2 does not describe a chaos–that is, the antithesis of cosmos (the currently prevalent interpretation, which draws on Babylonian parallels); rather, it describes the first step toward the order of the earthly cosmos, something like the preliminary rough sketch of the artist, which is later filled in with color and detail, or like the bare frame of a house before it is finished and furnished. The point is that there is no distortion of God's good creation before man's sin: formless means 'unformed,' not 'deformed.'" Wolters, *Creation Regained*, 22. Hoeksema frames it as follows: "Creation is from the beginning adapted to the final purpose of God's counsel, and every single creature is formed that it must serve God in this accomplishment of that counsel. At the creation of every separate and individual part of creation and again at the finishing and perfecting of the whole creation, God's declaration that what he made was very good (Gen 1:31) does not simply denote that there was no imperfection in the work of God as it stood at that very moment before his face, but denotes also that everything was adapted to the final purpose unto which God from the very beginning had created all things." Hoeksema, *Reformed Dogmatics*, 248.

This chapter is structured as follows: the first section presents some trends in the study of Genesis 1–3, while the second section unpacks the methodology utilized in analyzing the biblical text.

Some Trends in the Study of Genesis 1–3

Genesis 1–3 has, through the generations, been approached from different perspectives and with different methodologies that have yielded both complementary and contradictory results. I do not intend to offer a comprehensive analysis of the history of interpretations of Genesis 1–3; rather, I am more interested in the modern critical readings, synchronic and canonical readings, and postmodern readings.[4]

Modern Critical Readings of Genesis 1–3

Modern critical scholars, with the use of the historical-critical method, aimed at understanding the text from a rigorous historical perspective which implied that the Bible had to be set in its ancient setting and explained as a witness of its own time.[5] For historical-critical scholars, the Pentateuch lacked monologic unity; it was rather a juxtapositioning of multiple voices that originated from different historical settings.[6]

Diverse Literary, Historical, and Theological Contexts of the Creation Narratives

In the nineteenth century, with the rise of Documentary Theory, the Pentateuch came to be viewed as composed of four different strands of literary

---

4. In this analysis, I do not discuss, for example, feminist studies or debates regarding Genesis and science.

5. Historical critics operated with certain basic commitments or presuppositions: (a) study of Scripture must be free from doctrinal commitments; (b) Scripture must be studied like any other book; (c) man is the supreme judge for the interpretation of Scripture; (d) Scripture is interpreted for its meaning, not its truth; and (e) Scripture must be interpreted entirely within the natural realm. As Poythress points out, the historical-critical method "aspired to scientific objectivity, but in the nature of the case it could not succeed. In freeing biblical study from commitments of denominational doctrine, it made study subject to the philosophical commitments of rationalistic, antisupernatural historiography and metaphysics and to the ethical commitments of contemporary humanism. It did not give people pristine, absolute objectivity." Poythress, "Science and Hermeneutics," 442.

6. See Newsom, "Bakhtin, Bible," 290–306, 293.

traditions (Jahwist, Elohist, Deuteronomistic, and Priestly sources [JEDP]).[7] This laid a foundation for later critics to develop theologies of these independent traditions, which originated at different periods in Israel's history ranging from the beginning of the monarchy to the postexilic period (J c. 840 B.C.; E c. 700 B.C.; D c. 623 B.C.; P c. 500–450 B.C.), with each having its own particular characteristics.[8] Within this scheme, Genesis 1–3 came to be viewed as two independent stories – Genesis 1:1–2:4a was attributed to the Priestly source (P), whereas Genesis 2:4b–3:24 was attributed to the Yahwistic source (J).[9] Genesis 1:1–2:4a and Genesis 2:4b–3:24 were now each understood within the literary, historical, and ideological or theological context of its respective strand of tradition.[10] In this model, Genesis 1:1–2:4a is later than J's version, Genesis 2:4b–3:24, which is dated to the ninth century B.C.[11]

Concern with the Formation Process of the Creation Narratives

Toward the end of the nineteenth century, scholars turned their attention to the preliterary stage of the Pentateuch sources. Two factors contributed

---

7. The "Newer Documentary Theory" (JEDP) was popularized by Wellhausen, who published a number of articles on the issue culminating in the publication of his monumental book on the development of Israel's history. See Wellhausen, "Die Composition des Hexateuchs," 392–450; repr. *Die Composition des Hexateuchs*; *Geschichte Israels*; E.T. *Prolegomena*.

8. It has often been argued that the sources can easily be distinguished from each other. See, for example, Wellhausen, *Prolegomena*; Holzinger, *Einleitung in den Hexateuch*, 332; Driver, *Introduction to Literature*, 129; Schmidt, *Einführung*; Smend, *Die Entstehung*, 49; Friedman, *Exile and Biblical Narrative*, 44.

9. Wellhausen, *Prolegomena*, 297–308.

10. For example, Von Rad states regarding these two creation narratives, "the difference between P and J is very great. Their traditions, which are obviously derived from very different *milieux*, are not only different in the way in which they present the material, but also in the subject in which they are interested: P is concerned with the "world" and man within it, while J shows the construction of man's immediate environment and defines his relationship to it." Von Rad, *Old Testament Theology*, 1:150. In the Documentary Theory, Genesis 1:1–2:4a is a later version of creation proceeding from the Priestly redactor of the Pentateuch, who often placed his own versions alongside JED narratives (for e.g., P's Gen 17 alongside E's Gen 15 [Covenant with Abraham], P's Exod 6 alongside J's Exod 3–4 [Moses' call], P's Num 27 alongside D's Deut 31 [Joshua's commissioning] etc.) Nicholson, *Pentateuch in Twentieth Century*, 25.

11. Carr makes the following synthesis of this position: "The formation process of this text [Gen 1–4a] started with the writing of the non-P creation account, a depiction of the negative consequences of human movement toward godlikeness (Gen 2:4b–3:24). Next, the P creation account was written (Gen. 1:1–2:3). This account's description of humanity contradicts the negative claim of its non-P precursor. Only later did the P-strand creation account come to be placed before the non-P narrative it corrected. Now the non-P narrative (Gen. 2:4b–3:24) is no longer replaced but serves as a partial renarration of and corrective sequel to the P-strand creation account." Carr, *Reading Fractures of Genesis*, 67.

to this move: (1) the discovery of ancient Near Eastern documents like the *Enuma Elish*, *Atrahasis*, and the *Gilgamesh Epic* in the 1870s and their use to elucidate the origin and meaning of the biblical text; and (2) the recognition that behind the formation of the independent sources of the Pentateuch stands a long and complex process of transmission of tradition. Gunkel, in his *Schöpfung und Chaos in Urzeit und Endzeit* (1895), was the first to bring these two factors together in an attempt to understand the two creation narratives in Genesis 1–3.[12] Gunkel made two main arguments regarding the creation narratives: First, he argues that Genesis 1 is "a quite peculiar mixture of very ancient and very recent motifs which can only be explained by a long history of tradition."[13] This laid the foundation for scholars to probe further into the sources underlying these two independent creation narratives.[14] This further led to the realization of the redactional roles of P and J in shaping their material. Second, Gunkel argued that Genesis 1 was dependent on the ancient Babylonian creation myth – a conclusion he arrived at by drawing parallels

---

12. Gunkel, *Schöpfung*; Gunkel, *Creation and Chaos*. For an abridged translation of this work, see "Influence of Babylonian Mythology," 25–52. Gunkel's commentary on Genesis first appeared in HKAT in 1901. The third edition of his commentary appeared in 1910 and the fourth through the sixth (1964) editions were reprints.

13. Gunkel, *Schöpfung*, 129.

14. In the case of Genesis 1:1–2:4a, Morgenstern argued that two creation traditions underlie this creation story: creation by word and creation by action. Morgenstern, "Sources of Creation Story," 169–212). Similarly, Lambert made a distinction between an "action-account" and a "command-account." Lambert, "Study of First Chapter," 3–12. This approach reached its climax in Schmidt, who distinguished five other traditions underlying Genesis 1 besides the creation-by-word tradition and the creation-by-action tradition: (1) the water cosmogony, (2) the myth of separation, (3) the motif of emergence, (4) the theme of God at work, and (5) the theme of Mother Earth. However, for Schmidt, these traditions are still recognizable despite the Priestly reshaping through the creation-by-word tradition. Schmidt, *Die Schöpfungshymnus*, 49–187. In the case of Genesis 2:4b–3:24, some argued that "the tree of life" tradition was a later insertion to the original text, which only had one tree, "the tree of the knowledge of good and evil." The aim here was to restore the original text before the insertion of the distortions. See Budde, *Die biblische Urgeschichte*, 1883; Holzinger, *Genesis, II*, 24–45. Following Budde and Holzinger, the two-source theory underlying Genesis 2:4b–3:23 became widely accepted, although some argued for even more sources. See Smend, *Die Erzählung*; Essifeldt, *Einleitung*; Schmidt, "Die Geschichte; Zimmerli, *I. Mose 1–11*; Lefèvre, "Bulletin d'exégèse," 455–80; Dus, "Zwei Schichten," 162–72; Haag, "Die Komposition," 1–7. Gunkel did not follow Budde's suggestion of sources that spoke of two trees underlying Genesis 2–3; rather, he argued that behind it lie two oral traditions: a creation tradition and a paradise tradition. Gunkel, *Genesis*, 4–40. Gunkel's distinction finds support in Westermann, who divides Genesis 2–3 in two: the creation story (Gen 2:4b–8, [10–14], 15a, 18–24), and the paradise narrative (Gen 2:9, 16–17, 25; 3:1–24). Like Gunkel, Westermann is convinced that there are other earlier traditions behind these two traditions, which were merged by J. Westermann, *Genesis 1–11*, 259–61.

between Genesis 1 and the Babylonian epic in *Enuma Elish*. Since Gunkel, the motif of the mythical battle between the creator god and the opposing powers of chaos, so-called *Chaoskampf* mythology, has served for many commentators as the basis of exegesis of Genesis 1. In the case of Genesis 2–3, scholars have also argued for a non-Israelite origin of some of the motifs present in this creation narrative.[15]

Marginality of the Creation Narratives

In the Wellhausenian JEDP model, Genesis 1:1–2:4a is a later version of creation proceeding from the Priestly redactor of the Pentateuch, who often placed his own versions alongside JED narratives (for example: Genesis 17 alongside E's Genesis 15 [Covenant with Abraham], P's Exodus 6 alongside J's Exodus 3–4 [Moses' call], P's Numbers 27 alongside D's Deuteronomy 31 [Joshua's commissioning] etc.).[16] In this model, Genesis 1:1–2:4a is later than J's version, Genesis 2:4b–3:24, which is dated to the ninth century B.C.[17] Blenkinsopp and Otto have challenged the classical position, arguing that Genesis 1:1–2:4a is earlier than Genesis 2:4b–3:24, which they regard as a redactional rewriting of Genesis 1:1–2:4a.[18] It is beyond our scope to reproduce the arguments of these scholars in their entirety. We simply note here that the arguments of these scholars are based on the intertextual associations between

---

15. See for example, Smith, *Chaldean Account of Genesis*, 305; Delitzsch, *Wo lag das Paradies?*, 83–94; Zimmern, *Biblische und babylonische*; Gunkel, *Genesis*, 4–40; Stade, "Der Mythus von Paradies," 172–79; Gressmann, "Mythische Reste," 345–67; Feldmann, *Paradies und Sündefall*; Landersdorfer, *Die sumerischen Parallelen*; Morgenstern, "Sources of Paradise Story," 105–23; Skinner, *Critical and Exegetical Commentary*; Deimel, "Die biblische Paradieserzahlung," 90–100; Heinisch, *Probleme der biblishcen*; Vriezen, *Onderzoek naar*; Cassuto, *Commentary on Genesis*; Chaine, *Le livre de Genèse*, 14; McKenzie, "Literary Characteristics of Genesis 2–3," 541–72; Pohl, "Der Schopfungshymnus der Bible," 252–66; Hvidberg, "Canaanite Background of Gen I–III," 285–94.

16. Nicholson, *Pentateuch in Twentieth Century*, 25.

17. Carr makes the following synthesis of this position: "The formation process of this text [Gen 1–4a] started with the writing of the non-P creation account, a depiction of the negative consequences of human movement toward godlikeness (Gen 2:4b–3:24). Next, the P creation account was written (Gen. 1:1–2:3). This account's description of humanity contradicts the negative claim of its non-P precursor. Only later did the P-strand creation account come to be placed before the non-P narrative it corrected. Now the non-P narrative (Gen. 2:4b–3:24) is no longer replaced but serves as a partial renarration of and corrective sequel to the P-strand creation account." Carr, *Reading Fractures of Genesis*, 67. See also Otto, "Die Paradieserzählung Genesis 2–3," 167–92.

18. Blenkinsopp, *Pentateuch: An Introduction*, 60–67; Otto, "Paradieserzählung Genesis 2–3," 173–88.

Genesis 2–3 and prophetic literature (Isa 51:3; Ezek 31:9, 16, 18; 36:35; Joel 2:3), wisdom literature (common motifs – the motif of tree of life [Prov 1–9], the motif of "returning to dust" [Job 4:19–20; 7:21; 10:19; 16:15l 17:16; 20:11; 21:26; 30:19; 34:15; 38:38; 40:13; 42:6]), and Deuteronomistic literature (Gen 2:15 and Deut 4:34; 12:9–11; Gen 2–3 and the succession narrative in 2 Sam 11–20 and 1 Kings 1–2). For these scholars, Genesis 2:4b–3:24 originated in the exilic or post-exilic period.[19] Hoffmann has recently argued that Genesis 1:1–2:4a had no canonical status for other biblical authors, as evidenced by the lack of citations, allusions, and references by other biblical books.[20] For Hoffmann, none of the similar motifs and expressions found between Genesis 1:1–2:4a and other texts like Psalms 33; 136; Jeremiah 4:23–27; Job 3 and Second Isaiah can be proved to be dependent on the former.[21]

Von Rad, in his influential essay in 1936, argued that Israel's faith is "based on the notion of election and therefore primarily concerned with redemption."[22] For von Rad, creation did not form part of Israel's earliest creedal statements (Deut 6:20–24; 26:5–9; Josh 24:2b–13). The doctrine of creation only came to attain its independence through the influence of wisdom literature, wherein it occupies a central position. Israel's greatest theological achievement, according to von Rad, was their ability to relate creation and the saving history – "and not with a present conceived in terms of myth."[23] For von Rad, Genesis 2–3, the opening section of the Yahwist (J), is marginal and achieves no identifiable reference from the prophets and psalms.[24] This view of Genesis 2–3 as marginal has been adopted by many scholars since von Rad.[25] As Stordalen points out, it is surprising that these scholars dismiss

---

19. For an argument against this position, see Vervenne, "Genesis 1, 1–2, 4," 60–64.
20. Hoffman, "First Creation Story," 32–53.
21. Hoffman, 50.
22. Von Rad, "Das theologische Problem," 138–47; English Translation of this edition: "Theological Problem of Old Testament. Von Rad was not the first to relegate the idea of creation to the margin; Herman Schultz in his *Old Testament Theology*, which appeared at the second half of the nineteenth century, thought that the primitive Semitic tribes had no idea of creation. Schultz, *Alttestamentliche Theologie*; English Translation of the 4th edition: *Old Testament Theology*.
23. Von Rad, *Old Testament Theology*, 1:136.
24. Von Rad, *Genesis*, 74.
25. Stordalen, *Echoes of Eden*, 21. This view is reflected, for example, in the following works: Cothenet, "Paradis," 1177–1220; Haag, *Der Mensch am Anfang*; Pritchard, "Man's Predicament in Eden," 5–23; McKenzie, "Literary Characteristics"; Pedersen, "Fall of Man,"

the use of prophetic and other literature in reading Genesis 2–3 on the basis of mere chronology, in spite of a number of passages that refer, allude, and are similar to it.[26]

The final redactor of the Hexateuch, for von Rad, as was for Gunkel, was not a creative author, as he "adds nothing essentially new to the discussion"; he simply combines the independent sources together.[27] With the works of von Rad on the Hexateuch and Noth on the Deuteronomistic history, the stage was set for those who came after them to start probing on the role of the redactors.

The attempt by historical critics to split the biblical text into sources is fraught with difficulties. As Whybray argues, the approach presumes that the original sources were non-contradictory, consistent in terms of language, style, and theology, and not repetitious, whereas the present text, which is an amalgamation of sources, will have contradictions, inconsistencies, and repetitions. The hallmark of the redactors is the inconsistencies in the text in its final form.[28]

Synchronic and Canonical Readings of Genesis 1–3

During the second half of the twentieth century, scholars were becoming more and more dissatisfied with the historical-critical approach for its neglect of the text in its final form, as critics were more interested in fragmenting the text

---

167–72; Hartman, "Sin in Paradise," 26–40, 26; Brueggemann, *Genesis*, 41; Wenham, *Genesis 1–15*, 90; Milne, "Patriarchal Stamp of Scripture," 17–34; repr. with an afterword in Brenner, *Feminist Companion to Genesis*, 149; Bechtel, "Rethinking Interpretation of Genesis 2–3," 78; Bird, "Genesis 3," 3; Morris, "Walk in the Garden," 25.

26. Stordalen, *Echoes of Eden*, 22–23.

27. Concerning the relationship between Genesis 1 (P) and Genesis 2–3 (J), Von Rad's position is clear from his viewpoint regarding the sources: "The process by which E and P are superimposed on J, as well as their relationship to one another, is a purely literary question, which adds nothing essentially new to the discussion so far as form-criticism is concerned. The form of the Hexateuch had already been finally determined by the Yahwist. The Elohist and the Priestly writer do not diverge from the pattern in this respect: their writings are no more than variations upon the massive theme of the Yahwist's conception, despite their admittedly great theological originality." Von Rad, "Form Critical Problem," 55. The Yahwist, as Van Seters points out, was for Von Rad not an editor (or redactor); rather, he was an author and a historian who brought together "a body of scattered oral traditions into a unified literary work." See Van Seters, "Author or Redactor?" For further debates regarding authors and redactors of the Hebrew Scriptures, see Van Seters, *Edited Bible*; "Redactor in Biblical Studies," 1–19; "An Ironic Circle," 487–500; Ska, "Plea on Behalf," 4–18; Otto, "Review of John Van Seters"; Levin, "Yahwist," 209–30; *Der Jahwist*.

28. Whybray, *Making of the Pentateuch*, 18–19, 47–51.

and in diachronic issues. In an attempt to address the weaknesses and limitations of the historical-critical approach, two developments were underway.

The first development was the synchronic analysis of the text. In 1968, James A. Muilenburg in his Society of Biblical Literature (SBL) presidential address called for a move beyond form criticism by directing attention to rhetorical criticism.[29] This meant paying attention to the text itself – what the text says and how it goes about saying it. In 1975, Robert Alter also called for a "literary approach to the Bible" that pays attention to the artful use of language and to the shifting play of ideas, convention, tone, sound, imagery, syntax, narrative, viewpoint, compositional units, and much more.[30] Following Muilenburg's and Alter's calls, a number of studies on Genesis have been produced, focusing on the literary features of Genesis 1–3, and demonstrating the text's artistic unity,[31] its unity with the Primeval History (Gen 1–11),[32] its unity with the whole book of Genesis,[33] its unity with rest of the Pentateuch,[34] and its unity with the Primary History (Gen–2 Kgs).[35] In such studies, the unity of the biblical text is often presupposed; the critic in this regard is interested in showing the creativity of the author(s) (or redactor[s]) by setting forth the linguistic style of such things as chiasmus, structure, and themes. The ambiguities, complexities, and ironies are regarded as cardinal virtues of a work, and the task of the critic is to show how these are resolved in a unified text.[36] In such studies, issues of compositional art are at best ignored. Despite the waning significance of the documentary hypothesis, a number of

---

29. Muilenburg, "Form Criticism and Beyond," 1–18.

30. Alter, "Literary Approach to the Bible," 70–77. This article is the first chapter of Alter's *Art of Biblical Narrative*, 3–22. See also Alter and Kermode, *Literary Guide to the Bible*; Sternberg, *Poetics of Biblical Narrative*.

31. See Patrick and Scult, *Rhetoric and Biblical Interpretation*, 105–25; Shea, "Literary Structural Parallels," 49–68.

32. Kikawada and Quinn, *Before Abraham Was*; Anderson, "From Analysis to Synthesis," 23–39; Smith; "Structure and Purpose," 307–19; Clines, "Theme in Genesis 1–11," 483–507.

33. Robinson, "Literary Functions of Genealogies," 595–608; Steinberg, "Genealogical Framework," 41–50; Wiseman, *Ancient Records*; Baker, "Diversity and Unity," 189–205; Hart, "Genesis 1:1–2:3," 315–36; Fox, "Can Genesis Be Read?" 31–40; Rendsburg, *Redaction of Genesis*.

34. Clines, *Theme of Pentateuch*; Sailhamer, "Exegetical Notes," 73–82; Rendtorff, "Covenant as a Structuring Concept," 385–93.

35. Clines, *What Does Eve Do?*, 49–66; Turner, *Announcements of Plot*.

36. Clines, 54; Mathewson, "Critical Binarism," 3–28, 27.

studies are still being produced that emphasize the distinctiveness of Genesis 1 and Genesis 2–3 in terms of vocabulary, style, structure, and content.[37]

Some scholars have applied synchronic techniques, which analyze the biblical text as an autonomous entity completely divorced from its author, history, and audience. At the beginning of the twentieth century, Driver in his commentary on Genesis called for an approach that clearly distinguishes "between narrative itself, the scenery and incidents, as such, and the spiritual teaching which they are intended to convey."[38] As Morris points out, "in that the concern is with the text itself, it is unfortunate that there appears to be little interest in anything else!"[39] During the 1970s and early 1980s, North American biblical scholars developed approaches derived from linguists such as Saussure, Levi-Strauss, Propp, Greimas, and Roland Barthes. As Aichele et al. point out, it was during this time that the journal *Semeia* was generated, and the Structuralism and Exegesis Group in the Society of Biblical Literature was established under the leadership of Patte.[40] *Semeia* 18 (1980) contained a collection of articles on structural exegeses particularly focused on Genesis 2–3.[41] Common to the synchronic structuralist analysis is the goal of analyzing the text in a purely synchronic and structural fashion free from any context. There are several weaknesses that may be identified in the structural exegeses of Genesis 1–3: (1) The biblical text is treated as an ahistorical autonomous entity; for that reason the critic focuses on the structures within the text. (2) There is a tendency to disregard other ancient Near Eastern texts that may help to shed light on the biblical creation narratives. (3) The results of structural exegesis are not purely objective. As Kovacs points out, they "are not and probably cannot be purely synchronic and structural as such. While the structure is pre-hermeneutic, the report of the structure is not."[42]

---

37. See for example, Westermann, *Genesis 1:1*; Anderson, "Stylistic Study," 148–62; Boomershine, "Structure and Narrative Rhetoric," 31–49; Culley, "Action Sequences in Genesis 2–3," 51–60; Dohmen, *Schöpfung und Tod*; Jobling, "Structural Analysis of Genesis," 61–69; Schmidt, *Die Schöpfungsgeschichte*; Steck, *Der Schöpfungsbericht*; Trible, *God and Rhetoric*, 77–143; Van Wolde, *Semiotic Analysis of Genesis*.

38. Driver, *Book of Genesis*, 51.

39. Morris, "Walk in the Garden," 26.

40. Aichele et al., *Postmodern Bible*, 82.

41. For other structural exegeses on Genesis 2–3, see Engell, "'Knowledge' and 'Life,'" 103–19; Leach, *Genesis as Myth*, 7–23; Walsh, "Genesis 2:4b–3:24," 167–77; Rosenberg, "Garden Story Forward," 1–27.

42. Kovacs, "Structure and Narrative Rhetoric," 141.

The second development was the canonical approach, a concern with the theological intention of the canonical shapers. Childs has criticized historical criticism for its lack of interest in the final form of the canon and its failure to bridge the gap between the canon and the church, the community of faith for whom the canon is the authoritative and definite word of God.[43] Childs suggested that the "canon of the Church is the most appropriate context from which to do biblical theology."[44] The object of study in Childs's canonical approach is the Bible in its final form. In this approach, the historical-critical concerns are not dismissed; rather, they serve to expose critical or problematic issues in the text that are to be considered in determining the theological intentionality of the final redactor(s). In his treatment of Genesis 1–3, Childs accepts the historical distinction of the sources into J and P; however, he then proceeds to pay attention to the formal features in the text in order to discern the canonical shaping of the text.[45] Childs argues that the redactor joined the two creation accounts through the genealogical formula in Genesis 2:4a. This, however, is not a juxtaposition of two parallel creation narratives; rather,

> the introductory formula in 2:4 makes it clear that J's account has now been subordinated to P's account of the creation. What now follows proceeds from the creation in the analogy of a son to his father. Mankind is the vehicle of the *toledot*. Thus in spite of the partial overlapping in the description of creation, ch. 2 performs basically a different role from ch. 1 in unfolding the history of mankind as the intended offspring of the creation of the heavens and the earth.[46]

Thus, for Childs continuing "to speak of the 'two creation accounts in Genesis' the interpreter disregards the canonical shaping and threatens its role both as literature and as scripture."[47] If the historical-critical concerns entail

---

43. Childs, *Biblical Theology in Crisis*.

44. Childs, 99. Childs laid out the details of his canonical approach in his *Introduction Old Testament*, 1–31.

45. Childs, *Biblical Theology in Crisis*, 148–50; see also Childs, *Biblical Theology*, 107–13.

46. Childs, *Biblical Theology in Crisis*, 150.

47. Childs, 150. Barton criticized Childs for flattening the text by attempting to harmonize or smooth over the disagreements in Genesis 1–2. For Barton, Childs's canonical approach has close affinities with redaction criticism. Regarding redaction criticism of Genesis 1–2, Barton states, "If, say, Genesis 2 follows on so naturally from Genesis 1, then this is indeed evidence

such a "disregard" to the canonical shape and intentionality, it is surprising to find Childs himself taking such concerns as his starting point.

Postmodern Interpretation

In contrast to the previous approaches, postmodern biblical interpretation views the text as having potential for multiple meanings, with readers actively participating in the construction of meaning. According to Vanhoozer, a point of agreement for almost all secular postmodernists (Derrida – nihilist; Rorty and Fish – pragmatists; Gadamer and Ricoeur – hermeneuticists; Wittgenstein and MacIntyre – nonfoundationalists) is that "language, in different ways, *situates* us."[48] The postmodern contribution to biblical interpretation "is the awareness of language's irreducibility and plurality."[49] For some examples of postmodern readings of Genesis 1–3, see Bal, Fewell, Rashkow, Landy, Jobling, Pardes, van Wolde, Kimelman, Rutledge, Goldingay, Miscall, and others.[50]

This study may be classified under the postmodern category for two reasons: First, I will be adopting an approach that some would consider postmodern or perhaps more accurately as anticipating postmodernity, dialogism. Second, my approach is based on the conviction that the biblical text is open to several possible meanings, but not to just any possible meaning. To use Bakhtin's term, the biblical text remains "unfinalized."[51]

---

for the skill of the redactor *if we know that Genesis 1 and 2 were originally distinct*; but the only ground we have for thinking that they were is the observation that Genesis 2 does *not* follow on naturally from Genesis 1. Thus, if redaction criticism plays its hand too confidently, we end up with a piece of writing so coherent that no division into sources is warranted any longer; and the sources and the redactor vanish together in a puff of smoke, leaving a single, freely composed narrative with, no doubt, a single author." Barton, *Reading Old Testament*, 49, 57.

48. Vanhoozer, "Pilgrim's Digress," 76. For Vanhoozer, postmodernity is so preoccupied with human situatedness in history, social class, gender, culture, and religion that postmoderns cannot get beyond it.

49. Vanhoozer, 77.

50. Bal, "Sexuality, Sin, and Sorrow," 317–38; Fewell, "Reading Bible Ideologically," 237–51; Fewell and Gunn, "Genesis 2–3," 194–205; Rashkow, *Phallacy of Genesis*; Landy, *Paradoxes of Paradise*; Jobling, "Myth and Its Limits," 17–43; Pardes, *Countertraditions*; Van Wolde, *Words Become Worlds*; Kimmelman, "Seduction of Eve," 1–39; Rutledge, *Reading Marginally*; Slivniak, "Garden of Double Messages," 439–60; Goldingay, "Postmodernizing Eve and Adam"; Miscall, "Jacques Derrida," 1–9.

51. I am convinced that the postmodern turn is under God's sovereignty and as such, it poses both opportunities and challenges for biblical interpreters. Adopting a postmodern reading strategy does not mean turning away from a Christian philosophy to a postmodern

Methodology: Canonical-Dialogic Reading

Genesis 1–3 is a highly complex and ambiguous narrative, saying as much as it conceals and thereby generating answers and questions that go far beyond itself. My approach in the reading of Genesis 1–3 will be a conflation of two reading strategies, "canonical" and "dialogic," and so "a canonical-dialogic approach." The canonical-dialogical approach that I am adopting for this study calls for creative understanding, which is the dialogical notion of textual interpretation. In this approach, the author, text, and the reader are all important components in activating the intentional potentiality and textual possibilities.

Canonical aspect puts emphasis on the canon's final literary form as an object for theological reflection. This approach is dialogic insofar as I will be adopting Mikhail M. Bakhtin's theory of language and dialogism philosophy, which will provide us with a model of reading the canon dialogically. The canonical-dialogical approach, I am convinced, provides us with a viable model of handling the monologic and the polyphonic nature of the canonical content.

Canonical Approach

The term "canonical" used methodologically can mean a wide range of things, and therefore, it is necessary to clarify how the term is understood and used in this study. The term "canonical" is used in this study specifically with reference to the final or full literary context under which Genesis 1–3 will be considered – that is, the canonical context. The term "canonical context," however, is used by canonical critics with different emphasis and focus.

Canonical Context

Sanders's canonical criticism is focused more on the process through which the faith community adopted and adapted the received tradition in new contexts.[52] For Sanders, canonical context is a three-dimensional situation encompassing ancient traditions (texts), situations (contexts), and

---

philosophy of life, in which there is no truth, no absolute, and no transcendence, and in which reality is a social construction and metanarratives (for example, the biblical metanarrative) are simply human constructs.

52. See Sanders, *Torah and Canon*; *Canon and Authority*; *From Sacred Story*.

hermeneutics.⁵³ The canonical context, in this sense, is not solely the text in its final form; rather, it includes both the process of adoption and adaptation of traditions. This process constitutes an attempt to discern the traditions included in the canon and the hermeneutic process behind the traditions. Sanders also makes it clear that he most often uses the term "canonical" to refer to the historical context, rather than the final form of the text.⁵⁴

Childs's canonical approach, although not excluding the canonical process, puts emphasis on the text in its final form.⁵⁵ Childs insists that he uses the term *canonical* not to refer to a new exegetical technique, but rather to a context from which literature is being understood.⁵⁶ The text in its final form is the final stage in the shaping of Israel's tradition to form a normative scripture.⁵⁷ The significance of the final form, as Childs argues, is that "it alone bears witness to the full history of revelation. . . . It is only in the final form of the biblical text in which the normative history has reached an end that the full effect of this revelatory history can be perceived."⁵⁸ The ultimate end of the revelatory history, for Childs, is in the New Testament canon, which sets the parameters for theological reflection; thus the canonical context encompasses both the Old Testament and the New Testament.⁵⁹ In this study, focus is limited to the Old Testament canon as the canonical context for theological reflection; this, however, does not imply that it is the only canonical context as Old Testament texts may also be understood within the context of the Christian canon.

Canonical Diversity

Scripture is characterized by both unity and diversity (or diversity and unity) – unity does not preclude diversity, nor diversity unity.⁶⁰ In a more postmodern

---

53. See Sanders, "Hermeneutics in True," 21.
54. Sanders, "Canonical Context," 173–97, 186–87.
55. Childs, *Introduction to Old Testament*, 73.
56. Childs, 16.
57. Childs, 77.
58. Childs, 76.
59. Childs, *Old Testament Theology*, 9.
60. As Coleridge points out, "the Bible insists upon a common narrative, but one which includes a diversity of voices; many stories comprise the story. God's story is both single and several. It also insists upon a narrative which at times is most disjointed and the connectedness of which is perceived only by way of struggle." Coleridge, "Life in Crypt," 148.

fashion, as Brueggemann argues, the Old Testament has a "plurality of the testimonies" which do not necessarily have to be reconciled or arranged in any single or unilateral pattern.[61] Brueggemann uses the courtroom metaphor as an organizing principle to handle the Old Testament's diversity and thus speaks of testimony, dispute, and advocacy. For him, Israel's testimonies are allowed to stand without an attempt to reconcile them. Brueggemann's court case is of an Israel who is divided against itself – offering testimonies and countering its own testimony in a court which has no intention of making a ruling, a court that is left open without a final closure.[62] The canonical-dialogic reading does not intend to resolve canonical diversity as if it were a problem; rather, it is an attempt to tap into the plenitude that the canonical diversity presents.[63]

The dialogic dimension, as will be argued below, not only allows us to appreciate the canon as God's communication to us; it is also a reading that allows us to appreciate the heterogeneous nature of the canon, to observe and analyze the dialogue that is inherent in canon, and it allows the reader to engage in a play with the text by engaging the multiple canonical voices in a dialogue.

Dialogism

Bakhtinian theory of language was developed in reaction against formalist literary theory and Saussurean linguistics. The Bakhtinian circle was displeased with formalist treatment of literary work, accusing formalism of divorcing the literary work from the subjectivity of its reader and the author/poet, and cutting it off from its social world and ideological world.[64] They accused

---

61. Brueggemann, *Theology of Old Testament*, 205–12, 707–20.

62. Brueggemann argues, "the text itself is remarkably open and refuses a simple or firm cognitive closure, that is, the text is available for many readings of particular texts, and seems at many points to delight in a playful ambiguity that precludes certitudes." Brueggemann, *Theology of Old Testament*, 110.

63. As Birch, Brueggemann, Fretheim, and Petersen argue, "The presence of such diversity in the same Hebrew canon is an invitation to consider the voices in relation to one another and as witness to diverse, even inconsistent, experiences of the same God. Such an invitation draws us into dialogue with these voices. We cannot settle for atomistic descriptions of each witness in isolation but are drawn to consider how so many diverse stories are collected into a canon that insists these stories be in dialogue together." Birch et al., *Theological Introduction*, 29–30.

64. Bakhtin and Medvedev, *Formal Method*, 145. According to Bakhtin and Medvedev, "their fear of meaning in art led the formalists to reduce the poetic construction to the peripheral,

Saussure's linguistics for its "abstract objectivism," as it sought to explain language as a synchronic system:

> Linguistics, as Saussure conceived it, cannot have the utterance as its object of study. What constitutes the linguistic element in the utterance are the normatively identical forms of language present in it. Everything else is "accessory and random" ... language stands in opposition to utterance in the same way as does that which is social to that which is individual. The utterance, therefore, is considered a thoroughly individual entity.[65]

For Bakhtin and Medvedev, these two schools of thought fail to realize that "language exists in specific social situations and is thus bound up with specific social evaluations."[66] In the Bakhtinian circle, "language acquires life and historically evolves ... in concrete verbal communication, and not in abstract linguistic system of language, nor in the individual psyche of speakers."[67] For Bakhtin, an "utterance" is the unit of "living language." For that reason he often speaks of "speech life" or "the life signs" to indicate that language and communication take place in real concrete social situations.

Bakhtin maintains that all utterances are dialogical in nature. As Reed points out, "Dialogue for Bakhtin is not merely the phenomenon of two people speaking back and forth to one another; it is the linguistic precondition for all communication whatsoever, and its interactive awareness of the utterance of others, before and after, is inscribed in every utterance a person makes."[68] Unlike Saussure's *langue*, an utterance is never neutral; rather, it receives specific meaning that flows from the concrete situations in which an exchange occurs between addresser and addressee; however, this exchange is one that is connected to previous utterances – the addresser and addressee derive meaning from the already-established patterns of meaning and to

---

outer surface of the work. The work lost its depth, three-dimensionality, and fullness." Bakhtin and Medvedev, 118.

65. Bakhtin and Volosinov, *Marxism*, 60–61. For Bakhtin and Volosinov, "there is no real moment in time when a synchronic system of language can be constructed." Bakhtin and Volosinov, 66.

66. Allen, *Intertextuality*, 16.

67. Bakhtin and Volosinov, *Marxism*, 95.

68. Reed, *Dialogue of Word*, 13.

future utterances – the reception of the utterance by others in the future.[69] According to Bakhtin,

> the speaker is not the biblical Adam, dealing only with virgin and still unnamed objects, giving them names for the first time.... In reality . . . any utterance, in addition to its own theme, always responds (in the broad sense of the word) in one form or another to others' utterances that precede it.... The utterance is not only addressed to its object, but also to others' speech about it.[70]

As Todorov explains, "the most important feature of the utterance, or at least the most neglected, is its *dialogism*, that is, its intertextual dimension. After Adam, there are no nameless objects nor any unused words. Intentionality or not, all discourse is in dialogue with prior discourse, as well as with discourse yet to come, whose reaction it foresees and anticipates."[71] Dialogic relationship, as Bakhtin further argues, cannot be confined to utterances; rather, such dialogic relationship can also be observed in such things as language styles, social dialects, and cultures.[72] No utterance exists in isolation.

Another aspect of utterance, important for Bakhtin's dialogism, is that every utterance is "double-voiced" – it is a response to previous utterances and anticipates rejoinder (future responses). Bakhtin describes "double-voiced discourse" as follows: "It serves two speakers at the same time and expresses simultaneously two different intentions: the direct intention of the character who is speaking, and the refracted intention of the author. In such discourse there are two voices, two meanings and two expressions."[73] This aspect of dialogism shows the transactional nature of utterances or individual texts. Bakhtin, however, also insists that double-voice in poetry or monological discourse is not the same as that found in novel or polyphonic discourse. Double-voice in poetic forms remains on the level of singular consciousness and is evidenced by such things as individualized dissonances, misunderstanding, and contradictions.

---

69. Bakhtin, *Problems of Dostoevsky's Poetics*, 201.
70. Bakhtin, *Speech Genres*, 93–94.
71. Todorov, *Mikhail Bakhtin*, x.
72. Bakhtin, *Problems of Dostoevsky's Poetics*, 184.
73. Bakhtin, *Dialogic Imagination*, 324.

Canon as a Monologic and Polyphonic Text

Bakhtin regarded Dostoevsky's work as groundbreaking, going where no other has gone before. For Bakhtin, what distinguishes Dostoevsky's work was his ability to create a "polyphonic novel," thereby creating a completely new "novelistic genre."[74] Bakhtin also criticized previous critics of Dostoevsky for being enslaved by philosophical monologization – attempts to analyze a work as corresponding to the single and unified consciousness of the author, thereby reducing plurality of unmerged voices. Dostoevsky's genius, according to Bakhtin, is that "what unfolds in his work is not a multitude of characters and fates in a single objective world, illuminated by a single authorial consciousness; rather in a plurality of consciousness, with equal rights and each with its own world, combine but are not merged in the unity or the event."[75] I am not concerned here with the correctness of Bakhtin's analysis of Dostoevsky, although I remain unconvinced by his analysis; nonetheless, he offers an alternative perspective of viewing Dostoevsky. I am convinced that the distinction he makes between monologic and polyphonic work yields potential and so is worth noting.

Monologic poetic genre or literature has as its conditions the unity of language and the author's individuality or an individual consciousness, which is reflected in their language and speech.[76] In his criticism of Tolstoy's work, *Three Deaths* (1859), Bakhtin states,

> thus, despite the multiple levels in Tolstoy's story, it contains neither polyphony nor (in our sense) counterpoint. It contains only *one cognitive subject*, all else being merely *objects* of its cognition. Here a dialogic relationship of the author to his heroes is impossible, and thus there is no *"great dialogue"* in which characters and author participate with equal rights; there are only the objectivized dialogues of characters, compositionally expressed within the author's field of vision.[77]

In monologic literature, an author has what Bakhtin calls an "essential surplus of meaning"; that is, he is located outside of the story and enjoys an

---

74. Bakhtin, *Problems of Dostoevsky's Poetics*, 7.
75. Bakhtin, 6.
76. Bakhtin, *Problems of Dostoevsky's Poetics*, 9–10; *Dialogic Imagination*, 264.
77. Bakhtin, *Problems of Dostoevsky's Poetics*, 71.

external position from which he can give definitive meaning. Thus, from this external position, the author enjoys an all-encompassing vision.[78] As Morson and Emerson point out, "authors enjoy an immense surplus of vision with respect to their characters, but the characters do not have the same surplus – indeed, often no surplus at all – with respect to the author."[79]

Bakhtin criticizes not only monologic literature but also the Western thought which has been dominated by monologic conception of truth. Monologic conception of truth is built upon the following ideological elements: First, it presents us with a set of propositions, assertions, or what Bakhtin calls "separate thought." These "separate thoughts" or propositions offer an accurate description of the world, and their source is of no significance to the determination of their authority. These, as Bakhtin conceives them, are "no-man's thoughts."[80] Second, it "gravitates toward a system as toward an ultimate whole." Unity and coherence are the ultimate values, as the "system is put together out of separate thoughts."[81] Third, it has faith in the self-sufficiency of single and unified consciousness. As Bakhtin argues, "all ideological creative acts are conceived and perceived as possible expressions of a single consciousness, a single spirit. Even when one is dealing with a collective, with a multiplicity of creating forces, unity is nevertheless illustrated through the image of a single consciousness: the spirit of the nation, the spirit of the people, the spirit of history, and so forth."[82]

In contrast to monologic literature, polyphonic literature is a combination of "plurality of independent and unmerged voices and consciousnesses, a genuine polyphony of fully valid voices."[83] In a polyphonic work the author's essential surplus of meaning is renounced.[84] Polyphonic literature operates

---

78. Bakhtin, 70.
79. Morson and Emerson, *Mikhail Bakhtin*, 241.
80. Bakhtin, *Problems of Dostoevsky's Poetics*, 93.
81. Bakhtin, 93.
82. Bakhtin, 82.
83. Bakhtin, 240. As Morson and Emerson point out, "Using another favorite analogy, Bakhtin characterizes the monologic world as 'Ptolemaic': the earth, representing the author's consciousness, is the center around which all other consciousness revolve. The polyphonic world is Copernican; as the earth is but one of many planets, the author's consciousness is but one of many consciousnesses. . . . Bakhtin likens the polyphonic world to the universe of Einstein, in which one finds a 'multiplicity of measurement' . . . that in principle cannot be reduced to a single system." Morson and Emerson, *Mikhail Bakhtin*, 240.
84. Bakhtin, *Problems of Dostoevsky's Poetics*, 243.

with another form of ideology, namely, dialogic truth. Unlike in monologic truth, the cardinal virtues here are plurality and separateness. It is this plurality and separateness that is essential to the dialogue. This plurality and separateness is one that cannot be contained in a single consciousness; rather, it requires a plurality of consciousness. However, this does not make dialogic truth an un-unified truth or plural truth: "It is quite possible to imagine and postulate a unified truth that requires plurality of consciousness, one that cannot in principle be fitted into the bounds of single consciousness, one that is, so to speak, by its very nature *full of event potential* and is born at a point of contact among various consciousness" [emphasis in original].[85] The "unity" of truth, as Morson and Emerson points out, is "the unified 'feel' of a conversation, not the unity of a single proposition, however, complex, that may result from it."[86] Unity in this regard is a result not of a "system" but rather of an "event," which refers to "a concrete event made up of organized human orientations and voices."[87] It should be realized, however, that Bakhtin is talking here of the characters and ideas in a polyphonic work. As Bakhtin points out, "[Dostoevsky] brought together ideas and worldviews, which in real life were absolutely estranged and deaf to one another, and forced them to quarrel."[88]

Dialogic distinction between monologic and polyphonic discourse provides us with two trajectories that are both applicable to the canon. For those who believe in the Bible as a divine book, the canon is in a sense a monologic discourse – it has a single consciousness, a single author, whose thoughts hold it together from beginning to end. This is in contrast to Newsom, who in her adoption of Bakhtin dialogism claims, "the Bible certainly is not a monologic text. There is not a single 'author' who coordinates and controls meaning across the whole. One can easily identify a plurality of unmerged voices in the Bible."[89] For Bakhtin, monologic authors enjoy an immense surplus of meaning which would finalize an objective dialogue. The belief that the Bible is a sacred book with God as the prime author of the words of

---

85. Bakhtin, 81.
86. Morson and Emerson, *Mikhail Bakhtin*, 237.
87. Bakhtin, *Problems of Dostoevsky's Poetics*, 93.
88. Bakhtin, 91.
89. Newsom, "Bakhtin, Bible," 296.

Scripture and the ultimate source of meaning gives stability to meaning and sense.[90] As Poythress argues, God is able to do so, because, first, he exists as the source of meaning, second, he is an interpreter of his own words, and third, meaning and application coinhere.[91]

The monologic nature of the canon does not imply that the canon cannot be regarded as a polyphonic text or be read dialogically. On the contrary, Scripture, as already observed, is characterized by both unity and diversity. It can be agreed with Newsom that the plurality of the Bible is easily noticeable – it is a collection of books which originated on different occasions at different historical moments by different authors over a long period of time; thus, we have, at this macro level, a "plurality of consciousness." From the perspective that the Bible has God as its divine author, therefore, the Scriptures fit within the single divine consciousness.[92] It can be presumed from this perspective that later revelation will interact with earlier revelation, later authors with earlier authors. At this level, dialogic reading will cross roads with many intertextual studies or studies on inner biblical interpretation, which particularly pays attention to how later texts echo, allude, or evoke earlier texts or how earlier traditions are adopted and adapted to newer situations. As Bakhtin argues, every utterance is double-voiced. Such an approach, however, exhibits a diachronic understanding of the dialogic nature of texts as the concern is with observing the dialogue already occurring within the canon.[93] This

---

90. Poythress, *God-Centered Biblical Interpretation*, 76.

91. Poythress, 76.

92. *Pace* Bakhtin's claim that the plurality of consciousness "cannot be fitted within the bounds of a single consciousness." Bakhtin, *Problems of Dostoesvsky's Poetics*, 81. Vanhoozer rightly points out, "Bakhtin's claim that Dostoevsky invented polyphony; the truth is, he was two millennia too late. The canon is not only polyphonic but consists of two choirs singing in antiphonal witness. Or, to use George Caird's image, the canon is a kind of conference table around which a number of different authors/actors are seated. The Bible is not a book but a library. Each canonical voice represents a distinct point of view in time, space, and culture. Indeed, even within a single book, such as the Psalter, there are multiple authorial voices." Vanhoozer, *Drama of Doctrine*, 272.

93. Claassens, "Biblical Theology as Dialogue," 127–44, 134–35. For an example of such a diachronic appropriation of Bakhtin's dialogic theory, see Willey, *Remember Former Things*. Willey investigates how "Second Isaiah, by recollecting the voices of others, organizes and manages the variety of viewpoints present at the end of the exile." Willey, *Remember Former Things*, 3, 7. The concern, as Willey argues elsewhere, "the question is not whether any speech is intertextually laden, but rather with whose speech it is laden, and how it uses that speech." Willey, "Rhetoric of Recollection," 76. The advantage of Bakhtinian dialogism in biblical interpretation, as Reed argues, is that "it encourages the perception of more than one kind of formal ordering and more than one level of significant shaping in the canonical text. . . .

approach has some limitations. First, it tends to presume a chronological succession which is not always easily discernible in some cases – especially within the Old Testament. Second, it tends to be unidirectional as it tends to be a kind of back-draft from later to earlier.[94]

The biblical canon, as already observed, is characterized by a twofold division: Old and New Testament – the two discrete voices which already stand in a dialogic relationship with each other. There is a two-way relationship between the Old and the New Testament.[95] These two testaments are set in a dialogic relationship with each other in which they mutually enrich each other. Each discrete voice retains its historical particularity and theological significance. This, however, does not obliterate other attempts to identify the inner relationship between the two testaments in terms of promise-fulfillment, salvation history, law-gospel, and topology as these do offer alternative perspectives of establishing the relationship.[96] Childs rightly states, "The Christian canon maintains the integrity of the Old Testament in its own right as scripture of the church. However, it sets it within a new canonical context in a dialectical relation with the New Testament."[97] Thus the two discrete voices do not have to be collapsed as each discrete voice should be allowed to have its own relative distinctive perspective.

Dialogic reading, however, does not have to be limited to the issue of use or the dialogue already occurring in the canon; rather, it can be used

---

Bakhtin allows the literary critic to attend to the final form of the Bible without disregard for the analysis of intermediate stages of the formation of the Bible's formation – or attend to an intermediate stage without ignoring the final form of the text."

94. See Claassens, "Biblical Theology as Dialogue," 134.

95. Eichrodt, *Theology of Old Testament*, 1.26.

96. For further discussion on the relationship between the Old and New Testament, see Gunneweg, *Understanding Old Testament*; Baker, *Two Testaments, One Bible*; Childs, "Nature of Christian Bible," 115–25; Motyer, "Two Testaments," 143–64.

97. Childs, *Old Testament Theology*, 9. Elsewhere Childs notes: "Although the New Testament has in part Christianized the Old Testament in rendering its witness to Jesus Christ, the Christian church has rightly retained within its canon of authoritative scripture the unaltered voice of Ancient Israel as a response to its experience of the living God." Childs, *Biblical Theology*, 445. As to why this was necessary, Childs offers the following reasons: First, the Old Testament remains a lasting witness to the truth that Israel's existence depends solely upon the divine mercy and initiative; Second, the relationship between Israel and God was toward the purpose of shaping this people into a holy and righteous vehicle by which to reconcile himself to the world, a purpose which remains valid for the New Testament church; Third, Israel's voice in the Psalter remains the authentic response of the people of God by which the New Testament witness is also to be tested. Childs, *Biblical Theology*, 445.

alternatively as a synchronic reading that is especially concerned with reading the unmerged canonical voices in dialogue with each other.[98] In this model, the interpreter especially pays attention to the iconic pointers which link together the unmerged canonical voices. The iconic pointers or the shared features between the unmerged voices may be such things as repetitions of words and semantic fields; similarities in style and structure; similarities in genre, theme, and motif; analogies in character descriptions; and similarities in narratological representation.[99] These relationships, as van Wolde argues, are not so much indexical relationships, but potential relationships.[100] The potential shared elements, as van Wolde argues, "permit the individual autonomous text to dialogue with other texts without allowing itself to be absorbed by them or absorbing them itself."[101] In a synchronic dialogic reading, the intention is not to collapse or renounce the historical and cultural distance between the texts; rather, it is to engage canonical voices, which have distinct perspectives and originating from different historical, cultural and literary contexts, in a conversation.[102] The conversation or the dialogue among the canonical voices is mutual – these voices influence each other reciprocally in such a way that neither is left untouched by the interaction.[103] The truth produced in such a conversation is "unified truth that requires plurality of consciousness." Bakhtin, as already observed, terms the truth or the message produced "event potential." As Thiselton argues,

> the notion "event potential" denotes a particularity within a temporal process that is not exhausted by its own moment of existence, and in this sense is not "finalized." The development of the biblical canon and its continuity is a coherent plurality that generates Christian tradition and doctrine reflects this plurality-in-coherence that characterizes a hermeneutic of doctrine. A hermeneutic of doctrine prevents doctrine from becoming

---

98. See Claassens, "Biblical Theology as Dialogue," 134.
99. Van Wolde, "Intertextuality," 432–33.
100. Van Wolde, 432.
101. Van Wolde, 432.
102. See Claassens, "Biblical Theology as Dialogue," 136; Newsom, "Bakhtin, Bible," 305; Green, *Mikhail Bakhtin*, 27, 61.
103. Claassens, 136.

only monologic discourse; a hermeneutic of doctrine prevents hermeneutics from becoming only relativistic.[104]

It follows that the unmerged voices cannot do without each other. As Morson and Emerson point out, "their separateness is essential to dialogue. Even when they agree, they do so from different perspectives and different senses of the word."[105] As will be observed subsequently, the reader plays an active role in orchestrating the dialogue.

The distinction between monologic and polyphonic/dialogic also pertains to the issue of truth. For Bakhtin, dialogic truth is preferred over monological truth. In contrast to Bakhtin, the two do not necessarily need to be held as antithetical to each other. A polyphonic text requires a plurality of voices, which implies a plurality of monologues. The truth that emerges when these voices intersect does not necessarily render monological truth invalid. Biblical truth, as already observed, did not come all at once, as Vos points out: "Truth comes in the form of growing truth, not truth at rest."[106]

God did not just reveal himself through a multiplicity of acts; he also wanted his acts to be presented from a multiplicity of perspectives. God did not reveal himself at once, once for all; rather it is revelation that came through a series of God's acts. Many of God's acts are presented from a multiplicity of perspectives. Most notable are the following examples: the Primary History (Gen–2 Kings) and the Secondary History (1–2 Chron) on Israel's history from creation to Babylonian exile; Daniel, Esther, Ezra-Nehemiah, and the post-exilic prophets (Haggai, Zechariah, Malachi) on the return from exile, rebuilding, and settlement; the Gospels (Matthew, Mark, Luke, John) on Jesus's ministry.

Canonical truth did not come all at once; the truths in the unmerged voices of the canon are no less truth, although not the whole truth, as they form part of something larger. I concur with Vanhoozer's observation that, if no one point of view – any single voice, perspective, literary genre, or conceptual scheme – can adequately articulate the whole truth of the text, then "the essence of [canonical] drama is dialogical action. The question of propositionalism, then, is whether its monologic conception of truth does

---

104. Thiselton, *Hermeneutics of Doctrine*, 136.
105. Morson and Emerson, *Mikhail Bakhtin*, 237.
106. Vos, "Idea of Biblical Theology," 10.

not end up losing the very dialogical quality that makes the drama, and the canonical script, what it is. Dialogical form cannot be reduced to monological substance."[107] Rather than monologic truth and dialogic truth being polar opposites, in Poythress's terms, each of these is "a perspective on the other."[108]

Canonical Potentiality

The reader cannot claim to have exhausted the "semantic treasures" of the biblical canon; even less can the reader claim to have exhausted its potential intentionality or meaning potentiality. Reading Scripture in light of the broader canonical context has implications on the conception of meaning. Scripture, as already argued, is both a divine and human book, and, as Poythress argues, the two do not simply stand side by side; rather, they point to each other and affirm the presence of the other.[109] This dual authorship of the Scripture points also to the potentiality, which may not be simply derived from attending to the human authors at the neglect of the divine author. The omniscient God not only knows the meaning of the words at the point of writing but also knows all the implications they carry to his other words past and future, and the implications they will have for all future generations.

The biblical canon is divine revelation which did not come all at once. If the New Testament is taken into consideration, it is a revelation which came over a long period of time and reached its culmination, although not its finality, in the revelation of Christ. As Vos argues, historic progressiveness is one characteristic feature of divine revelation: "The self-revelation of God is a work covering ages, proceeding in a sequence of revealing words and acts, appearing in a long perspective of time. Truth comes in the form of growing truth, not truth at rest."[110] This understanding of revelation implies that our conception of meaning cannot simply rest on the individual words, sentences, author, or book without taking into consideration the dynamic and relational character these may have in the context of a larger story. As Poythress points out, responsible biblical interpretation cannot be content with a grammatical historical exegesis of Scripture, which self-consciously pays attention to each

---

107. Vanhoozer, *Drama of Doctrine*, 270.
108. See Poythress, *Symphonic Theology*.
109. Poythress, "What Does God Say?" 83.
110. See Vos, "Idea of Biblical Theology," 10.

book as a product of a human author in its historical setting. Poythress offers the following reasons amongst others: First, the biblical human authors intended their words to also be received as the words of the Holy Spirit; Second, an intertextual reading of Scripture can help provide synthesis which goes well beyond what a text can say in isolation.[111] The potential intentionality of God's revealed words continued to widen as revelation progressively accumulated.

The canon's potential intentionality is not only evidenced by its nature as a monologue, a divine book, or its polyphonic nature as cumulative revelation; it is also evidenced by its most important dialogue, that between the Old Testament and the New Testament. Vanhoozer calls it a *canonically bounded dialogue*.[112] Each of these two voices retains its particularity, yet they stand with each other in dialogue in which they are mutually enriched. The potential intentionality of the canon is enhanced by the dialogue between the two testaments. A canonical-dialogic reading attends to the conversation between these two testaments. The two testaments shed light on each other in their answer and question, their agreement and disagreement, and their continuity and discontinuity. In the current study, the focus is solely in the Old Testament, and therefore, I will not venture into the New Testament.

Creative Understanding of the Canon

We have so far dealt with the various levels at which a reader or biblical interpreter may engage texts in a dialogue. In dialogic reading, the biblical interpreter plays an active role in orchestrating the dialogue by engaging the biblical voices in a conversation, thereby tapping into the potential intentionality of the text. Dialogism, as already observed, calls for "creative understanding" by the biblical interpreter. The creativity in this regard is not creation *ex nihilo*. Neither is it simply a reading out of the text nor a reading into the text. As Vanhoozer notes, Gadamer's "fusion of horizon" falls short compared to Bakhtin's "creative understanding." Gadamer's fusion of horizon is monologic "because instead of preserving the particularity of each of the two horizons, it collapses them into one."[113] In creative understanding,

---

111. Poythress, "What Does God Say?" 99.
112. Vanhoozer, *Drama of Doctrine*, 291.
113. Vanhoozer, 352.

"each [of the two horizons] retains its own unity and open totality, but they are mutually enriched."[114]

In this dialogic encounter, the interpreter or the outsider to the text "does not renounce itself, its own place in time, its own culture; and it forgets nothing."[115] Olson argues that a provisional step in a dialogic creative understanding occurs when the interpreter brings their own formative traditions or interpretive framework into the dialogic encounter with the ancient or foreign text.[116] A Christian interpreter will likely bring into this dialogue a constellation of voices from their Christian doctrinal tradition, as these provide fruitful prejudices in interpreting the Scripture, whereas a Jewish interpreter will also engage in an exclusively Jewish reading of the Scripture.[117] Provisional monologization, as Olson argues, is entirely appropriate, as it allows the interpreters to bring their own set of philosophical commitments and traditions into dialogue with Scripture.[118] Like Morson and Emerson who have called attention to incarnational analogy, Bakhtin also used incarnational analogy to explain this dynamic: "[Bakhtin] envisaged Christ as the One who performed a live entering into the world without ever losing his divine outsideness."[119]

In dialogism, the interpreter is not regarded as an isolated figure; rather, he/she is a member of a community constantly involved in the interaction between the centripetal and centrifugal forces. The centripetal forces seek coherence, centralization, and unity of meaning. The centripetal forces are necessary for creating a shared basis of communication. The individual making utterances is part of a community, and thus, our use of language is predetermined by the ideology of our society or the dictates of our community. Equally significant is the centrifugal force, which "disrupts any homogenizing procedure and ensures that ideology remains open to different views."[120]

---

114. Bakhtin, *Speech Genres*, 69.

115. Bakhtin, 7.

116. Olson, "Biblical Theology," 175.

117. Olson, 175.

118. Olson states, "Scripture is always in dialogue with some tradition in the act of interpretation." Olson, "Biblical Theology," 178.

119. Morson and Emerson, *Mikhail Bakhtin*, 61.

120. Sellers, *Myth and Fairy Tale*, 43. Baxter points out that for Bakhtin the "centripetal-centrifugal tension is dialectal but not in the Hegelian sense of a thesis, which produces its opposite in an antithesis, which then culminates in a synthesis. . . . To Bakhtin, the centripetal-

As Sellers points out, behind this centrifugal dynamic is "'heteroglossia' or the presence of multiple narratives, a process that enables the mapping of discourses as their contours are outlined in relation to each other, and which thus relativises any claim to a monopoly."[121]

The individual, unlike in Fish's reader response theory, is not an irredeemable product of his own community; the community is not a closed entity. As Ray points out,

> Fish's reader knows no anguish, can provoke no change in himself. Theoretically capable of persuading others, he can never outflank the beliefs of the institutions that define him; he can trigger no revolutions; the discipline will always have already understood, assimilated, indeed produced, any arguments for its realignment he might generate.[122]

As Shepherd points out, in Bakhtin the authority of the community is "less happily benign," unlike Fish's notorious interpretive community.[123] The dialogism within the community cannot be reduced to monologism; the community and the individual reciprocally influence each other in a dialogic relationship.

Unfinalizability of the Canon

Bakhtin's concept of "unfinalizability" should not be confused with the poststructuralist notion of "undecidability" – the idea that every reading is a misreading because to decide on one meaning would be to elevate it over other meanings. The canon remains open or unfinalized for the following reasons, amongst others. First, the canon has the potentiality to communicate in ever-changing contexts – the canon is always ready to address the coming generations of readers, and its potentiality can never be exhausted. The prophet Isaiah states regarding the word of God, "The grass withers and the flowers fall, but the word of God stands forever" (Isa 40:8; cf. 1 Pet 1:23–25).

---

centrifugal dialectic is a dynamic, fluid, and ongoing process whose particular shape varies chronotopically, or contextually." Baxter, "Dialogues of Relating," 114.

121. Sellers, 43.
122. Ray, *Literary Meaning*, 169.
123. Shepherd, "Bakhtin and the Reader," 100.

Second, readers re-accentuate the canon from different contexts and from different points of view or perspectives. In Bakhtin's terms, "every age re-accentuates in its own way." As Bakhtin argues, re-accentuation is an inevitable and organic further development of the image or a text as it serves as a continuation of the potential already embedded in the image or text.[124] Every age and every interpreter of the canon has a *surplus of vision* in relation to other generations, and other interpreters yet remain unfinalized, as it is impossible for finite human beings to understand another totally – there is no Archimedean point of view. Our horizons of interpreting the canon look forward to the eschatological horizon – the final context in which everything will be made clear. The eschatological horizon in biblical interpretation is not yet fully realized; the final context in which everything will be made clear is still to come: "Now I know in part; then I shall understand fully, even as I have been fully understood" (1 Cor 13:12, RSV).

The notion of "unfinalizability" does not necessarily imply that the canon has no determinate meaning. As already observed, for Bakhtin, "*the word is a two-sided act*. It is determined equally by *whose* word it is and *for whom* it is meant." Bakhtin's notion of the instability of meaning is based on human finiteness. For him, human authors are not in full command of all the implications their words or works will have. The goal of interpretation is not to reduplicate the probable intention of the author or editor at the time of writing. Reading merely to discover the authorial intention encloses the text. Biblical human authors are not little gods who are fully in command of their words. The stability of the meaning of biblical texts cannot be established by appealing to the intentions of human authors. It is only God, the divine author, who is in full command of canonical words. Poythress is pointed in this regard:

> God plans and intends that his words should have the effects on readers that they have. This intention includes all details of all the applications throughout history. The applications are part of God's intention. Hence, in the usual approach that identifies meaning with authorial intention, all the applications are part of the meaning. Conversely, each application, if it is an application

---

124. Bakhtin, *Dialogic Imagination*, 409–10.

at all, is an application of something: it is an expression or instantiation of the intention of God, an intention that covers more than one application. Hence, the very idea of application presupposes a unity of meaning thoughout the unity of God's plan.[125]

The canon as God's word is a "great work" of the past – a work which outgrows its epoch of creation, a work whose efficacy and significance cannot be confined to "small time" – its own epoch; it is a work of "great time" – it is in the true sense of the word an "infinite and unfinalized dialogue in which no meaning dies."

Viable Trajectories for Dialogic Reading

There are a number of viable trajectories through which biblical texts may be read dialogically. Dialogic reading may be utilized to build on the results of the historical-critical approach. For the historical critics, the Pentateuch was not a product of a single consciousness; rather, it was a juxtapositioning of a plurality of voices. Historical critics, however, had a monologic conception of truth; that is, the plural voices had to be separated from each other so that each individual monologic voice could be heard independent of the others.[126] Dialogic reading would not deny that apparent contradictions, obscurities, ambiguities, incoherencies, discontinuities, ellipses, interruptions, and repetitions may point to a plurality of voices in a text. Furthermore, dialogic reading would not even deny that these plural voices stem from particular contexts or settings; the aim, however, in dialogic reading is not to reconstruct the prehistory of the text, nor is the aim a duplication of the original meaning of the plural voices. Dialogic reading would insist that the first order of meaning is the dialogical effect when the plural voices are read together. The plurality of voices in a work such as the Pentateuch or other biblical books does not necessarily have to be attributed to a multiplicity of sources, as historical critics tended to think. The plurality of voices may just as well be consistent with the purpose of the author in weaving his text.

Dialogues, thus, can also be found within a single author's work, and so we can speak of "inner dialogue" or "internal dialogue." Dialogue in the canon should not only be viewed as interaction or conversation amongst different

---

125. Poythress, *God-Centered*, 76.
126. Newsom, "Bakhtin, Bible," 293.

sources or different authors. Dialogue, as Reed points out, "is not merely the phenomenon of two people speaking back and forth to one another; it is the linguistic precondition of all communication whatsoever, and its interactive awareness of the utterances of others, before and after, is inscribed in every utterance a person speaks."[127] In Bakhtin's dialogism, a text with a plurality of voices is viewed as an artistic work by an author.[128] A polyphonic text, in a Bakthinian sense, is what Newsom calls "an intentional artistic presentation of the dialogic nature of an idea."[129] A biblical example of Bakhtin's polyphonic text is the book of Job, if one assumes a single author, who has completely given up his privileged position and subsumed himself in the text, thereby allowing his ideas to engage in dialogue with those of his characters and thus resulting in a plurality of unmerged voices.[130] A polyphonic text or "a literary dialogue," as Sternberg calls it, "entails indirection by its very form, because in staging it the artist communicates with the audience through the communication held among his speaking characters, the dialogists."[131] For Sternberg, this indirect communication requires, on the one hand, an attempt to make sense of the artist's mind by analyzing the discourse assigned to the characters and, on the other hand, an attempt to make sense of what the narrator opts to reveal or conceal during the dialogue.[132] The omniscient narrator, as the maker of dialogue, may choose to communicate freely – thus turning the story into a monologue by using their privileged position to give all overt guidance, elucidating everything they tell, and thereby finalizing the text. By contrast, the dialogic narrator "chooses to play, indeed to outplay," by holding back the kinds of aids and shortcuts that would otherwise finalize

---

127. Reed, *Dialogues of the Word*, 13.

128. Bakhtin states, concerning Dostoevsky, "Thus the new artistic position of the author with regard to the hero in Dostoevsky's polyphonic novel is a fully-realized and thoroughly consistent dialogic position, one that affirms the independence, internal freedom, unfinalizability, and indeterminacy of the hero. For the author the hero is not 'he' and not 'I' but a fully valid 'thou,' that is, another and autonomous 'I' ('thou-art')." Bakhtin, *Problems of Dostoevsky's Poetics*, 63.

129. Newsom, "Bakhtin, Bible," 297.

130. See Newsom, 297–98; Newsom, "Book of Job," 87–108.

131. Sternberg, "Double Cave," 28.

132. Sternberg, 28–29.

the text. This, as Sternberg argues, puts heavy demands on interpretation, as the reader has to wonder about the point of it all.[133]

It should also be noted, however, that the goal of dialogic reading is not a pursuit of contradictions; rather, the focus is on questions and answers, agreements, and disagreements. As Bakhtin argues, even where there is agreement, from a dialogical perspective, the voices in agreement are not identical.[134] The two utterances "life is good" and "life is good" are identical, but they can also be viewed as phrases uttered from two spatially separated people who are probably in agreement with each other. The first utterance may be regarded as a statement, and the second as a confirmation. The confirmation is not mere repetition; rather, it is made from the perspective of another, who arrived at the same conclusion having gone through a different life experience. In this way, the first utterance is unfinalized and is dialogically expanded by the second, which widens its meaning. On the other hand, the two utterances "life is good" and "life is not good" may be regarded as opposite judgments: one is a negation of the other. These two utterances are in a dialogic relation of disagreement that exists between different speakers. If these judgments proceed from a single subject on a particular question, the relationship is dialectic, not dialogic. For Bakhtin, dialogic relations arise where two different utterances are uttered by two different subjects. Bakhtin's attempt to rule out "internal dialogue" within a single consciousness is unconvincing. Dialogic relationships do not necessarily have to be confined to different people in communication. It is quite possible for one and the same subject to attend to the same question from completely different perspectives, emphasizing different aspects relating to the same question. For example, historical critics have argued that Genesis 1–3 was composed of two stories of creation that allegedly have different origins and do not share the same style, expression, and theology. Genesis 1:1–2:4a was attributed to the Priestly source (P), whereas Genesis 2:4b–3:6 was attributed to the Yahwistic source (J). However, such an approach is monologic at best, as it does not aim at reading the two stories in a dialogic relationship. The two stories may be read as the work of a single writer who approached the same subject from different perspectives, thereby putting them in a dialogic relationship with each other.

---

133. Sternberg, 52–53.
134. Bakhtin, *Problems of Dostoevsky's Poetics*, 183–84.

Dialogic reading also intersects with narrative criticism (or literary criticism). Both approaches do pay due attention to the plot of the narrative; however, the emphases differ. Narrative critics concern themselves with the aesthetic value of the plot, as it is a means through which a single consciousness artfully manages their story and finalizes it. As Reed points out, the presence of the plot implies "a definite beginning, middle, and end, of whose individual fates, realistic or symbolic, freely chosen or predetermined, are the primary determinants of the action of the text as a whole."[135] In dialogic reading, the plot serves the dialogic idea. The role of the reader is no longer simply to analyze the plot; rather, the reader, as Newsom frames it, is "more like a bystander suddenly caught up in the quarrel."[136] Thus, a dialogic reading of the biblical canon is not necessarily a violation of the biblical plot at either the micro or the macro level. For example, at the macro level of the biblical metanarrative, our dialogic reading of texts from the Old Testament and the New Testament will take into consideration the fact that the canon as a whole presents us with a coherent message at the climax of which stands Jesus Christ.

Furthermore, dialogic reading, like narrative criticism, also pays attention to techniques of repetition such as, *leitwort*, motif, theme, type-scene, sequence action, and parallelism, and even more broadly to intertextual relations through echoes, allusion, and typology. A dialogic reading of the intersecting texts presumes that these texts influence each other and that neither text is left untouched by the interaction. As already pointed out, even where there is agreement, the meaning is widened. Dialogical reading is not an irresponsible juxtapositioning of texts, as Green argues: "Bakhtin's devotion to and skill at playing the many textual cues dispel or discourage any reading that is arbitrary or irresponsible, and his example invites other interpreters to be explicit about their own strategies."[137] Great literary works, as Bakhtin argues with respect to those of Shakespeare, are rich in embedded "semantic treasure," which the reader cannot exhaust:

> They were created and collected through the centuries and even millennia: they lay hidden in the language, and not only in the literary language, but also in those strata of the popular language

---

135. Reed, *Dialogues of the Word*, 12.
136. Newsom, "Book of Job," 93.
137. Green, *Mikhail Bakhtin*, 64.

that before Shakespeare's time had not entered literature, in the diverse genres and forms of speech communication, in the forms of a mighty national culture (primarily carnival forms) that were shaped through millennia, in the theatre-spectacle genres (mystery plays, farces, and so forth), in plots whose roots go back to prehistoric antiquity.[138]

The richness of Shakespeare's work, it should be stated, is nothing compared to the riches of the Bible as a book of faith. The richness of language is not simply derived from its long and complex history. Perhaps, even better, "human language mirrors divine language. We may expect that it has a derivative richness mirroring the richness of divine language."[139]

A canonical-dialogical reading of Genesis 1–3 will allow us to approach this passage as part of a larger story in which it is amplified and illumined in new and unexpected ways.[140] This makes it impossible to simply read this text only as a text about creation. Genesis 1–3 is telling a story whose continuation is far beyond itself. This should be expected because Scripture is cumulative and as such it is intertextual.

In chapter 2, I will read Genesis 1–3 as a polyphonic text with an internal dialogue that remains unfinalized. The following questions will be addressed: The first creation is "good," but in contrast to what? Does the language of good have overtones of perfection? What is the goodness of creation? Is Genesis 3 part of the resumption of the activities that occurred within the creation week or not?

The Old Testament has a multiplicity of voices that offer different perspectives, which when read dialogically illuminate each other. In chapters 3 and 4, Genesis 1–3 is read in dialogue with other Old Testament voices. In chapter 3, I will engage Genesis 1–3 in dialogue with other Old Testament creation fragments, especially pertaining to the creation conflict motif. A distinction will be made between creation through conflict and conflicts within the creation. I will also explore the significance of this distinction pertaining to our understanding of the first creation in its original state. In chapter 4, I will explore the motif of uncreation and re-creation. Genesis 1–3,

---

138. Bakhtin, *Speech Genre*, 5.
139. Poythress, *God-Centered*, 77.
140. See Hays, "Reading Scripture," 233.

as we will observe, functions as a paradigm for eschatological uncreation and re-creation – the bad and the good.

Therefore, I will explore the potential intentiality of the Genesis 1–3 text in the following chapters. Ultimately, this book introduces an alternative model of making sense of the canonical story.

CHAPTER 2

Internal Dialogue in Genesis 1:1–2:4a: God Saw That It Was Good, But Not All Was Good

Introduction

The anonymous author of Genesis speaks in this narrative in voices other than his own; in Sternberg's terms, he is like a "scriptwriter and stage manager rolled in one," speaking "through voices and words and obliquities of his own devising."[1] In Bakhtin's terms, he is a polyphonic author who gives up his privileged position, completely immersing himself in his narrative. This author is in a literary sense an omniscient narrator, as he narrates events that precede human history, and yet he does so with authority.[2]

Genesis 1–3 may be read dialogically in many different ways by focusing on the different rhetorical plays in the text. My dialogic reading will be focused on one dialogic opposition: good and bad. This text, I am convinced, builds up this dialogic opposition by what it says and what it does not say (or its silence) through its narrative flow and language use. The story invites the reader's participation and exposes itself to dialogic reading by leaving questions and ambiguities either purposefully or accidentally. The gaps and

---

1. See Sternberg, "Double Cave," 28.
2. Fokkelman, *Reading Biblical Narrative*, 56. The authority with which the writer speaks, as Fokkelman argues, "is a result of his position as narrator." Fokkelman, 56.

the ambiguities in the story create openness for the readers to keep on coming back to it to make sense of it, as Goldingay argues, "it can be creatively provocative, evidently part of God's purpose."[3]

In this chapter, I will focus on the internal dialogue within Genesis 1:1–2:4a. I will argue that the narrative progression in this creation narrative is developed through the projection of a dialogic opposition of bad and good. Therefore, the creation process is presented as moving creation from a "bad" state, a "non-functional state," to a "good" state, that is a "functional state." The dialogic idea in Genesis 1:1–2:4a, as I argue elsewhere, "is not so much a result of the interaction between the characters; rather it is the result of the narrator's play by leaving gaps and fissures through which the text communicates, whether purposefully or accidentally."[4]

The Good Creation – "God Saw That It Was Good"

Genesis 1:1–2:4a is dominated by two voices, the narrator's voice and the voice of God (*Elohim*). The narrator, however, is the one who is in control of the narrative – he decides what to tell, he even knows the mind of God, and also explicates the words of God. The dialogic idea in this narrative does not so much result from the interaction between the characters; such interaction is minimal at best[5] – rather it is the result of the gaps and the fissures through which the text communicates with the reader.

The narrator repeatedly gives the reader glimpses of what happened in God's mind during the creative activity by unveiling God's thoughts to the reader. In Genesis 1:1–2:4a, we find God's continual evaluation of his creation acts. The refrain "and God saw that it was good" is repeated in 1:4, 10, 12, 18, 21, and 31. The final refrain on the sixth day (1:31), "so God saw all that he

---

3. Goldingay, "How Far Do Readers?", 6.
4. Ramantswana, "From Bad to Good," 238.
5. In this narrative, God's speech is monological. God's speech is creative speech – he speaks and things come into being: "Let there be . . ." (Gen 1:3, 6, 9, 11, 14, 20, 24). In Genesis 1:26–27, God urges other unidentified beings to join in the creation of mankind: "*Let us* make man *in our image, in our likeness.*" Is this dialogic act communication with the heavenly host, or intradivine? However, no response is forthcoming, and as the story goes, God gets it his way: "So God created man *in his own image, in the image of God* he created him," thus making the whole creative enterprise a monologic activity. Following the creation of mankind, God blesses mankind and instructs them concerning their livelihood (Gen 1:28–29); however, in this interaction too, mankind offers no response.

had made and behold it was very good," (ESV) seems to suggest that God was satisfied not only with some aspects of his creation, but also with the whole of creation. All is good, and even more so "very good," or so it seems. This repetitious detail in the narrative apparently builds in intensification through indirection (implication, silence, difficult coherence), thereby requiring the reader to draw inferences.[6] What is this "goodness" of creation, and what exactly does it mean?

Some suggest that these refrains, especially the final refrain, function as a declaration of perfection over creation.[7] Those who read this refrain as a declaration of perfection on creation intend to avoid positing any metaphysical dualism to the world. From this perspective, "good" has priority over bad; evil is not ontological but is a consequence of the fall(s).[8] The problem with this argument is that, on the one hand, it cannot be fully supported by Genesis 1–3, and, on the other, it idealizes the pre-fall creation by declaring it perfect. The argument put forward is that to opt for a metaphysical dualism necessarily makes God the author of sin and evil. In the fear of making God the author of evil, interpreters thus end up flattening Genesis 1–3 by overlooking the clues that point to the internal dialogue within this narrative. The internal

---

6. On the subject of indirection, see Sternberg, "Double Cave," 28, 52.

7. Wenham regards the modification of the refrain in v. 31 as emphasizing the perfection of the final work. He states that the formula in aesthetic judgment in Genesis 1:31 modifies the previous formulas (vv. 4, 10, 12, 18, 21, 25) in three ways to emphasize the perfection of the final work: (1) it is applied to the whole creation; (2) the use of והנה instead of כי suggests God's enthusiasm as he completed his work; (3) the whole finished work is said to be "very good" not merely "good." Wenham, *Genesis 1–15*, 34. Atkinson, prioritizing the good over the bad, states, "Before anything is said about evil, or pain, or sin, or disorder, we need first to hear this note of excited pleasure. What God made is good." Atkinson, *Message of Genesis 1–11*, 42. According to Von Rad, "No evil was laid upon the world by God's hand, neither was his omnipotence limited by any kind of opposing power whatever. When faith speaks of creation, and in so doing directs its eye toward God, then it can only say that God created the world perfect." Von Rad, *Genesis: A Commentary*, 61. Childs states, "God pronounced his workmanship good and blessed it. The creation rested in its perfection; no further work was needed." Childs, *Biblical Theology*, 385. Sarna, a Jewish interpreter, states, "The formula of divine approbation, 'God saw that [it] was good,' affirms the consummate perfection of God's creation, an idea that has important consequences for the religion of Israel. Reality is imbued with God's goodness. The pagan notion of inherent, primordial evil is banished. Henceforth, evil is to be apprehended on the moral and not the mythological plane." Sarna, *Genesis*, 7. Another Jewish scholar, Cassuto, speaks of God's completed work: "For both in detail and in its entirety it had emerged perfect from his hand." Cassuto, *Commentary on Genesis*, 1:59. See also Gilkey, *Maker of Heaven*, 48–49.

8. For a detailed discussion on this issue see Sponheim, "Sin and Evil," 1:385–403.

dialogue within this narrative, as will become evident, does not necessarily result in a metaphysical dualism.

Genesis 1–3, speaking more broadly, seems to undermine any claim for hierarchical opposition or attempts at prioritizing "good" over "bad." The text also suggests and puts forward points of breakdown or points susceptible to breakdown in the good creation. This text seems to suggest, on the one hand, that there is a sense that the bad precedes the good; and on the other hand, that the bad is coexistent with the good.

Genesis 1:1–2:4a – Good in Contrast to What?

In dialogic reading, the narrative flow or plot serves the dialogic idea. The question to ask of the narrative flow, especially pertaining to the aesthetic judgment on the part of God, is: "Good in contrast to what?"

From an Unproductive and Uninhabited Earth to a Productive and Inhabited Earth

"In the beginning God created the heavens and the earth. The earth was formless and empty, darkness was over the surface of the deep, and the Spirit of God was hovering over the waters" (Gen 1:1–2, NIV). These two verses pose intriguing grammatical and interpretive problems. There are four main options for understanding these verses.[9] According to the first option, Genesis 1:1 is the initial creation in its original state of perfection, whereas Genesis 1:2 describes creation in a state of judgment, a chaotic state, a state associated with the fall of angels.[10] In the second option, all of creation falls within the seven-day framework, Genesis 1:1 is the first act of creation on day one; Genesis 1:2 describes the initial state of creation prior to the creation of light.[11]

---

9. For detailed discussion on some of the options below, see Hasel, "Recent Translations of Genesis," 156–67; Waltke, *Creation and Chaos*; Barr, "Was Everything That God?", 55–65.

10. This option is traditionally called the "gap theory" and gained support through the *Scofield Reference Bible*, which contains the following note on Genesis 1:2, "Jeremiah 4:23–26; Isaiah 24:1 and 45:18, clearly indicate that the earth had undergone a cataclysmic change as the result of the divine judgment. The earth bears everywhere the marks of such a catastrophe. There are not wanting intimations which connect it with a previous testing and fall of angels. See Ezekiel 28:12–15 and Isaiah 14:9–14, which certainly go beyond the kings of Tyre and Babylon." *Scofield Reference Bible*, 3.

11. This is the more traditional Christian understanding of these verses and has been influential in arguing for the doctrine of creation *ex nihilo*. On this view, God began by creating

In the third option, Genesis 1:1 is regarded as a temporal clause, and Genesis 1:2 as a circumstantial clause, therefore suggesting that we read, for example: "In the beginning of God's preparing the heavens and the earth – the earth hath existed waste and void, and darkness *is* on the face of the deep, and the Spirit of God fluttering on the face of the waters" (YLT), or "When God began to create heaven and earth – the earth being unformed and void, with darkness over the surface of the deep and wind from God sweeping over the water" (NJPS).[12] In the fourth option, Genesis 1:1 is regarded as a summary statement of God's total work of creation followed by a detailed account of the creation process.[13]

I follow the second option above, and so I interpret Genesis 1:1–5 as a narration of the events of the first day of creation. This is a day whose duration only comes to an end with the separation of darkness and light inaugurating a cyclical pattern of night and day. It is, therefore, impossible to say how long the first day lasted; its duration is only limited by its coming to an end.[14] I regard Genesis 1:1 to be the first act of creation: God created the upper realm/abode – the heaven(s), which is the dwelling of God, and the lower realm – earth, humanity's dwelling place. The bipartite division of the world is well attested in the Old Testament, and it is found especially in text describing

---

the universe (heaven and earth) as shapeless, unformed mass, or an empty chaos. This view has received much criticism for presenting a double creation: the creation of the raw material and subsequent shaping of the raw material by ordering it and forming other things. For a recent affirmation of this position, see Collins, *Genesis 1-4*, 42–43; Sailhamer, *Genesis Unbound*, esp. 37–45, 99–108.

12. See also the following modern translations: "In the beginning, when God created the heavens and earth, the earth was a formless wasteland, and darkness covered the abyss, while a mighty wind swept over the waters" (NAB); "In the beginning of creation, when God made heaven and earth, the earth was without form and void, with darkness over the face of the abyss, and a mighty wind that swept over the surface of the waters" (NEB). Two main arguments have been advanced in support of this option: First, it is similar to other creation stories, for example, Genesis 2:4b reads, "In the day that the LORD God made the earth and the heavens . . ." and the Mesopotamian *Enuma Elish* begins, "When above the heaven had not been named. . . ." Second, the grammatical argument that the Hebrew בְּרֵאשִׁית functions in this regard as a construct, therefore suggesting that we read "in the beginning of" (cf. Hos 1:2).

13. The phrase "the heavens and the earth" is taken as hendiadys referring to the universe as an ordered or organized entity. See Waltke, "Literary Genre of Genesis," 3–4; Westermann, *Genesis 1-11*, 93–94, 97; Young, *Studies in Genesis One*, 9–11, 14.

14. I do not intend to engage here in a debate regarding the meaning of *day* in Genesis 1 or the duration of the day. It should be noted, however, that the only point in the narrative wherein we can perhaps begin to speak of a normal day is perhaps on the fifth day, as it was only then that the normal lights, which mark seasons, had been created; days were only created at some point on the fourth day (Gen 1:14).

creation or the greatness of the creator God (Gen 14:19, 22; 24:3; Pss 89:12[11]; 146:6; Isa 66:1) – heaven and earth in their totality belong to God. It should be noted that Hebrew does not have a specific word for universe, or world, or cosmos; rather it speaks of "all things" (e.g., Eccl 11:5; Isa 44:24; Jer 10:16; 51:19) and/or "heaven and earth" (e.g., Exod 20:11; 31:17; Deut 10:14; 2 Kgs 19:15; 2 Chr 2:12; Ezra 5:11; Pss 115:15; 121:12; 124:8; 134:3; 146:6; Isa 37:16).[15] The two realms, heaven and earth, are also described in terms of their occupants. Psalm 115:16 states, "The heavens are the LORD's heavens, but the earth he has given to the sons of men." Thus, I consider "heaven and earth" in Genesis 1:1 to be referring to "two fundamental realms,"[16] the heavenly realm, God's realm,[17] and the earthly realm, humankind's realm.[18] It should be noted, however, that at this point humankind is yet to be created.

Genesis 1:2 describes creation in its initial state prior to God's creation activities. Interpreters usually interpret the expression תֹהוּ וָבֹהוּ (*tōhû wābōhû*) as an expression of chaos, confusion, disorder, formlessness, shapelessness, or nothingness.[19] For Gunkel and his followers, Genesis 1:2 describes the

---

15. Fretheim, *Suffering of God*, 37.

16. Knierim argues, "We should assume that *the formula 'heaven and earth' reflect an elementary need for distinguishing between two fundamental realms within creation. This need leads to a systematic understanding of creation as bipartite, or bipolar, universal space. Our formula is the expression of this understanding. Under the influence of this understanding, the expression of the bipartite structure of creation was more important than the assumed unity, and the other cosmological options were subjected to it at the same time. The paradigmatic text for this phenomenon is undoubtedly Gen 1:1–2:4a.*" Knierim, *Task of Old Testament*, 190–91.

17. In the Old Testament, heaven is generally considered to be a dwelling place or abode of God (Deut 26:15; 1 Kgs 8:30–52), where he sits on his throne (Pss 2:4; 103:9), from whence he speaks (Gen 21:17; 22:11, 15; Exod 20:22; Deut 4:36; 2 Sam 22:14), where he hears (1 Kgs 8:30, 32, 34, 36, 39, 43, 45, 49; 2 Chr 6:21, 23), and from whence he looks down (Pss 14:2; 33:13; 80:14; Isa 63:15; Lam 3:50); yet he is an uncontainable God (1 Kgs 8:27; 2 Chr 2:6; 6:18; Jer 23:24).

18. In the Old Testament, the earth is the dwelling place of man (Gen 1:28–30; 9:1–3; Jer 27:5–6).

19. Luther reads this expression as implying "a shapeless lump, or mass." Luther, *Luther's Commentary on Genesis*, 10. For Calvin, this expression was used to express something that is "empty and confused, or vain, and nothing worth"; however, Calvin further goes on to say that "undoubtedly Moses placed them both in opposition to all those created objects which pertain to the form, the ornament and the perfection of the world." Calvin, *Commentaries*, 73. For Cassuto, creation in its initial state was an "undifferentiated, unorganized, confused and lifeless agglomeration," which he describes as a "chaotic mass, without order or life." Cassuto, *Commentary on Genesis*, 1:23. For Westermann, the expression *tōhû wābōhû* is analogous to the Greek *chaos*, by which he means "a desert waste." Westermann, *Genesis 1–11*, 8. For Waltke, it expresses "utter chaos," by which he means "unformed and unfilled," which he regards as an antonym of "heaven and earth" in Genesis 1:1. Waltke redefines *chaos* to mean "unformed and unfilled." Waltke, "Literary Genre of Genesis," 4.

precosmic chaos, that is, the terms *tōhû wābōhû* and *těhôm* are terms for the "watery chaos," which symbolize an opponent to Yahweh's creation will.[20] Both positions regard the initial state of creation or the precosmic state of creation as a negative one. The key difference between these two positions is that in the former position, the initial state of creation is regarded to be an inactive undesirable state, whereas in the latter position, the precosmic state is an active one that is marked by conflict between God and the personified *těhôm*.

Creation in its initial state, rather than refer to it as "chaos" in whatever sense, may be properly referred to as "bad." The negative term "bad," in Hebrew רַע, is functionally a better contrastive term to the positive term "good," Hebrew טוֹב (cf. Gen 2:9), which is repeated in Genesis 1.[21] The narrative flow of Genesis 1 serves the dialogic idea. The creation process is described as a series of activities that are deemed good, that is, a gradual transformation process of creation from one state to another – from "bad" to "good," or in extreme terms, from "very bad" to "very good."

The word-pair *tōhû wābōhû* that is used for creation in its initial state occurs three times in the Old Testament (Gen 1:2; Isa 34:11; Jer 4:23). In both Isaiah 34:11 and Jeremiah 4:23, the context is that of judgment. In the former text, God threatens to bring about the destruction of the land of Edom, and in the latter, the destruction of the land of Israel. In the case of Isaiah 34, the immediate context is specifically that of human habitation, "from generation to generation; it will lie desolate [תֶּחֱרָב], no one will ever pass through it" (v. 10) – thus the land of Edom will be an uninhabited or deserted dangerous desert-like territory, a forbidden zone inhabited by desert birds and desert creatures (vv. 11–16). In Jeremiah 4, there is immediate reference to the

---

20. Gunkel, "Influence of Babylonian Mythology," 25–52. Among the followers of Gunkel, Childs states, "the Old Testament writer struggles to contrast the creation, not with the background of empty neutrality, but with an active chaos standing in opposition to the will of God. . . . The chaos is a reality rejected by God." Childs, *Myth and Reality*, 42. Elswhere, Childs describes the state of creation in Genesis 1:2 as "the mystery of a primordial threat against creation, uncreated without form and void, which God strove to overcome." Childs, *Old Testament Theology*, 223–24. Anderson writes, "Genesis 1 begins by portraying a precreation condition of watery chaos. Indeed, the Hebrew word for deep (Gen 1:2: Tehom) appears here without the definite article (elsewhere it is in the feminine gender), as though it were a distant echo of the mythical battle with Tiamat, the female personification of the powers of chaos." Anderson, *Creation versus Chaos*, 39. Further discussion on Gunkel's theory will follow subsequently and in chapter 3.

21. For more on the contrastive terms רַע and טוֹב (good), see Ramantswana, "From Bad to Good," 247–50.

emptiness of the land, with no human beings and no birds (v. 25), and to the fruitful land becoming desert-like or unproductive (v. 26).²² Thus, the land is a *tōhû wābōhû*, implying that it is, on the one hand, an unfruitful land, barren, or desert-like, a *tōhû*; on the other hand, it is uninhabited, or empty, a *bōhû*. By using this creation language or by invoking a picture of the reversal of creation, the prophets were pointing to the severe nature of the destruction which would come on both these lands.

Jeremiah 4:23–26 provides a close parallel to Genesis 1. In Genesis 1, the third, fifth and sixth days are set as climaxes in the framework of this creation story, with the creation of humankind on the sixth day as the grand climax. On the third day, the unproductive land becomes productive: "The land produced vegetation: plants bearing seed according to their kinds and trees bearing fruit and seed in it according to their kinds. And God saw that it was good" (v. 12, NIV). On the fifth and sixth days, God creates living creatures, sea creatures, birds (fifth day), and earth creatures and human beings (sixth day), to increase and fill the waters and the earth – the uninhabited land or empty land becomes populated with living creatures.²³ Tsumura rightly suggests we render *tōhû wābōhû* as "an unproductive and uninhabited place."²⁴ Thus, *tōhû wābōhû* is not utter chaos, confusion, disorder, formlessness, shapelessness, or nothingness, but unproductiveness and uninhabitedness. The earth was, so to speak, like the barren womb of Sarah, unproductive and unfruitful, as good as dead.²⁵ The progression of the creation narrative is like a pretold story of Israelite history – a story that progresses from the

---

22. Jeremiah 4:23–24:
   I looked at the earth, and it was **formless and empty** (תֹהוּ וָבֹהוּ);
   and at the heavens, and their light was gone.
   I looked at the mountains, and they were quaking;
   all the hills were swaying.
   I looked, and **there were no people** (וְהִנֵּה אֵין הָאָדָם);
   every bird in the sky had flown away.
   I looked, and **the fruitful land** (הַכַּרְמֶל) **was a desert** (הַמִּדְבָּר);
   all its towns lay in ruins before the Lord, before his fierce anger. (NIV)

23. See also, Wenham, *Genesis 1–15*, 6; Anderson, *Creation versus Chaos*, 187–88. See also Young, *Studies in Genesis One*, 99. Tsumura, *Creation and Destruction*, 34.

24. Tsumura, *Creation and Destruction*, 35; see also Tsumura, *Earth and Waters*, 41–43.

25. In the words of Hebrews 11:11–12, "By faith he received power of procreation, even though he was too old – and Sarah herself was barren – because he considered him faithful who had promised. Therefore from one person [Sarah], and this one as good as dead, descendants were born as many as the stars of heaven and as the innumerable grains of sand by the seashore" (NRSV).

laughable, hopeless situation of an aged couple, the barren wife already past childbearing age, conceiving and their descendants becoming fruitful and multiplying greatly and becoming exceedingly numerous "so that the land was filled with them" (Gen 17:15–22, ESV; 18:13; Exod 1:7). Israel's story is the story of the God of creation.

Creation in its initial state was in a "bad" state in contrast to the "good" state in which it was on the sixth day of creation activity – that is, the productive earth, conducive to life, and inhabited. Waltke rightly observes: "The situation of verse 2 is not good, nor is it ever called good."[26] This progression from bad to good is one that was purposed and planned by God. Thus, in this narrative, the positive term "good" does not seem to have priority over the negative term "bad" in terms of the narrative progression. The positive term, however, does have qualitative priority, as the creation order progresses from unproductive to productive, from uninhabitable to inhabitable, or, so to speak, from lifelessness to life. The idea of a habitable creation clearly comes out in Isaiah 45:18:

> For thus says Yahweh, who created the heavens,
>> He is God, who formed the earth and made it,
> He established it;
> He did not create it to be empty [*tōhû*],
> But formed it to be inhabited.
>> I am Yahweh and there is no other.

The term *tōhû* is used here in the context of a description of the purpose of creation. In contrast to the common renderings of the term *tōhû* as formless (KJV, NIV, NRSV, NLT), without form (RSV, NKJV, ESV, NCV), unformed (NJPS), without shape (NET Bible), as Walton argues, considering all its occurrences in the Old Testament has nothing to do with material form;[27] rather, it is used to describe "that which is nonfunctional, having no purpose and generally unproductive in human terms."[28] Thus, in negative terms, the purpose of creation was not for creation to remain empty, that is,

---

26. Waltke, *Creation and Chaos*, 58. For a similar position, see Ross, *Creation and Blessing*, 106, 722; Heward, "And Earth Was," 13–37, 16; Gibson, *Genesis*, 29.

27. See Deut 32:10; 1 Sam 12:21; Job 6:18; 12:24; 26:7; Ps 107:40; Isa 24:10; 29:21; 34:11; 40:17; 40:23; 41:29; 44:9; 45:18–19; 49:4; 59:4; Jer 4:23.

28. I am indebted here to Walton, *Lost World of Genesis*, 47–51, esp. 47–49.

nonfunctional; in positive terms, the purpose of creation was for the creation to be inhabited, that is, functional.

Creation in its initial state was unproductive and uninhabited because it was flooded and in a state of darkness that made it inhospitable to life. Furthermore, the earth remained in a bad state, or nonfunctional at least during the first two days of creation. In those days, the land was still unproductive and uninhabited. This is clear in Job 26:7: "He spreads out the northern skies over empty space [*tōhû*]; he suspends the earth over nothing" (NIV). We have in Job 26:7 a parallel construction in which the second colon sharpens the meaning of *tōhû* in the first colon. In the second colon, the primordial condition of a flooded earthly realm is regarded as "nothing." In this case, as Walton argues, the term *tōhû* refers to the nonfunctional primordial waters, or the "'nonexistent' cosmic waters above and below."[29]

The author of Genesis 1 was communicating to his audience about "God's creation of the functional cosmos."[30] This, as Walton argues, is a common phenomenon reflected in other ancient Near Eastern cosmological mythologies, whose concern is not to communicate the material or structure of the cosmos.[31] In ancient cosmologies, the cosmos begins in a nonfunctional state, a state often symbolized by the primeval waters.[32] In this state as Walton points out, there is "no operational system in place," that is a state of singularity in which there is no differentiation.[33] The separation and naming of the created items make them functional.[34]

Similarly, the creation account in Genesis 1 begins with a nonfunctional cosmos. Creation in its initial state was in a state of lifelessness, a *tōhû wābōhû*,

---

29. Walton, *Lost World of Genesis*, 49–50.
30. Walton, *Genesis*, 85.
31. Walton, Genesis, 85.
32. Walton, *Lost World of Genesis*, 31.
33. Walton writes, "Egyptian texts talk about a singularity – nothing having yet been separated out. All is inert and undifferentiated. Similarly, one Sumerian text speaks of a time when there was darkness, no flow of water, nothing being produced, no rituals performed, and heaven and earth were still joined together. Even the gods were not yet there. For an example in Egyptian literature, the god Atum is conceptualized as the primordial monad – the singularity embodying all the potential of the cosmos, from whom all things were separated and thereby were created." Walton, *Lost World of Genesis*.
34. See also Bronner, *Biblical Personalities and Archaeology*, 85; Clifford, *Creation Accounts*, 7; Plumley, "Cosmology of Ancient Egypt," 38.

that is, nonfunctional – unproductive and uninhabited.[35] The aesthetic judgment that everything in creation is "good" simply expresses God's satisfaction with his work. As Walton argues, the purpose of Genesis 1 as a whole is that "God made everything just right and set it up to function properly within his purposes."[36] God created everything and assigned to each its place in order that it might perform its appointed role in serving and glorifying him. At the end of the sixth day, creation was fully functional – it was productive and inhabited, and so it was "very good."

Two analogies can be drawn from this. First, God did his creative work as a priest, making distinctions, assigning things to their proper categories, and assessing their fitness: heaven and earth, darkness and light, the waters above and the waters below, land and sea, animals and plants according to their kinds, sun to govern the day and moon the night, and humanity: male and female.[37] Second, God, like a craftsman, stands back and looks at what he has made and declares his satisfaction (cf. Isa 41:7).[38]

In Genesis 1:2, in consideration of the triple meaning of *rûaḥ* as spirit or wind or breath, the imagery of the *rûaḥ* hovering over the surface of the deep is better understood as God's manifestation of his glory on earth. This implies that the *rûaḥ* in Genesis 1:2 is not a mighty storm or wind that somehow was contributing to the lifelessness of the earthly realm; rather, it was a symbol of God's creative presence in the earthly realm. This, as Middleton notes,

> would be consistent with the connection between God's creative word and breath according to Psalm 33:6: "By the word of YHWH the heavens were made/and all their hosts by the breath [*rûaḥ*] of his mouth." It is significant that the section of this psalm that deals with creation (33:6–9) recapitulates precisely the pattern of Gen 2 in moving from the heavens (days 1 and 4) to the waters (days 2 and 5) to the earth (days 3 and 6).[39]

Furthermore, there is correspondence between *rûaḥ* activity at creation and *rûaḥ* activity in the construction of the tabernacle. "Bezazel's Spirit-filled

---

35. See also Walton, *Lost World of Genesis*, 47–53.
36. Walton, *Genesis*, 91.
37. Levenson, *Creation and Persistence of Evil*, 127.
38. Gordon, "טוב" in *NIDOTTE* 2:353–57.
39. Middleton, *Liberating Image*, 86. See also Sarna, *Genesis*, 6, 9.

craftsmanship, which imitates God's primordial wise design and construction of the cosmos, is functionally equivalent to the imago Dei" (Exod 31:2–3; 35:30–31).[40] The differences between the theophanic manifestation in Genesis 1:2 and all other subsequent manifestations of the *rûaḥ* of God are two: First, the *rûaḥ* of God was at this point in creation active in a nonfunctional cosmos.[41] Second, prior to day two of creation, there was no barrier set up between the heavenly realm and the earthly realm. All theophanic manifestations subsequent to the second day of creation presume a separation between the heavenly realm and the earthly realm.

It may be concluded that the progression from the first day of creation to the sixth day of creation is from bad to good, from unproductive and uninhabited, or from nonfunctional to functional. There is also the sense, however, that the good coexists with the bad in creation.

Coexistence of the Good with the Bad

The earth in its initial state was dark and gloomy; it was at this point flooded and covered in darkness, and, probably to keep things under control, the *rûaḥ* of God was hovering over the waters (Gen 1:2). The other daily creation activities in the first and the subsequent days were also aimed at dismantling this duopoly of the darkness and the deep. The only thing that is pronounced "good" within the first two days of creation is the "light" created on the first day.

Coexistence of Darkness and Light. In Scripture, darkness has both positive and negative connotations. In the case of Genesis 1:2, darkness appears to have a negative connotation, though some regard darkness in this instance as having a positive connotation: Wyatt regards darkness as a figure for the invisibility, out of which God's word is uttered, initiating the creative process and the manifestation of his glory.[42] In its more immediate syntactic context, darkness stands in relation to the deep, and these two factors appear to contribute to the nonfunctionality of the earth.

---

40. Middleton, 87.

41. Walton, *Lost World of Genesis*, 85.

42. Wyatt, "Darkness of Genesis 1:2," 548. Wyatt cites the following Scripture passages in support of this positive connotation: Deut 4:11, 23; 2 Sam 22:12; Ps 18:2.

In Genesis 1:3–5, God begins with his creative activity. The first thing that God creates through his utterance is "light" (אוֹר). This light precedes the light that proceeds from the heavenly luminaries – the sun, the moon, and stars, which serve as signs to mark seasons, days, and years created on the fourth day (Gen 1:14–19). The formula of approval in Genesis 1:4a, וַיַּרְא אֱלֹהִים אֶת־הָאוֹר כִּי־טוֹב, is unlike the regular formula of approval in verses 10b, 12b, 18b, 21b, 25b, וַיַּרְא אֱלֹהִים כִּי־טוֹב. The formula in Genesis 1:4a is exceptional in that the object is included in the formula, thus making the light itself to receive the predicate טוֹב.[43] Of all the works of creation, this light is singled out as "good" (Gen 1:4). In its immediate context, the light is set in a dialogic relation of contrast with the darkness. This dialogic contrast between the darkness and the light may be understood in terms of the dialogic opposition of the terms bad and good, which is implied by the absence of an aesthetic judgment concerning the darkness. The darkness precedes light; it is not good, but the light is good. The light does not completely banish the darkness; rather, it pushes it back to its place – "night" (לַיְלָה) – and light takes its place as "day" (יוֹם). As Noord notes, "In the separation from the light and in the name-giving, Elohim demonstrates his power over darkness. Darkness is no longer boundless, but is given its place in the rhythm of time."[44] Walton argues, "The basis for time is the invariable alteration between periods of light and periods of darkness. This is a creative act, but it is creation in a functional sense, not a material sense."[45] Furthermore, Walton states, "If creation is understood in functional terms . . . Time is much more important than the sun – in fact, the sun is not a function, it only has functions. It is a mere functionary."[46]

The light of Genesis 1:3 is mysterious. This light does not proceed from the heavenly luminaries, sun, moon, and stars. From whence does it proceed? This question may seem unnecessary, as our passage does indicate that God through his divine speech brought the light into being – creation through the word. However, as Smith has recently argued, there are reasons to suspect as the ancient interpreters (Philo, *Creation* 31, 35, *4 Ezra* 6:40; *2 En.* 25:3; Aristobulus frg. 3) did, that the light of Genesis 1:3 was a special

---

43. Noord, "Creation of Light," 8.
44. Noord, 19.
45. Walton, *Lost World of Genesis*, 56.
46. Walton, 56.

light, a primordial divine light.[47] Among the reasons given by Smith, we note here only three.

First, considering the parallels between the creation of the cosmos and the erection of the tabernacle, the light of Genesis 1:3 may be equated with the *kābôd* ("glory") in Exodus 40. "In contrast to Exodus 40, where the divine *kābôd* goes into the tabernacle, in Genesis 1 it is the creation in days two through six that follows from divine *'ôr* of day one."[48] This is particularly so, if we take into consideration that the divine *kābôd* is sometimes described in categories of light (Exod 34:29; Ps 104:2; Ezek 1:26–28),[49] or as in some cases the *kābôd* stands in a parallelistic relationship with *'ôr* in which the one points to the other (Isa 58:8; 60:1, 19). It should also be added that in the tabernacle in which the divine *kābôd* dwelt, apparently light had to be kept burning continually or permanently (Exod 27:20; Lev 24:2–4).

Second, there is a close parallel between Genesis 1:3 and Psalm 104:1b–2: "You were clothed with splendor and majesty, wrapped in light as with a garment; you stretched out the heavens like a curtain." (Own translation). Von Rad regarded these two texts to be making two completely different claims; for him, the light in Genesis 1:3 is created, whereas the light in Psalm 104:1–2 is uncreated.[50] In contrast to von Rad's attempt to dissociate the light in Psalm 104:1b–2 and the light in Genesis 1:3, the two passages seem to have much commonality.[51] Both texts appear to envision the same creation order – the creation or an overflow of light prior to the creation of the heavens or the *rāqîaʿ*. In both texts, the light that precedes the creation of the heavens is a special light – in Genesis 1:3, God himself is the only source of the light and in Psalm 104:1b–2, the light is regarded as a theophanic element. As Smith argues, "Gen 1:3 elevates the cosmic divine light, experienced not as a theophany in conventional Priestly terms of *kābôd*, as in Exodus 39–40 and Ezekiel 43. Instead, this light follows in the wake of divine speech."[52]

---

47. Smith, 125–34.
48. Smith, 128.
49. Noort, "Creation of Light," 17.
50. In Von Rad's words, "In contrast to a few freer poetic declarations (Ps. 104.2), here [Gen 1:3] the creatureliness even of light is emphasized unmistakably. It is not somehow an overflow of the essence of deity but rather an object, even though preferential, of God's creation." Von Rad, *Genesis*, 49.
51. Smith, "Light in Genesis 1:3," 129.
52. Smith, 131.

Third, there is a correspondence between the light in Genesis 1:3 and the light emanating from the gods in *Enuma Elish* tablet 1, lines 101–104[53] and tablet IV, lines 57–58.[54] In *Enuma Elish*, the light that precedes creation is associated with the deity's own light.[55] As Smith argues, "the comparison of this presentation with biblical treatments of the theme should be taken seriously, especially given the use of **lbš* both in *Enuma Elish* I 103 and in Ps 104:2 (cf. BH **lbš* in Isa 59:17; 63:1; and Ps 93:1)."[56]

The evidence from *Enuma Elish* and other Old Testament texts may suggest that the author of Genesis 1 was well aware of the theme of uncreated divine light and adapted this primordial element to be assimilated in the creation process.[57] I am more inclined, however, to think of this light as an outflow of the heavenly light that enlightens God's heavenly dwelling. The fact that the tabernacle, the earthly replica of the heavenly reality, was somewhat regarded as a locus of permanent light suggests also that God's heavenly dwelling was regarded as a locus of permanent light.

The creation of light or the flow of light at the wake of divine speech in Genesis 1:3–4 is the first act of God that brings life to a lifeless earth. The creation of light brings about a progression in time that climaxes on the seventh day of creation. With the creation of light, creation began, not an aimless cyclical movement of days or night and day, but rather a cyclical movement toward its goal – the seventh day, that is, the day which may be described as the fullness of time, a holy and blessed day. As Levenson points out, "the priority of 'evening' over 'day' reminds us of that which is primordial and recalls again that chaos in the form of darkness has not been eliminated,

---

53. Translation below taken from Foster, "Epic of Creation (1.111)," in *COS* 1:392, Tablet I, lines 101–04:
    "The son Utu, the son Utu,
    The son, the sun, the sunlight of the gods!"
    He wore [*labiš*] (on his body) auras of ten gods,
    Had (them) wrapped on his head too,
    Fifty glories were heaped upon him.

54. See Foster, "Epic of Creation (1.111)," in *COS* 1.397, Tablet IV, lines 57–58:
    He was garbed in a ghastly armored garment,
    On his head he was covered with terrifying auras.

55. Smith, "Light in Genesis 1:3," 130.

56. Smith, 130–31.

57. Smith, 131.

but only confined to its place through the alternation."[58] In each of the six days of creation, creation is making its move toward the dawn of day not to return again to the night. Thus, there is progression from complete darkness to fullness of light. Or do we already have here a prophetic narrative – an encapsulation of the world history from beginning to end, world history moving toward its goal – a day in which there will be no darkness? In Isaiah 60:19-20 the picture of the *endzeit* reverses the order of *urzeit*: "No longer shall the sun serve as your light by day, nor for brightness shall the moon provide light for you; the LORD will serve you as an eternal light, your God, as your glory."[59] It should be noted, however, that the *endzeit* is not a return to primordial conditions wherein the light coexisted with the darkness; rather, it is a new era of eternal light proceeding from God himself.

The Deep Not Eliminated but Bounded. The תְהוֹם (*těhôm* – "deep") appears to be another contributing factor in the state of unproductiveness and uninhabitability of the earth. The nature of the *těhôm* has been a subject of great debate. Since Gunkel, the motif of the mythical battle between the creator god and the opposing powers of chaos – so-called *Chaoskampf* mythology – served for many as the basis for the exegesis of Genesis 1. This theory has recently come under heavy criticsm, and many argue for the abandonment of the term "chaos" with regard to Genesis and the rest of the Old Testament.[60] The theory that the *těhôm* in Genesis 1 posed a threat in God's work of creation and its alleged connection with the Akkadian *Tiamat* is unconvincing. I do not intend to rehearse here all the findings regarding the impossibilities of such connections. What is important for us to note that in Genesis 1 the great deep posed no challenge at all to the creator God, nor is it personified at all. The absence of the battle theme or the conflict theme points to the lack of the personification of the *těhôm*.[61] As Watson points out,

---

58. Levenson, *Creation and Persistence of Evil*, 123.

59. Smith, "Light in Genesis 1:3," 129.

60. See Tsumura, *Creation and Destruction*; Watson, *Chaos Uncreated*.

61. See Smith, *Memoirs of God*, 97; Day, *God's Conflict*, 50; Cassuto, *Commentary on Genesis*, 1:24, 31–33; Steck, *Der Schöpfunsbericht*, 231–32; Wyatt, *Myths of Power*, 200; Niditch, *Chaos to Cosmos*, 20. For a comprehensive list of reasons why the *těhôm* should not be identified with mythological conflicts, see Tsumura, *Earth and Waters*, 62–65; *Creation and Destruction*, 75.

here [Gen 1] is a highly monotheistic creation account in which there is no trace of combat, no personification of waters, yet at the same time it understandably reflects a common ancient cosmological structure in which there was water and darkness at the beginning of the world, the waters being separated from the waters for the dry land to appear.[62]

The negative nature of the *tĕhôm* is not a result of its connection with mythological conflicts, but rather its contribution to the lifelessness of the earth. On the second day of creation, God deals with the *tĕhôm*. God separates the waters by setting a separator or *rāqîaʿ* in the midst of the waters to separate the waters above from those below it. As already observed, the situation of day two was still bad, the earth was still flooded, and the land remained invisible and unproductive. It is only on the third day that something good finally happens: the waters below the divider, which are the waters on earth, are pushed back to their place to form the sea, and dry land starts to appear, thereby resulting in the potential of the earth to start being productive.

The deep itself, in its initial stage, had no life within it. It was only on the fifth day that the waters of the deep started to teem with life under the command of God. However, the deadly nature of the great deep is never forgotten. The destructive nature of the *tĕhôm* is apparent in Genesis 7:11 when all the springs of the "great deep" (תְּהוֹם רַבָּה) burst forth when God threatens the reversal of creation by annihilating the distinctions made in Genesis 1.[63] In the Old Testament, God is constantly presented as holding back the *tĕhôm* in its place, lest the waters of the deep transgress their boundaries (Job 38:8–11; Pss 33:7; 104:9; Prov 8:29; Jer 5:22). These Scriptures should be understood as God's way of keeping his promise: "Never again shall all flesh be cut off by the waters of the flood; never again will there be a flood to destroy the earth" (Gen 9:11, ESV).

---

62. Watson, *Chaos Uncreated*, 271.

63. See also Gen 8:2; Exod 8; Pss 36:7; 71:20; 106:9; 107:26; Isa 51:10; 63:16; Ezek 26:19; Amos 7:4; Jonah 2:6. However, the word *tĕhôm* does not always have such sinister nuances. There are other instances where it carries the positive nuance of blessing (Gen 49:25; Deut 8:7; 33:15; Ps 78:15; Ezek 31:4), even when used in parallel with the sea (Job 28:14; 38:16, 30; Pss 33:7; 104:6; Hab 3:10). For the threat of the reversal of creation, see Clines, "Theology of Flood Narrative," 128–42; "Themes in Genesis 1–11," 499–502.

In Genesis 1:2, darkness should be taken as working together with the *tĕhôm* to generate a state of lifelessness on earth. This is not to suggest that darkness and the *tĕhôm* served as opposing forces that God had to wrestle with as he engaged in his creation activities. The darkness and *tĕhôm* were under God's mastery, and he utilized them as he willed in the creation process. However, these elements characterized the primordial state of the earth; they were not completely annihilated, but were simply pushed back. Thus, creation even in its original state is characterized by both the good and the bad.

Second Day – A Separator between Heaven and Earth

One of the most notable things in the progression of this creation narrative is that the second day is not pronounced "good." Why is the second day not pronounced good? Or more specifically, why is the *rāqia'* not pronounced good?[64] It should be noted, however, that the Septuagint (LXX) adds aesthetic formula "and God saw that it was good." The LXX addition, however, does not find support from any other ancient text. The Greek translator probably added the refrain "for the sake of mechanical uniformity";[65] hence, the Masoretic Text is to be preferred over the LXX.

The narrator's silence with regard to the second day of creation is probably another signal of our dialogic idea. The absence of the refrain breaks the uniformity of the second day with the other creation days. Many suggest that the reason for the omission of the refrain is that the work of second day was left incomplete only to be completed on the third day, resulting in the double expression of the refrain on the third day. However, it is not just a matter of an unfinished business that the second day is not pronounced good. As we have already noted, the earth was at this point still flooded and therefore still unproductive and uninhabitable. Sailhamer argues that the second day is not pronounced good because nothing beneficial for humanity was created on that day: "When and only when the land was ready for man could God call it good."[66] While it is true that the earth was not yet habitable, it is not true that nothing beneficial for humanity was created on this day. The second day

---

64. For more detailed study on why the *rāqia'* is not pronounced good, see Ramantswana, "Day Two of Creation," 101–23.

65. Cassuto, *Commentary on Genesis*, 1:34.

66. Sailhamer, "Genesis," 2:26; *Genesis Unbound*, 118–19.

brings about the possibility of rain, which will be beneficial for humanity. Sarna rightly suggests that this day is not pronounced good because rain would have had no value on a flooded earth.[67] Rain, as Genesis 2:4b–5 suggests, is the necessary condition for a productive and inhabited earth.

I do think, however, that there is another potential reason why the second day is not pronounced good. The setting of *rāqîaʿ* appears to be a major factor. This is not to suggest that *rāqîaʿ* only has negative connotation; as already observed, its establishment brings about the possibility of rain. The negative impact of the *rāqîaʿ* has to do with its function as a separator, by default a separator between the heavenly realm and the earthly realm.

Genesis, like other ancient Near East texts, conceived the world as a flat disc with the ocean surrounding the land; all of this was covered by the sky (firmament), a rock-solid dome over the earth supporting the heavenly ocean.[68] There are similarities and differences between Genesis and *Enuma Elish* in this regard: First, the creation of the firmament follows the creation of light. Second, they both mention the separation of the waters into two parts by the sky or firmament. See *Enuma Elis*h Table IV, lines 137–39:

> He split her into two, like a fish for drying, [cf. Gen 1:6]
> Half of her he set up and made as a cover, heaven [cf. Gen 1:8, 14]
> He stretched out the hide and assigned watchmen,
> And ordered them not to let her waters escape [cf. Gen 1:7].[69]

In *Enuma Elish*, Marduk slew Tiamat, split her into two halves, and used half of her to make the firmament that keeps the waters above from escaping. In Genesis, however, the separation did not result from a conflict among the gods, nor was God using the corpse of a slain god to spread out the firmament; rather, God was simply creating through his word and ordering his

---

67. Sarna, *Genesis*, 8.

68. Walton states, "We have no reason to suppose that the Israelites thought about the composition of the sky any differently than those around them. We know from Exodus 24:10 that they shared the idea of a pavement in God's abode – and it is even of sapphire, as in the Mesopotamian text." Walton, *Ancient Near Eastern Thought*, 169. Elsewhere, the Old Testament speaks of the "four corners of the earth" (Isa 11:12; Ezek 7:12) and the "ends of the earth" (Deut 13:8; 28:64; Ps 135:7; Isa 5:26), which fall within this dome.

69. Translation taken from Foster, "Epic of Creation," (*Enuma Elish*), in *COS*, 1.111:398.

creation in accordance to his will. The material used for the firmament is also not specified.

In Genesis 1:6–8, *rāqîaʿ* carries the notion of something hard or solid, and in this context it functions as a rock-solid dome separating the waters above from the waters below. The idea of a solid firmament is also found in Genesis 7:11–12, which speaks of the "windows of heaven opened" in the time of Noah. Job 37:18 speaks of God spreading out the skies, which are "hard as a mirror of cast bronze." Isaiah 40:22 states, "He [God] sits enthroned above the circle of the earth, and its people are like grasshoppers. He stretches out the heavens like a canopy, and spreads them out like a tent to live in." The waters above the firmament were conceived not as clouds, or atmosphere, or vapor, but rather as an ocean. The flood waters above are referred to as the *mabbûl* in Genesis 9:11, and in Psalm 29:10 Yahweh sits enthroned over the *mabbûl*.[70]

The similar patterns of separation discernable elsewhere in the Old Testament are possible reapplications of this creation motif in Israel's self-understanding. This is particularly so, when the Old Testament correspondences between the cosmos and Israel's sanctuaries, the tabernacle and later the temple, are taken into consideration.[71] As Levenson points out, "the Temple and the world were considered congeneric," meaning that the creation of the cosmos parallels the creation of the tabernacle and later the temple, as evidenced by the manifold correspondences between the creation account (Gen 1:1—2:4a) and the tabernacle construction (Exod 25–40) and the temple (1 Kings 6:38b; 8:1–66).[72] As Kline argues, "in harmony with the identification of heaven and earth as a macrocosmic temple, the earthly tabernacle and temple appear in redemptive re-creation symbolism . . . to be a microcosmic

---

70. Walton, *Ancient Near Eastern Thought*, 170.

71. The correspondence between the cosmos and the temple or earlier tabernacle is presented clearly in Yahweh's own words in Isaiah 66:1: "Heaven is my throne, and the earth is my footstool. Where is the house you will build for me? Where will my resting place be? Has not my hand made all these things, and so they came into being." In this text, as Walton notes, "we can see the elements of a cosmos-sized temple, a connection between temple and rest, and a connection between creation and temple. This in itself is sufficient to see that the cosmos can be viewed as a temple." Walton, *Lost World of Genesis*, 83–84.

72. Levenson, "Temple and the World," 286–91; see also Levenson, *Creation and Persistence of Evil*, 86–88. See also Weinfeld, "Sabbath, Temple, and Enthronement," 501–12; Blenkinsopp, *Prophecy and Canon*, 56–69. For the most recent work, see Walton, *Lost World of Genesis*, 78–86.

representation of heaven and earth."[73] Thus, the Mosaic tabernacle and the later temple were not just replicas or a תַּבְנִית ("pattern," Exod 25:9, 40; 1 Chr 28:19) of the invisible heavenly reality, they are also better understood as "microcosmic representation[s] of heaven and earth."[74]

I am here particularly interested in the correspondence between the *rāqiaʿ* and the פָּרֹכֶת, the inner tabernacle or temple veil. Of all the tabernacle veils, the פָּרֹכֶת is the only veil whose function is clearly explained in Exod 26:33c:

וְהִבְדִּילָה הַפָּרֹכֶת לָכֶם בֵּין הַקֹּדֶשׁ וּבֵין קֹדֶשׁ הַקֳּדָשִׁים

"the veil shall separate for you the holy place and the most holy place."

As Seely points out, the meaning of the word *separate* [בָּדַל] in Genesis 1:6–7 "is illustrated in Exodus 26:33 where the task of the veil [פָּרֹכֶת] in the Tabernacle is to separate the Holy Place from the Holiest Place."[75] The פָּרֹכֶת functioned as a barrier to heaven – the throne room of Yahweh or Yahweh's dwelling. This idea is particularly evidenced by the fact that inside the holy of holies was the golden כַּפֹּרֶת, "atonement cover," that is, a footstool that supported Yahweh's throne, that is, the two cherubs upon which Yahweh sits enthroned (1 Sam 4:4; 2 Sam 6:2; 2 Kgs 19:15; 1 Chr 13:6; Pss 80:1; 99:1; Isa 37:16). The holy of holies was a replica of the heavenly reality, so to speak, the heavenly throne room (Ps 103:19; 2 Chr 20:6; Isa 14:13–14; 66:1) or Yahweh's dwelling (Pss 2:4; 14:2; 53:2; 80:14; Eccl 5:2; Lam 3:1; Dan 2:28). In the postexilic period, God is often referred to as the "God of heaven" (2 Chr 36:23; Ezra 1:2; 5:11–12; 6:9–10; 7:12, 21, 23; Neh 1:4–5; 2:4, 20; Ps 136:26; Dan 2:18–19, 37, 44; 5:23). This congruence is clearly captured in Psalm 11:4ab, "The LORD is in his holy temple; the LORD's throne is in heaven" (ESV, cf. Isa 6).

The tabernacle and later the temple mediated God's presence in the earthly realm. The tabernacle and later the temple, however, did not overcome the dualism established at creation – heaven as God's dwelling and the earth as humankind's dwelling. Even with these majestic symbols, Israel continued to lift its eyes, voice, and hands into the heavens in praise, imploring God

---

73. Kline, "Creation in Image," 258.
74. Kline, 258.
75. Seely, "Firmament and Water Above," Part II, 40; Seely, "Firmament and Water Above," Part I, 227–40.

to look down or come down to help. In Isaiah 64:1 [MT 63:19], the prophet calls upon God, saying, "Oh, that you may tear open (קָרַע) the heavens and come down" (NRSV). Thus, we may conclude that the firmament stood as a separator between heaven and earth.

The *rāqîaʿ* is both good and bad for humankind. It is good because it opens the possibility of the showers of blessings, that is, rain; however, it is bad because it separates the heavenly realm, the dwelling of God, from the earthly realm, the dwelling of humankind.

Conclusion

God was willing to evaluate his creation as very good despite the inherent bad that already accompanied the good in his creation and despite the inbuilt potentialities for either good or bad. The created order contained the elements that God did not pronounce good: the sea, the darkness, and the firmament.

It may be concluded so far that creation at the end of the sixth day was indeed very good compared to its initial state in day one of creation. In its initial state, creation was unproductive and uninhabited because it was completely flooded and completely covered in darkness; thus, it was nonfunctional. At the end of the sixth day, creation was productive and inhabited because the *tĕhôm* and the darkness that made the earthly realm lifeless had been bounded, thereby making way for life to flourish in the earthly realm; thus, it was functional. However, the *tĕhôm*, the darkness, and the *rāqîaʿ* are good in so far as they are a necessary part of God's creation, but because they do not receive God's approval, they are not good.[76] The *tĕhôm* and the darkness are bad because the earth subsumed under them was lifeless, or nonexistent, or nonfunctional. The *rāqîaʿ* was bad because it separated the heavenly realm, God's dwelling, from the earthly realm, humankind's dwelling, thereby bringing about the dualism of creation. However, Genesis 1:1–2:4a is not the narrator's last word.

---

76. I am indebted here to Westermann, *Genesis 1–11*, 113.

CHAPTER 3

Genesis 1:1–2:4a in Dialogue with Genesis 2:4b–25: Paradisiacal Situation Not All That Good

Introduction

The second creation story (Gen 2:4b–3:24) is a retelling of the first creation. There is a sense in which the narrative progression in Genesis 1:1–3:24 is not progressive but dialogic, as Genesis 2:4b–3:24 retells how the universe came into being. In a sense, Genesis 2:4b–3:24 looks over the shoulder of Genesis 1:1–2:4a and offers an alternative perspective on creation. The second creation story, and in a limited sense, the pre-fall creation narrative (Gen 2:4b–3:5), seems to undermine the assertion that "God saw all that he made and behold it was very good." But does it?

In historical critical scholarship, as already noted, Genesis 1:4b–3:24 is considered to be composed of two creation narratives, which were penned down by different authors: Genesis 1:1–2:4a, the first creation narrative, is commonly regarded as part of P (the Priestly source), and Genesis 2:4–3:24, the second creation narrative, is commonly regarded as part of J (the Yahwistic source) or non-P (non-Priestly source). Concerning Genesis 2:4b–3:24, it is considered to be a combination of two independent traditions – the creation tradition, which is contained within Genesis 2:4b–25, and the paradise tradition, which extends from Genesis 2 to Genesis 3.[1] For Von Rad, the Genesis 2:4b–3:24 narrative has two independent traditions with one contained within Genesis 2:4b–25 and the other contained within Genesis 3:1–24 as distinct narratives "thematically" and "materially."[2] For Westermann, the Genesis 2:4b–3:24 narrative is a fusion of two traditions, the creation of humanity narrative, which is contained within Genesis 2:4b–25, and the narrative of crime and punishment. Similarly, Carr argues that the narrative in Genesis 3 is a redactional activity of the creation narrative contained in Genesis 2.[3] In this study, Genesis 2:4b–3:24 as a whole is considered a creation narrative. I concur with Carr's view that Genesis 2:4b–3:24 serves well as an elaboration and specification of Genesis 1:1–2:4a.[4]

Therefore, there are three key issues that informs my reading in this study: First, the second creation narrative, Genesis 2:4b–3:24, is for the most part a resumption of the Genesis 1:24–31 narrative, the sixth day of creation. Second, considering the final form of the text, the two creation naratives, Genesis 1:1–2:4a and Genesis 2:4b–3:24, stand in a dialogic relationship with each other – a dialogue that remains unfinalized and full of potential intentionality. Third, while Genesis 2:4b–3:24 as whole is a creation narrative, however, Genesis 2:25 functions as "a transition verse" or a "bridge verse" not from creation to post-creation events; rather, as a description of a transition within the creation process from a state of humankind in a state of "innocence" or prior to fall of humanity; therefore, the so-called "fall of humanity" or "the crime and punishment" narrative falls within the scope of creation.[5] The treatment of Genesis 2:4b–25 and Genesis 3:1–24 independently of each

---

1. For Budde, the Genesis 2:4b–3:24 story contains the following doublets: creation in complete dryness (Gen 2:5) and with rivers (Gen 2:10–14); the presence of two trees (the tree of life and the tree of the knowledge of good and bad, Gen 2:9, 16; 3:3, 24); the placing of humanity in the garden twice (Gen 2:8 and 2:15); the expulsion from paradise (Gen 3:23–24). Budde, *Die biblische Urgeschichte*. Gunkel also argued that Genesis 2:4b–3:24 contains "two bodies of material originally [that] had nothing to do with each other as a prelude or continuation. The two accounts were joined with each other because they both deal with the primeval period. A thorough division of sources and establishment is no longer possible, although a general separation of the bodies of material is. The paradise account surely included vv. 9, 15–17, 25; the creation account . . . vv. 7, 18–24." Gunkel, *Genesis*, 27.

2. Von Rad, *Genesis*, 85.
3. Carr, "Politics of Textual Subversion," 577–95.
4. Carr, *Reading Fractures of Genesis*, 63, 68.
5. See Ramantswana, "Humanity Not Pronounced Good," 804–18.

other is intended to accentuate the dialogic relationship between Genesis 1:1–2:4a and Genesis 2:4b–3:24. In this chapter, the focus is on the dialogic relationship between Genesis 1:1–2:4a and Genesis 2:4b–25, while in the next chapter, the focus is on the dialogic relationship between Genesis 1:1–2:4a and Genesis 3:1–24.

Below, we begin by examining the dialogic relationship between the two creation narratives, Genesis 1:1–2:4a and Genesis 2:4b–24, considering narrative styles of the two narratives. Then we proceed to examine the following dialogic points that seem to undermine the claim that all creation is as good as Genesis 1:1–2:4a seems to suggest. For the narrator, the first creation in its state of goodness or its paradisiacal situation is not all that good. We note in particular the following elements that raise suspicion that the pre-fall conditions are not ideal: (a) that the divine presence in the garden of Eden was a limited presence, (b) that Adam, though an image of God – was made from dust of the ground, (c) the presence of the tree of knowledge of good and bad in the garden of Eden, and (d) for a human being to be alone was "not good."

Dialogic Relationship Between Two Creation Narratives

Genesis 1:1–2:4a is dominated by positivity. Polak describes this narrative as "hymnic poetry" the purpose of which "is to praise and celebrate the mighty deeds of God."[6] Particularly noted is the repetitious refrain "and God saw that it was good" (וַיַּרְא אֱלֹהִים כִּי־טוֹב) in verses 10, 12, 18, 21, 25, which opens in verse 4 with "and God saw the light that it was good" (וַיַּרְא אֱלֹהִים אֶת־הָאוֹר כִּי־טוֹב), and closes in verse 31 with this praise: "and God saw everything that he made and it was very good" (וַיַּרְא אֱלֹהִים אֶת־כָּל־אֲשֶׁר עָשָׂה וְהִנֵּה־טוֹב מְאֹד). Westermann particularly notes that there is no tension built up in the progression of the narrative; rather, it is characterized by "its onward, irresistible and majestic flow that distinguishes it so clearly from the drama narrated in Genesis 2–3."[7] Miscall states regarding this narrative, "everything

---

6. Polak, "Poetic Style and Parallelism," 5. Others have also noted this narrative poetic pattern: Albright, "Refrain 'And God Saw,'" 22–26; Kselman, "Recovery of Poetic Fragments," 161–73; Loretz, "Wortbericht-Vorlage," 279–87; Anderson, "What Biblical Scholars Might," 52–74.

7. Westermann, *Genesis 1–11*, 80.

is positive. There is not a no, a not, a never, or such in the story. All is good and complete, and the completion is marked with repetition in the report of the seventh day."[8]

The Gen 2:4b–25 narrative begins with a series of circumstantial clauses that recapitulate creation activities and climaxes with the creation of humanity (Gen 2:4b–7). The creation activity is presented in these verses as an undoing of a series of negatives:

> When the LORD God made the earth and the heavens – and *no* shrub of the field had *yet* appeared on the earth and *no* plant of the field had *yet* sprung up, for the LORD God had *not yet* sent rain on the earth and there was *no* man to work the ground, but streams came up from the earth and watered the whole surface of the ground – the LORD God formed the man from the dust of the ground and breathed into his nostrils the breath of life, and the man became a living being. (Gen 2:4b–7)[9]

In contrast to this synopsis of the creation process in Genesis 2:4b–7, there is not a single negative in Genesis 1:1–2:4a. The four negatives in Genesis 2:4b–7 specifically pertain to an unproductive earth – no plants and no rain, and the absence of a caretaker – no human being. Creation is presented here as a series of problems to be solved. The problems are solved with a sense of immediacy by the watering of the land and the forming of a caretaker. Without much being said, the narrator gives us a tour of that very first day of humanity, the first day of the human being's first week, the sixth day of God's creation activity.

Humanity is created and placed in the garden of Eden (or "the garden of delight," or as some suggest, "the garden of abundance")[10] specifically prepared for him to work and take care of. The Edenic situation is presented as

---

8. Miscall, "Jacques Derrida," 3.

9. MT:
בְּיוֹם עֲשׂוֹת יְהוָה אֱלֹהִים אֶרֶץ וְשָׁמָיִם׃
וְכֹל ׀ שִׂיחַ הַשָּׂדֶה טֶרֶם יִהְיֶה בָאָרֶץ וְכָל־עֵשֶׂב הַשָּׂדֶה טֶרֶם יִצְמָח כִּי לֹא
הִמְטִיר יְהוָה אֱלֹהִים עַל־הָאָרֶץ וְאָדָם אַיִן לַעֲבֹד אֶת־הָאֲדָמָה׃
וְאֵד יַעֲלֶה מִן־הָאָרֶץ וְהִשְׁקָה אֶת־כָּל־פְּנֵי־הָאֲדָמָה׃
וַיִּיצֶר יְהוָה אֱלֹהִים אֶת־הָאָדָם עָפָר מִן־הָאֲדָמָה וַיִּפַּח בְּאַפָּיו נִשְׁמַת חַיִּים
וַיְהִי הָאָדָם לְנֶפֶשׁ חַיָּה׃

10. Tsumura, *Earth and Waters*, 123–37; Millard, "Etymology of Eden," 103–6.

a paradisiacal one; it was indeed a garden of delight – a garden at the center of the world, well watered, full of exotic trees, abundant with food, full of minerals, and harmonious relationships – between humanity and God, between humanity and animals, between man and woman, between humanity and land (cf. Ps 36:9-10; Ezek 28:13; 31:8-9, 16). The Septuagint refers to this primal situation as παράδεισον (paradise), a Greek transliteration of a Median loanword used in Hellenistic times to refer to the luxurious royal parks with many trees and suitable for walks.[11] The idea of royal gardens, however, is not exclusively Hellenistic; it goes back to earlier times. Some of the ancient Near Eastern kings boasted about their exotic gardens, among them Tiglath-pileser I (1114-1076 B.C.), Ashurnasirpal II (883-859 B.C.), Sennacherib (706-681 B.C.), Sargon II (721-705 B.C.), Merodach-Baladan II (721-710 B.C.).[12] The garden of Eden might just as well be described as a royal park specifically created for the earthly ruler, humankind, who is created as the radiance of God's glory – created in "the *image* of God in accordance to the *likeness* of God" (Gen 1:27-28).[13]

In the Old Testament, the garden of Eden has other associations as well. It is elsewhere also referred to as "the Garden of the LORD" or "the Garden of God" (Isa 51:3; Ezek 28:13; 31:8-9, 16). This description also suits well the

---

11. Bremmer, "Paradise," 18-19. As Bremmer argues, "behind the *paradeisos* of the heavenly king in the Septuagint version of Genesis, there loom the cultivated *paradeisoi* of the all too earthly rulers of contemporary Egypt." Bremmer, "Paradise," 19. In Ecclesiastes 2:4-5 (LXX) the same word is used by the speaker, who identifies himself as the "son of David, king in Jerusalem": "I undertook great works: I built myself houses and planted vineyards; I made myself gardens and parks [παράδεισους] and planted all kinds of fruit-trees in them; I made myself pools of water to irrigate a grove of growing trees." The term παράδεισος, however, is also used in the LXX in a general sense to refer to any garden (Isa 1:30; Jer 29:5).

12. As Gleason points out: "Kings boast of large parts of cities devoted to these parks, of great irrigation works that feed them, and of the distant lands from which the plants and animals are gathered. Tilgath-pileser I (1114-1076 BCE) created a combined zoological part and arboretum of exotic animals and trees. Ashurnsirpal II (883-859 BCE) created a garden or park at Nimrud (Kalhu) by diverting water from the Upper Zab River through a rock-cut channel for his impressive collection of foreign plants and animals. Sennacherib (704-681 BCE) makes a similar claim for Nineveh. Parks are beautifully represented on the reliefs from Sargon II's (721-705 BCE) palace at Khorsabad, in which a variety of trees and a small pavilion with proto-Doric columns are depicted. Other reliefs depict lion hunts and falconry in the parks. A clay tablet from Babylon names and locates vegetables and herbs in the garden of Merodach-Baladan II (721-710 BCE). In the palace reliefs of Ashurbanipal, the garden symbolizes the abundance and pleasures of peace after bravery in battle." Gleason, "Gardens in Preclassical Times," 383.

13. Bremmer, "Paradise," 19.

description of this garden in Genesis 2. It is the Lord, God, who has the ultimate authority over the garden – he created it and gave instructions regarding its keeping and use. In Ezekiel 28, the garden of Eden motif also has close association with the "holy mountain of God" motif that is very common in the ancient Near East. In Israel's traditions, the mountain of God is Mt. Sinai or Horeb (Exod 3:1; 18:5; 24:13) and later on Zion in Jerusalem (Ps 48:3) – the sacred space on which God made his dwelling.[14] The idea of the garden of Eden as the mountain of God may perhaps be derived from an idea that already exists in germinal form in Genesis 2:10–14. As Mettinger points out, "the idea of an elevated position for the garden is reflected in the notion of four rivers streaming forth from Eden in Genesis 2:10–14."[15] The Jerusalem temple is also envisioned as the fountain of life from which the waters flow for the benefit of humanity (Ps 36:8–9; Ezek 47:1–6, 12; cf. Joel 4:18; Zech 14:8). In Psalm 46:5, various motifs are intertwined – the mountain of God, the dwelling of God, and the primeval waters: "There is a river whose streams make glad the city of God, the holy place where the Most High dwells" (NIV). The garden, as Wyatt points out, is where different worlds meet; heaven and earth come together.[16] The garden of Eden was a place of intimate communion for the heavenly king and the earthly king. It is the sacred place where God spoke with human beings and walked to and fro. Presented as such, the initial situation of humans prior to the fall was indeed "good." However, the paradisiacal situation is also presented as a fragile one.

---

14. The mountain motif played an important role in the broader religious context of the ancient Near East. The gods held their divine assemblies on the mountains. The Ugar texts often refer to the mountains as the home of the gods. El and Baal, for example, were thought to live on individual mountains, and even Mot, the god of death, was associated with a subterranean mountain. Baal's home was on Mount Zaphon. The great gods of Mesopotamia like Enlil and Ashur could be addressed as "great mountain." The attachment of the ancient world to holy mountains could be explained by the expectation of the ancient peoples for the gods to continue to reveal their presence in certain localities where a theophany occurred in the past. Therefore, many peoples identified certain localities as dwelling places of the gods and erected altars there. For detailed discussions, see Lundquist, "Common Temple Ideology,", 59–60; Clifford, "Temple and Holy Mountain," 107–24.

15. Mettinger, *Eden Narrative*, 88.

16. Wyatt, *Myths of Power*, 70.

Paradiasical Situation Not All That Good

In the traditional reading of the Genesis 1–3 story, Genesis 1:1–2:25 is considered to be a presentation of God's "good" creation prior to the distortion or the fall of humanity. As Spykman notes, this methodologically implies "adopting a canonical order of Scripture, beginning with the Genesis narrative, which itself begins with creation."[17] However, as already noted, Genesis 3 should also be viewed as forming part of the creation process and not as narrating events subsequent to the completed creation process.

The paradiasical situation as projected in Genesis 2:4b–25 that will be highlighted below did not preclude the presence of the not good.

Limited Divine Presence in the Garden of Eden

There are several elements that further testify to the idea that the garden of Eden was a sphere of divine presence. We noted above that the garden of Eden was also regarded in the Old Testament as the garden of God. Furthermore, I have already alluded to some parallels between Eden and tabernacle and later the temple. Wenham writes,

> The Garden of Eden is not viewed by the author of Genesis simply as a piece of Mesopotamian farmland, but as an archetypal sanctuary, that is a place where God dwells and where man should worship him. Many of the features of the garden may also be found in later sanctuaries, particularly the tabernacle or Jerusalem. The parallels suggest that the garden itself is understood as a sort of sanctuary.[18]

The parallels between the garden of Eden and the Israelite tabernacle and temple later include among others the following: the iconography of flowers, trees, and cherubim in the later Israelite sanctuaries (Exod 25:18–22; 37:8; 1 Kgs 6:18, 24–26, 29, 32, 35; 7:18; 2 Chr 3:11–12); the eastward placement of the entrances to Eden and later Israelite sanctuaries from the east (Gen 3:24; Exod 25:18–22; 26:31; 36:35; I Kgs 6:23–39; 2 Chr 3:14); the tree of life probably symbolized by the lampstand in the holy place (Gen 2:9; 3:22; Exod 25:31–35); the provision of food in Eden symbolized by the "Bread of

---

17. Spykman, *Reformational Theology*, 144.
18. Wenham, "Sanctuary Symbolism," 19.

Presence" (Exod 25:30); and precious stones such as gold and onyx found in the garden of Eden (Gen 2:11–12; cf. Ezek 28:13) used in the decoration of Israel's sanctuaries (Exod 25:3; 26:6, 29, 32, 37; 28:5–36; 30:3, 5; 31:4; 32:2–4, 24, 31; 36:13, 34–38; 37:2–28; 39:2–25; Lev 24:4, 6; Num 7:86; 1 Kgs 6:21–35; 7:49–51; 1 Chr 29:2), and for the priestly rings and garments (Exod 25:7, 11, 17, 31; 28:20–27; 39:13–20).[19] For these reasons the garden of Eden may be regarded as the first earthly temple, standing as an archetype to subsequent Israelite sanctuaries.

Furthermore, as Beale argues, the garden of Eden may also be regarded as the holy of holies, the dwelling of God, with the outer regions of garden – the rest of creation, the land and the seas – as the Holy Place.[20] In the garden of Eden, humanity had the most intimate communion with God; this was the place where they walked and talked with God (Gen 3:8; cf. Lev 26:12; Deut 23:15; 2 Sam 7:6–7). In addition, the presence of the cherubim in the garden of Eden (Gen 3:24), which in Israel's sanctuaries symbolized God's throne in the holy of holies (Exod 25:20–22; 1 Kgs 6:27; cf. 1 Sam 4:4; 2 Sam 6:2; Pss 80:1; 99:1; Isa 37:16), also suggests that Eden be identified with the holy of holies. It should be noted, however, that the cherubim only took over the function as guards of the garden of Eden subsequent to humankind's failure to protect it, now guarding it against humankind's reentry (Gen 3:24). This primordial failure of humankind is, in turn, reflected in Israel's sanctuaries, however, with hope like a mustard seed. As Richter notes,

> the distinction between Eden and the Holy of Holies is that whereas 'Ādām was driven out with no hope of reentry, the Holy of Holies is designed to function as God's outpost in 'Ādām's world. Here, although guarded by his cherubim and set apart by means of the mediation of sacrifice and priestly staff, God once again dwells among his people.[21]

---

19. For a detailed discussion on the parallels between the Garden of Eden and Israel's tabernacle and later temple, see Wenham, "Sanctuary Symbolism," 19–25; Beale, *Temple and Church's Mission*, 66–80; Beale, "Final Vision of Apocalypse," 197–99; Beale, "Eden, Temple," 7–10; Stordalen, *Echoes of Eden*, 307–12; 457–59; Walton, *Lost World of Genesis*, 78–85; Meyers, *Tabernacle Menorah*, 162–72.

20. Beale, "Eden, Temple," 10–11; Beale, *Temple and Church's Mission*, 75. It should be noted, however, that the first explicit identification of Eden with the holy of holies comes from a Second Temple text, *Jub.* 3:12 and 8:19.

21. Richter, *Epic of Eden*, 124.

It was hope like a mustard seed because only the high priest could enter into the holy of holies and that also only once in a year on the Day of Atonement.

If the identification of the garden of Eden with Israel's sanctuaries and in particular the holy of holies is plausible, then God's presence in the garden of Eden is the first introduction of a dualistic notion of divine presence or divine dwelling. On the one hand, God created the heavens and earth as a macrocosmic temple with heaven as his dwelling place, and on the other hand, the microcosmic temple, the garden-temple, his miniature dwelling place, is not an end in and of itself; rather, it points to the heavenly dwelling that is veiled from human visibility by the heavenly curtain, the *rāqîaʿ*. Divine presence in the microcosmic temple may be described as a relative presence or a relative indwelling. It may be that the first human couple had unmediated communion and interaction with Yahweh in the sacred space; however, Yahweh's true dwelling was still heaven. The garden of Eden mediated God's presence in the earthly realm.

Furthermore, Yahweh's presence did not fill the entire earth; rather, it was limited to a secluded spot, the garden of Eden. Humankind was not supposed to remain "in the garden in a static situation"; rather, in accordance to the creation mandate humankind had to multiply, fill the earth, and subdue and rule the earth.[22] This, as Beale argues, implied that "he [humankind] was to extend the geographical boundaries [of] . . . the Garden of Eden until Eden extended throughout and covered the whole earth."[23] The extension of the boundaries of Eden would have implied a transformation of the entire earthly realm into a sphere of God's presence. However, as we will observe subsequently, this transformative goal of creation failed.

Thus, it may be concluded that creation even prior to the fall of humanity inasmuchas it was good, it was not ideal. God's presence was manifested in the earthly realm, though in a limited sense. The garden of Eden functioned as a type of the heavenly reality, and, in turn, the garden of Eden was a type of what the whole earthly realm was supposed to become, a sphere of God's presence, a garden of God. We may even speak of gradation in terms of holiness and beauty. The garden of Eden is a luxurious royal park for Yahweh, the cosmic king, and his earthly representative whereas the outer space, the

---

22. Walton, *Genesis*, 186.
23. Beale, "Eden, Temple," 10–11.

rest of the land and seas of the earth, is not. From the outside proceeding inwards, the outer space is good in that it is God's creation; however, non-ideal for God's dwelling. The garden of Eden is a sacred space separate from the outer space; it is Yahweh's dwelling where human beings perform their royal priestly functions by cultivating and guarding the garden.[24] It should be noted, however, that the garden of Eden as we will observe in the points below, still required to be rectified on several fronts.

Adam, Image of God – Dust from the Ground

The second creation narrative, as already noted, begins with a series of negatives climaxing with the mention of the absence of humankind (Gen 2:4b–5).[25] The creation of humankind is presented as the solution to the problem of creation: "There was no human being to till the ground" (Gen 2:5). Its solution is presented in the mandate of verse 15: "to cultivate it and to keep it" (לְעָבְדָהּ וּלְשָׁמְרָהּ). These two verbs in Genesis 2:15 may also be translated "serve and guard," and they occur elsewhere with reference to priests who "serve" God in the temple and "guard" the temple from having unclean things enter it (Num 3:7–8; 8:25–26; 1 Chr 23:32; Ezek 44:14).[26] Thus, the creation of humankind is good, because it solves the problem of creation: creation needs to be taken care of, and humankind is the creature for the job. In some sense there is agreement between the first creation narrative and second narrative. In the first creation narrative, humankind is created in the image of God in accordance to his likeness; he is created to be fruitful, multiply, and fill and subdue the earth (Gen 1:26–28). In Genesis 2, humankind's mandate is described in terms of servitude, whereas in Genesis 1 humankind's mandate is described in terms of domination and dominion.[27] It may be concluded that in the creation narratives, the creation of humankind is depicted in positive

---

24. I am indebted here to Beale, *Temple and Church's Mission*, 75.

25. See also White, *Narration and Discourse*, 117.

26. Beale, "Eden, Temple," 7–8. See also Kline, *Kingdom Prologue*, 54. Kline, who only sees that only the "guarding" as having any priestly connotations, particularly with the priestly "guarding" of the temple from the profane, cite Num 1:53; 3:8, 10, 32; 8:26; 18:3–32; 1 Sam 7:1; 2 Kgs 12:9; 1 Chr 23:32; 2 Chr 34:9; Ezek 44:15–31; 48:11.

27. In the creation intent, man's priority call is described as "to have dominion" (רָדָה). When the king is born, he is given the mandate "to be fruitful" (פָּרָה), "to multiply" (רָבָה) and "to fill" (מָלָה) the earth; and finally "to subdue" (כָּבַשׁ) and "to have dominion" (רָדָה) over the earth. In the expanded mandate in Genesis 1:28, "to have dominion" is mentioned last probably to remind man again of his high calling.

terms. Creation at the end of the sixth day is productive and inhabited and entrusted under the care of humankind – the servant king.

There is, however, for the narrator, both good and bad in the nature of humankind. In Genesis 1:26–28, humankind is created in the "image of God." The phrase "the image of God" has been the subject of debate for centuries, and I do not intend to engage with the varying interpretations and all the possible meanings conferred on it. I do intend, however, to make a few observations regarding the creation of humanity. First, humankind's creation is clearly distinguished from that of all other living creatures. Humankind, unlike animals, which are "created according to their kinds," is created in the image and likeness of God. There is a unique relationship between the creator God and the human beings he created. Second, humankind, as image of God, is given a unique role in creation, a royal office in which they function as divine representatives.[28]

In Psalm 8:5–6, probably an actualization of Genesis 1:26–28, humankind is described in similar terms:

> What is man that you are mindful of him,
>   and the son of man that you visit him?
> For you made him a little lower than the angels,
>   and you crowned him with glory and honor.
> You made him to have dominion over the works of your hands;
>   you have put all things under his feet.[29] (NKJV)

As Anderson points out, "this passage is extraordinarily interesting because it is the one passage in the Old Testament aside from the Priestly passages in Genesis (1:26–27; 5:3; 9:6), that mentions the divine image."[30] Psalm 8:6 [MT] also confers human beings the same dignity as in the Genesis tradition. On

---

28. For further discussion on kings as representatives of their gods in the ancient Near Eastern context, see, Wildberger, "Das Abbild Gottes," 481–501; Clines, "Image of God," 53–103; Curtis, *Man as Image*; Curtis, "Image of God (OT)," *ABD* 3.389–91.

29. MT:

מָה־אֱנוֹשׁ כִּי־תִזְכְּרֶנּוּ וּבֶן־אָדָם כִּי תִפְקְדֶנּוּ׃
וַתְּחַסְּרֵהוּ מְּעַט מֵאֱלֹהִים וְכָבוֹד וְהָדָר תְּעַטְּרֵהוּ׃
תַּמְשִׁילֵהוּ בְּמַעֲשֵׂי יָדֶיךָ כֹּל שַׁתָּה תַחַת־רַגְלָיו

30. Anderson, *From Creation to New*, 15.

the one hand, human beings are a little less than *e/Elohim* (אֱלֹהִים)[31] and on the other, they are endowed with dominion over the works of God. The Septuagint (LXX) translator of Psalm 8:6 interpreted *elohim* as angels (ἠλάττωσας αὐτὸν βραχύ τι παρ' ἀγγέλους, δόξῃ καὶ τιμῇ ἐστεφάνωσας αὐτόν·). Childs points out that the LXX translator offered an interpretation that does not in itself do an injustice to the Hebrew in consideration of the use of the word *elohim* in other contexts.[32] From the perspective of these texts, humankind has closer affinities to the divine than any other earthly creature.

In Genesis 2:7–9, humankind is described in his relation to the earth without any allusion to his being a divine image and given a position of servitude. Genesis 2:7 reads:

> The LORD God formed a human being from the dust of the ground and breathed into his nostrils the breath of life, and so a human being became a living creature. (Own translation)

הָאָדָם (the human being) is from עָפָר (dust) of הָאֲדָמָה (the ground). אָדָם and אֲדָמָה are derived from the same word, אֲדָמָה meaning primarily the surface of the earth and only secondarily the cultivated land.[33] The dust formula is found both in Genesis 2:7, which is pre-fall, and again in 3:19, which is post-fall, thereby forming a narrative *inclusio*.[34] The dust formula, pre-fall or post-fall, "is not a statement about curse, judgment, or indictment, so that the imposition of ashes is not related to guilt and sin."[35] There is a sense in which the dust formula indicates the elevation of humankind to kingship.[36] As Brueggemann notes, Genesis 2:7 has close association with 1 Kings 16:2–3, Psalm 113:7, and 1 Samuel 2:6–8 which "all speak of being raised from dust to power."[37] Dust in these cases represent "pre-royal status (1 Kgs. 16:2), poverty

---

31. Childs points out, "the Hebrew word for God (*elohim*) is somewhat ambiguous. Elohim is the general Semitic name for God, but it is also the name for that class of heavenly beings which serves God, especially the court beings which serve God, especially in the court." Childs, "Psalm 8," 20–31, 25.

32. Childs, 25.

33. Westermann, *Genesis 1–11*, 206.

34. Brueggemann, "Remember, You Are Dust," 3–4.

35. Brueggemann, 3–4.

36. Brueggemann, "From Dust to Kingship," 1–18.

37. Brueggemann, 4. See also Hamilton, *Book of Genesis*, 158.

(1 Sam 2:18; Ps. 113:7), and death (Isa 26:19; Dan 12:2)."[38] As Brueggemann argues, the dust formula "best makes sense if understood as an enthronement formula."[39] Understood in this manner, Genesis 2 stands in agreement with Genesis 1 that humankind is created to function as king over creation, a role that according to Genesis 2, humankind was to exercise from the garden of Eden, extending that garden to encompass the entire earth.

The dust formula, however, may also be understood as a formula of origin, thereby highlighting some aspects of human nature. First, humankind did not just happen to find themselves on earth. "Dust from the ground" did not fashion itself into a human being. Humanity was formed and fashioned by the creator God from dust of the ground. God out of his own free will planned and purposed the existence of humankind on the earth he created. Second, dust is the raw material from which humankind was created, as "rib" was the corresponding raw material for the woman.[40] Describing a human being as dust from the ground emphasizes the close tie between the human and the earth or land.[41] Thus, a human being is an earthly creature who is subject to the realities and limitations of the material composition.[42] Third, fashioned "dust of the ground" in and of itself is nothing but an inanimate and lifeless sculpture that cannot hear, see, feel, sense, talk, or walk.[43] A human is a living being because God breathed into him the breath of life; he thereby becomes a living being. A human being's vitality is dependent upon God's gracious gift of life from beginning (to end). We may conclude from this that a human is by nature finite.

There is one more important aspect of human nature, which only comes out in the context of the whole Eden narrative (Gen 2:4b–3:24) – the relationship between the dust formula and death. I have already alluded to Genesis 3:19 as forming an *inclusio* with Genesis 2:7. We ought to remember, however, that no one dies, at least not physically, in this narrative unless we are willing to introduce a dualism and speak about spiritual death and physical death. In

---

38. Hamilton, *Genesis 1–17*, 158.
39. Brueggemann, "From Dust to Kingship," 4.
40. Hamilton, *Genesis 1–17*, 158.
41. Westermann, *Genesis 1–11*, 202. The fact that man is created from dust is alluded to in many parts of the Old Testament (Job 10:9; Pss 90:3; 104:29; Isa 29:16).
42. Brueggemann, "Remember, You Are Dust," 4.
43. Brueggemann, 4.

Genesis 3:19, God states, "By the sweat of your brow you will eat your food *until you return to the ground*, since *from it* you were taken; *for dust you are* and *to dust you will return*" (NIV, emphasis added). This narrative seems to evince two views of death: first, death as a natural phenomenon of human's life, that is, the frailty of a human as dust from the ground, and second, death as a consequence of disobedience regarding the tree of the knowledge of good and bad.[44] It is, however, misleading to speak of two views or traditions regarding death in this narrative; rather, these two components are pieces of the same puzzle. The formula in Genesis 3:19 of humanity's material composition as being dust is a reaffirmation of human's status – human's creatureliness.[45] Genesis 3:19 does not demean humankind, yet it does point to the fact that humankind as dust of the ground is not an infinite creature – human beings by nature die.[46] In this sense, Genesis 3:19 does not simply reaffirm Genesis 2:7; rather, it is also in a sense a resumption of it – it tells what the other fails to tell. Thus, a fourth component of humankind as dust from the ground or his creatureliness is that he dies. There is no ontological change in the narrative from immortality to mortality. As Fretheim notes, "if they [the man and the woman] were created immortal, the tree of life would have been irrelevant."[47] I concur with Barr's thesis that the Eden narrative is "a story of how human immortality was almost gained, but in fact was lost" by human beings who are characterized by mortality from the beginning.[48]

The idea of unsuccessful quests for immortality is also found in the Gilgamesh epic and the Adapa myth. In both these myths, human representatives miss the chance to attain immortality. In the Adapa myth, Adapa, who was created mortal, is tricked by Ea, his creator, into refusing the heavenly meal offered him by Anu, the head of the pantheon, and thereby forfeiting his chance for immortality, a hallmark of the gods. In the Gilgamesh epic, though Utnapishtim and his wife, mortal beings, receive divine blessing, becoming recipient of immortality following their survival of the flood, Utnapishtim offers Gilgamesh a chance at immortality, but Gilgamesh fails the test. As

---

44. Mettinger, *Eden Narrative*, 131.
45. Brueggemann, "Remember, You Are Dust," 4–5.
46. Hamilton, *Genesis 1–17*, 158.
47. Fretheim, "Is Genesis 3?", 152.
48. Barr, *Garden of Eden*, 4.

Wallace points out, "immortality was not impossible for humankind, after all, Utnapishtim had gained it, but it only came by the decree of the divine council and in exceptional circumstances."[49]

The problem with the Akkadian mythologies is that immortality was not guaranteed for the gods either; the pantheon is not a harmonious family, but rather one of conspiracies, betrayals, and murders. The hope of becoming like the gods is not such a comforting idea after all. The uniqueness of Genesis in this regard lies in its concealment of the divine assembly and the activities that take place therein; however, there appears to be an allusion to the divine assembly participating in creation and in the deliberations regarding the actions of humankind: "*Let us* create man . . . , and "The man has become *like one of us*" (Gen 1:26; 3:22; ESV, emphasis added). In Genesis 2:4b–25, in contrast to Genesis 1:1–2:4a, the idea of humankind created in the image of God is not hinted at; instead, humankind is created from the dust of the ground – an earthly creature – and he is tempted to be like God.

In both Genesis 1 and Genesis 2, the creation of humankind is basically viewed positively – humankind is created as the image of God in order to function as a representative of God and mediator of his rule on the earthly realm, the top-down perspective (Gen 1). Or, from another perspective, humankind is elevated over all creation to serve as a representative of God and mediator of his rule on the earthly realm, from dust to king, the bottom-up perspective (Gen 2); and this is good, so to speak. If the representative function is taken seriously, it points to a dualism that is at the fabric of creation – Yahweh rules the cosmos from heaven, his throne room, whereas humankind exercises God's rule in the earthly realm. The separation of day two is functional; God does not exercise his rule from the earth; rather, his throne is in heaven. The narrator, however, also exposes in the pre-fall narrative, Genesis 2:4–3:5, the negative reality of being a human creature – as much as humankind is created in the image of God (Gen 1:26–28); humankind is also dust from the ground, an earthly creature, who dies, which is not good. For the narrator, the virtue that humankind is made in the image of God does not make him a heavenly being; humankind is in every sense of the word an earthly being. Thus, in dialog with Genesis 1, Genesis 2 emphasizes the earthliness of humankind as they relate to their creator. Thus, there are both

---

49. Wallace, *Eden Narrative*, 104.

correspondences and differences between the divine and the human. The divine is heavenly, whereas humankind is earthly, the two do not completely correspond.

The Good and the Bad in Paradise: The Tree of Life and the Tree of the Knowledge of Good and Bad

In Genesis 2:9 the narrator draws special attention to the trees in the garden – trees of all kinds, desirable trees and trees good for food. The narrator proceeds to draw attention to two unique trees in the midst of the garden: the tree of life and the tree of the knowledge of good and bad (Gen 2:9).[50] It has been highly debated as to whether there are two trees or one tree in the middle of the garden.[51] Scholarly interest has tended to fall on the tree of the knowledge of good and bad at the neglect of the tree of life.[52]

The two trees, unlike the rest of the trees in the garden, had potential to do more than simply satisfy physical pleasure and nourishment. The tree of life is mentioned only twice in Genesis 2:4b–3:24, first in Genesis 2:9 and again in 3:24, forming an *inclusio*. There is no indication that the tree of life was previously eaten from by humankind prior to the limitation in Genesis 3:24.[53] There are no instructions regarding the tree of life; the narrator does not tell us whether humankind was allowed or prohibited from eating from this tree. There is, however, a contrastive alternative to the tree of life presented by the presence of the tree of the knowledge of good and bad.

Humankind is commanded regarding the tree of the knowledge of good and bad, "You may freely eat of every tree of the garden; but of the tree of the knowledge of good and bad you shall not eat, for in the day that you eat of

---

50. Instead of the conventional translation "the tree of knowledge of good and evil," I choose to go with "the tree of the knowledge of good and bad," which provides a better contrast in this case and fits well with my overall framework.

51. For further discussion on this debate, see Mettinger, *Eden Narrative*, 5–11; Wallace, *Eden Narrative*, 101–41; Stordalen, *Echoes of Eden*; Van Wolde, *Semiotic Analysis*.

52. See Van Wolde, *Semiotic Analysis*, 32.

53. Barr's observation is pointed in this regard: "The phrase of 3:22, 'and now, lest he put forth his hand and take also of the tree of life and eat and live forever,' must mean that the fruit of the tree of life had not been previously eaten. By Hebrew grammar and meanings, I believe it cannot mean 'lest he continue to eat of the tree of life, as he has been doing all along.' In other words, the phrase which states the motivation of expulsion of humans from the garden is a phrase that excludes the idea that they might eat of the tree of life from the beginning." Barr, *Garden of Eden*, 58.

it you shall die" (2:16–17, own translation). The tree of the knowledge good and bad, in contrast to the tree of life, is the tree of death. This is evident by the curse attached to the tree of the knowledge of good and bad. If the human beings disobey God and eat from this tree, they will die. Described as such, the tree of life appears to be the "good" tree, whereas the tree of the knowledge of good and bad appears to be the "bad" tree. Thus, we have the good and the bad standing side by side in the earthly paradise.

But is the tree of the knowledge of good and bad altogether "bad"? Apparently not, this tree is in every sense of the word the tree of the knowledge of "good" and "bad"; it has potential for both "good" and "bad." As we have already observed, to this tree is attached a curse – death, the "bad"; however, although the blessing is not explicitly mentioned, it appears to be implied as being the opposite of the curse: human beings will live on the condition that they obey and do not eat from it – the "good." I concur with those who regard the instructions regarding the tree of the knowledge of good and bad as moral probation or testing; however, before we get to that, we do not have to miss the commandment motif attached to the tree of the knowledge of good and bad. The instruction in Genesis 2:16–17 is first and foremost a divine commandment; the specific term for testing (Hebrew verb נָסָה in the Piel) is not used in Genesis 2:4b–3:24.

> And the LORD God commanded [וַיְצַו] the man saying, "Of every tree of the garden you are free to eat; but of the tree of the knowledge of good and bad, you must not [לֹא] eat of it; for as soon as you eat of it, you shall die. (Gen 2:16–17, NJPS)

There are two notable things here. First, the use of the verb צָוָה, which has the same root as מִצְוָה, "commandment" (Exod 20:6; 34:28; Deut 4:13; 5:10, 22; 6:6; 9:10; 10:4; Josh 22:5). Second, the prohibition is expressed in an emphatic form as in the Decalogue (לֹא rather than אַל). Thus, we have here the first *torah* to which the Mosaic Torah has attached the choice between life and death: "This day I call heaven and earth as witnesses against you that I have set before you life and death, blessings and curses. Now choose life, so that you and your children may live" (Deut 30:19, NIV). The Mosaic Torah is, in turn, attached to the theme of creation – heaven and earth are called as witnesses against Israel. In Genesis 2 no witnesses are called; however, there is an indication that perhaps they were. The serpent's knowledge of the transaction between God and the human being is perhaps the one evidence of such witnesses having been called.

Some regard the pre-fall state of human beings described in covenantal terms as the covenant of works.[54] The covenantal idea has also found support in some critical scholars, for example, Lofhink, van Seters, and Otto; for these scholars, Genesis 2–3, generally attributed to J, is regarded as having close affinities with the Dueteronomistic covenantal tradition.[55] For these scholars, the Deuteronomic tradition lies behind Genesis 2–3, thereby deferring J to a later date. We are not concerned here with the dating of biblical sources; rather, we are concerned with the discernable parallels between Genesis chapters 2 and 3 and especially Deuteronomy. The motif of divine commandment pertaining to life and death and to choice between obedience and disobedience is echoed in the Deuteronomistic covenant theology. For example,[56]

> Be careful to follow every command I am giving you today, so that you may live and increase and may enter and possess the land that the LORD promised on oath to your forefathers. Remember how the LORD your God led you all the way in the desert these forty years, to humble you and to test you in order to know what was in your heart, whether or not you would keep his commands. He humbled you, causing you to hunger and then feeding you with manna, which neither you nor your fathers had known, to teach you that man does not live on bread alone but on every word that comes from the mouth of the LORD. (Deut 8:1–3, NIV)

---

54. Westminster Standards, 7.2: "The first covenant made with man was a Covenant of Works, wherein life was promised to Adam; and in him to his posterity, upon condition of perfect and personal obedience." Mettinger's view that divine test has not played any role in the history of exegesis is completely false. Mettinger makes this assessment: "With the prohibition of one of the two trees (2:17), God confronts man with a test, an important but surprisingly neglected feature of the text." Mettinger, *Eden Narrative*, 23. Mettinger further goes on to claim that the testing view cannot even be found with the church fathers. One cannot help but wonder which church fathers he consulted. For further discussion regarding the covenantal idea, see Karlberg, "Original State of Adam," 291–309.

55. Lohfink, *Das Siegeslied am Schilfmeer*, 90–95; Van Seters, *Prologue to History*, 127–29; Otto, "Die Paradieserzählung Genesis 2–3," 167–92.

56. Mettinger, *Eden Narrative*, 26–52.

See, *I am setting before you today a blessing and a curse*, the *blessing if you obey the commands* of the LORD your God that I am giving you today; the *curse if you disobey the commands* of the LORD your God and turn from the way that I command you today by following other gods, which you have not known. When the LORD your God has brought you into the land you are entering to possess, you are to proclaim on Mount Gerizim the blessings, and on Mount Ebal the curses. As you know, these mountains are across the Jordan, west of the road, toward the setting sun, near the great trees of Moreh, in the territory of those Canaanites living in the Arabah in the vicinity of Gilgal. You are about to cross the Jordan to enter and take possession of the land the LORD your God is giving you. When you have taken it over and are living there, be sure that you obey all the decrees and laws I am setting before you today. (Deut 11:26–28, NIV)

See, I set before you today life and prosperity [אֶת־הַחַיִּים וְאֶת־הַטּוֹב, lit. "life and good"], death and destruction [אֶת־הַמָּוֶת וְאֶת־הָרָע, lit. "death and bad"]. For I command you today to love the LORD your God, to walk in his ways, and to keep his commands, decrees and laws; then you will live and increase, and the LORD your God will bless you in the land you are entering to possess. But if your heart turns away and you are not obedient, and if you are drawn away to bow down to other gods and worship them, I declare to you this day that you will certainly be destroyed. You will not live long in the land you are crossing the Jordan to enter and possess. This day I call heaven and earth as witnesses against you that I have set before you life and death, blessings and curses. Now choose life, so that you and your children may live and that you may love the LORD your God, listen to his voice, and hold fast to him. For the LORD is your life, and he will give you many years in the land he swore to give to your fathers, Abraham, Isaac and Jacob. (Deut 30:15–20, NIV)

Most interesting to note is that the issue of obedience and disobedience, life and death, good and bad, blessings and curses, is attached to the theme of land. In the texts quoted above, obedience to God's commands is attached to life, the good, in which case is defined as possession of the land, and on the other hand, disobedience of God's command is attached to death, the curse, the bad, which is defined as loss of land. Similarly, the issue of obedience and disobedience, life and death, good and bad, blessings and curses in Genesis 2–3 is attached to the theme of land, the garden of Eden. Obedience to God's command by not eating of the tree of the knowledge of good and bad guarantees stability and life in the blessings of paradise, whereas disobedience results in curses on the earth and the loss of land, paradise, with no access to the tree of life. In both cases, of Israel and of the first human couple, death, that is the curse, is not so much physical death, although it is also envisioned; rather, it is the loss of land, a possession freely received from Yahweh. With regard to physical death, only from within the garden of Eden did humankind have a chance at immortality by eating of the tree of life, which is located therein. From outside of the garden any chance of immortality was lost to humankind.

The tree of the knowledge of good and bad suggests that even in their original state, humankind already had the potential to do good through the act of obedience or to do bad through the act of disobedience. Although the tree of life was available for humankind to eat from, apparently humankind could not have simply walked to the tree of life and eaten of its fruits without having had to face up to the challenge that the tree of the knowledge of good and bad posed. As the story of Job attests, the blameless and upright (תָּם וְיָשָׁר) are not exempt from testing, and for that reason testing is divinely intended. In the Reformed tradition, the tree of the knowledge of good and evil is regarded as symbolizing the probation for covenantal faithfulness or disobedience. The divine test motif is one that is found in other Old Testament Scriptures intended to reveal the inclination of the human heart or moral inclination.[57] It has also been regarded as the covenant of works, in that Adam's

---

57. For other Old Testament Scriptural examples, consider (1) the testing of Abraham in Genesis 22 – the offering of Isaac. In this test, following Abraham's obedience, God states, "Now I know that you fear God, because you did not withhold your son from me, your only son" (v. 12). As a result, Abraham and his descendants are blessed to be a blessing to all the nations "because you [Abraham] obeyed me [God]" (v. 18). (2) Israel's testing. First, the test at Marah – "There the Lord made a decree and a law for them, and there he tested them. He said, 'If you listen carefully to the voice of the Lord your God and do what is right in his eyes, if you pay attention to his commands and keep all his decrees, I will not bring on you any of the diseases I brought on the Egyptians, for I am the Lord, who heals you'" (Exod 15:25b–26, NIV). Second, the test at the Desert of Sin: "Then the Lord said to Moses, 'I will rain down

obedience will merit life for himself and all posterity, whereas disobedience will bring about death.

Whether it is a covenant, or simply a probation, the initial testing of humankind differs from Israel's testing in the wilderness in one important respect. In Genesis 2–3, the testing is set within the garden of Eden, a sacred land, and its result determines whether humankind gets to remain in the garden of Eden, the sacred land, or is cast out. Israel's test, on the other hand, is set in the wilderness, and its result determines whether Israel would remain outside or enter the holy land. The story of Israel's entrance into the holy land may relatively be understood as a reversal of the initial story of disobedience and expulsion.

In the garden of Eden or paradise, the tree of the knowledge of good and bad coexisted with the tree of life – the bad and the good, the former representing death and the latter representing life. However, no one physically dies in the garden of Eden following humankind's rebellion by eating from the tree of the knowledge of good and bad; instead, humankind is expelled from the garden. The paradisiacal situation, it may be concluded, was good, but not eternally guaranteed. Humankind had to pass the fidelity test first in order to show worthiness to remain in paradise or fail and be cast out.

It may be concluded that the tree of the knowledge of good and bad was good insofar as it was part of God's creation and part of the garden of Eden. Like other trees in the garden, the tree of the knowledge of good and bad was desirable; however, unlike the tree of life and the other trees in the garden, the tree of the knowledge of good and bad was a prohibited tree. The tree was unclean food to which was attached the threat of death if humankind ate or touched it. Thus, paradise was good, but not everything in it was good for

---

bread from heaven for you. The people are to go out each day and gather enough for that day. In this way I will test them and see whether they will follow my instructions'" (Exod 16:4). Third, forty years of testing in Deut 8:10–3: "This entire commandment that I command you today you must diligently observe, so that you may live and increase. . . . Remember the long way that the LORD your God has led you these forty years in the wilderness, in order to humble you, testing you to know what was in your heart, whether or not you would keep his commandments . . . in order to make you understand that one does not live by bread alone, but by every word that comes from the mouth of God." (3) The testing of Job: Job is described as a blameless and righteous man who feared God; however, he is tested to see if he fears God for nothing (Job 1:9).

humankind. The unclean tree posed a great danger to the priests who served within the royal garden-temple.[58]

Creation of Woman as a Correction of a "Not Good" Situation and the Separation from God

In the Genesis 2:18–25, the narrator takes up the point made in Genesis 1:27 that humankind was created "male and female." Man was at first alone in the paradisiacal garden; however, the beauty and the pleasures that the garden offered were not totally satisfying. Man was alone, and God himself admits that lack: "The LORD God said, '*It is not good* for the man to be alone. I will make for him a helper who corresponds with him" (2:18, emphasis added, own translation). This aesthetic judgment, as Miscall argues, is the climax of the contrast between Genesis 1:1–2:4a and Genesis 2:4b–25, in that "good itself is negated" – *it is not good*.[59] Following the failure of the animals to undo the aloneness of the man, that aloneness is remedied by the creation of the woman (Gen 2:19–22).

Genesis 2:18 is helpful in determining what the goodness of creation implies by investigating what it means when God says "it is not good."[60] In this context, it is the aloneness of the man that God pronounces as not good. This pronouncement, as Walton argues, "has nothing to do with moral perfection or quality of workmanship – it is a comment concerning function."[61] This implies that the divine purpose of creation cannot be achieved if the human being is alone.

The goodness of the solution was dependent on the man's judgment – the void to be filled was his. In the first instance, animals were created and brought to him, but no suitable helper was found. In Genesis 1:25–26 the creation of animals is pronounced good, whereas in Genesis 2:19–20 the animals fail to succeed in the purpose for which they were created – they do not functionally

---

58. Alexander writes, "Leviticus consistently underlines the danger posed by uncleanness to those who are holy or pure. This danger is greatest for the priests who work within the tabernacle, a holy area, and handle the tabernacle furniture, holy objects. For a priest to serve in the tabernacle, he must remain holy. If he becomes unclean, he can no longer carry out his duties; to do so without being cleansed and sanctified means death." Alexander, *From Eden*, 144–45.

59. Miscall, "Jacques Derrida," 5.

60. Walton, *Lost World of Genesis*, 51.

61. Walton, 51.

complete humankind. In the second instance, the creation of the woman from the rib of the man, it is man who pronounces the success of this attempt: The man says, "This is now bone of my bones and flesh of my flesh; she shall be called 'woman,' for she was taken out of man" (Gen 2:23 NIV). In Genesis 1, the term "human/human being" (אָדָם) or "the human being" (הָאָדָם) is used collectively to refer to both male (זָכָר) and female (נְקֵבָה), and there is no hierarchy involved (Gen 1:27). This is sometimes called the neutral position of primeval unity between male and female (or man and woman).[62] In the second creation story, the human being (הָאָדָם), later called אִישׁ ("man"), is created first, and woman (אִשָּׁה) is created second from the rib of the man.[63] The woman is in this sense the second Adam, "a suitable helper." In this sense, the woman may even be regarded as the climax of creation.[64] The two, the man and the woman, functionally complement each other. This, however, was only part of the divine purpose for humankind. As Clines argues, the kind of help that the text has in mind has to do with fulfilling the creation mandate, "Be fruitful and multiply, and fill the earth" (Gen 1:28, NRSV), which is the only thing that the man cannot do by himself.[65] Furthermore, it is the man who names the woman, thereby designating her function – "And Adam named his wife Eve, because she was the mother of all living" (Gen 3:20, NIV).[66] In Genesis 1:31, the creation activities are pronounced "very good," specifically having the creation of first human pair, male and female, in view. Creation is "very good" because it is through the human couple that the divine purposes of creation can be achieved.

It should be noted, however, in Genesis 2:24 the narrator adds that this successful creation of the first human pair also has its costs: "For this reason a man will leave his father and mother and be united to his wife, and they will

---

62. Cf. Gen 2:23–24.

63. The opposition between man and woman (or male and female) has also resulted in two opposing readings: patriarchal (androcentric) and matriarchal (gynocentric). The patriarchal position is that man was created first with woman created second (or later) in subordination to man. Woman is held responsible for the entrance of evil on earth. This position has been blamed for the male chauvinistic and misogynist message it carries. The matriarchal position, originating from the feminist circles, is that the woman is superior to man just as the human is superior to the ground from which man is taken, for she is the mother of all beings.

64. Trible, *God and Rhetoric*, 72–143; Trible, "Depatriarchalizing in Biblical Interpretation," 36.

65. Clines, "What Does Eve Do?", 34–36.

66. Clines, 36.

become one flesh" (Gen 2:24, NIV). Two things I would like to highlight from this statement. First is the unity of the first human couple: a man and woman would become "one flesh" (לְבָשָׂר אֶחָד). The unity of the two is important in this narrative for two reasons: first, the prohibition regarding the tree of the knowledge of good and bad by default applies to both of them because they are one, and second, the two are inseparable in taking responsibility for their actions in the garden.

Second, the creation of the woman is creation through separation that climaxes in unity between the man and the woman; this unity in turn requires separation. The woman was made from the rib that God had taken out of the man (Gen 2:22). This separation climaxes in unity between the man and the woman, a marriage covenant (Gen 2:23–25). However, the unity between the man and the woman is one which required separation from their parents.

In speaking of the separation between man and his parents, is the narrator prophetically speaking about subsequent relationships, or does he also have this first human couple in mind? There is a sense in which this separation also applies to the first human beings. The first human beings, the man and the woman had no flesh-and-blood parents; their only father and mother in the story so far is God – he gave birth to the first man and woman. God had to give the first human pair their relative autonomy. In the words of Hick, "the world must be to men, to some extent at least, etsi deus non daretur, 'as if there were no God.' God must be hidden deity, veiled by his creation."[67] The earthly realm was created for humankind and into humankind's hands it was entrusted: "Be fruitful and multiply, and fill the earth and subdue it. Rule over the fish of the sea and over the birds of the sky and over every living creature that moves on the earth" (NASB).

The issue in the separation of the human couple from their creator is both spatial and epistemic. Divine presence in the garden of Eden, as I already argued, was a limited presence. In the narrative flow, God does not appear on the scene until after the temptation and the fall. This, on one hand, points to spatial distance, although this kind of distance is a relative one as God claims every square inch of the universe (Ps 139:7–10; Isa 66:1–2; Jer 23:23–24); and on the other hand, it points to epistemic distance – human freedom in relation to their creator. Humankind had already received instructions

---

67. Hick, *Evil and God*, 317.

from God regarding the tree of the knowledge of good and bad; thus, God's will was known to humankind. What was left was for humankind to freely respond in "an uncompelled interpretive activity" to God's instructions.[68] If divine presence was fully manifested in the garden of Eden, it would have completely overwhelmed human freedom, so divine presence had to remain relatively veiled.

The creation of the woman is presented as good because the man alone was functionally incomplete. The man alone was incapable of fulfilling the creation mandate. However, in creating a human couple to fulfill the creation mandate, God relatively separated himself from the first human couple both spatially and epistemically.

Conclusion

Even prior to the fall, humankind had the potential to obey or disobey God, as evidenced by the tree of the knowledge of good and bad. The bad, embodied by the serpent, was even given room to operate, violating God's sanctuary; thus, the earthly paradise could potentially be violated, and violated it was. Furthermore, creation in its state of goodness is fallen. The goodness of creation does not necessarily have to be tied with the notion of perfection.[69] As Fretheim argues, "goodness can certainly entail a fundamental integrity short of perfection."[70] The first creation in its state of goodness does not have to be idealized. God does not idealize it, and neither should we. Creation was very good because God had through the creation activities moved it from a non-functional state to a functional state, and it was well moving toward its goal.

So how "not all that good" was the creation prior to the fall of humanity? Genesis 2:4b–3:5, the pre-fall narrative, focuses mainly on the creation of humankind and their placement in the garden of Eden or paradise and the chain of events climaxing in dialogic encounters in Genesis 3. The human condition and the paradisiacal condition are presented as ones which require improvement, because the conditions are not ideal. Regarding the conditions of humankind: First, humankind is an earthly creature, dust from the ground,

---

68. Hick, 317.
69. Barr, *Garden of Eden*, 92; Fretheim, "Is Genesis 3?", 147.
70. Fretheim, 147.

who dies. Second, humankind in its unison is relatively separated from God both spatially and epistemologically. The condition of the earth and paradise are also not ideal: First, the garden of Eden is a prototype for humankind of what the whole earth was supposed to be, which implies that the conditions outside of the boundaries of Eden are not qualitatively the same as inside Eden; whereas the garden of Eden is a luxurious royal park, the rest of the earth is not. Second, Eden was itself also a type of the heavenly dwelling of God, whereas the rest of the earth is not, and as a type of the heavenly reality, Eden is not God's ultimate dwelling. God's dwelling and humankind's dwelling are ultimately one; humankind's dwelling and God's dwelling are separated spatially. Third, in the garden of Eden stands the tree of the knowledge of good and bad to which is attached the threat of death, in contrast to the tree of life, which represents life. The tree of the knowledge of good and bad is unclean food that would defile humankind if it were eaten or touched.

The non-ideal character of the creation in its pre-fallen state and even more broadly in its original state of goodness, as we will observe in the subsequent chapters, clearly comes out in comparison with the conditions of the eschatological new heaven and new earth. The eschatological new heaven and new earth is not simply a reversal of the fall and a return to things as they were at the beginning; rather, it is a radical improvement or transformation of the non-ideal primordial conditions. Thus, creation prior to the fall of humanity is not creation in "all its perfection"; rather, it is creation in anticipation of a radical transformation. The dialogic encounter between the serpent and humankind was that point of creation at which creation could be radically transformed for either the worse or the better.

CHAPTER 4

Genesis 1:24–2:4a in Dialogue with Genesis 3:1–24 (Fall Creation Story): The Fall of Humanity within the Scope of God's Very Good Creation

Introduction

We have already noted that some regard the aesthetic judgment(s) in Genesis 1:1–2:4b to be an expression of "perfection." God's creation was "good," so it had to be "perfect." The claim for perfection is, to a large extent, based on reading Genesis 1:1–3:24 by following the narrative flow; consequently this narrative is usually structured as follows:

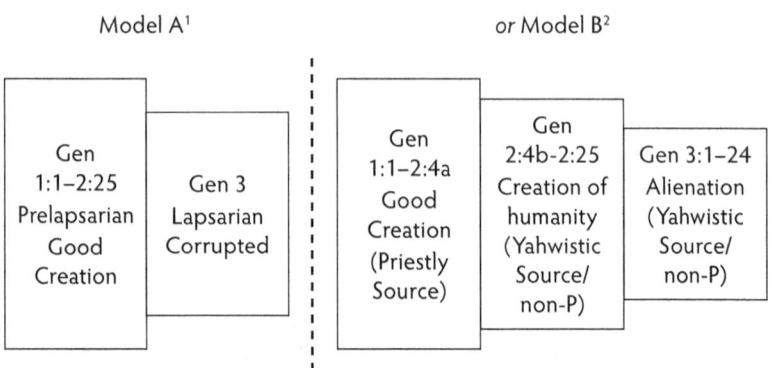

Figure 1: Progressive Reading Models of Genesis 1–3

The two models above are not far apart from each other, except for that the first model admits that we have two creation narratives. Model A and Model B both have a progressive understanding of the unfolding of events as narrated in Genesis 1:1–3:24, and both place the fall outside of the scope of the original good creation. Humankind's rebellion is understood as causing disruption on a creation that was originally perfect.[3] As Fretheim observes, if creation

---

1. This model reflects the most common systematic model: creation and fall. The fall of man is regarded as a corruption of God's good creation.

2. This model reflects the modern tendency of isolating different strands of traditions or sources from each other. Genesis 1:1–2:4a, as already noted, is regarded as from the Priestly source, whereas Genesis 2–3 is regarded as from the Yahwistic source. The Yahwistic source of Genesis 2–3 is further understood as a unification of two narratives that were originally separate. Both dealt with the subject of humanity in primordial times: one narrative dealt with the creation of humanity and the other narrative dealt with the alienation of humanity from their creator. For detailed arguments of the distinction between Genesis 2 and 3, see Westermann, *Genesis 1–11*, 190–96.

3. Wolters articulates this position as follows: "The crucial biblical teaching [is] that creation before and apart from sin is wholly and unambiguously good. On seven different occasions in the Genesis 1 account of creation, God pronounces his works of creation to be good, climaxing in the last verse with the words 'And God saw everything that he had made, and behold, it was very good.' God does not make junk, and we dishonor the creator if we take a negative view of the work of his hands when he himself takes such a positive view. In fact, so positive a view did he take of what he had created that he refused to scrap it when mankind spoiled it, but determined instead, at the cost of his Son's life, to make it new and good again. God does not make junk, and he does not junk what he has made." Wolters, *Creation Regained*, 48–49. Pannenberg writes, "God made the world good, but creatures – and especially humans, in whom the goodness of creation reached its climax – have corrupted it. Since an original perfection is ascribed to creation, the evil that is present in the world had to come later." Pannenberg, *Systematic Theology*, 163.

was "perfect" as claimed, how could anything go wrong?[4] As already noted in the previous chapter, there are a number of factors that make it implausible to regard the first creation in its original state as perfect, especially if Genesis 1:1–2:4a is invoked or implicated as a whole.

Genesis 2:4b–3:24 may be regarded as a retelling of the creation story in general; however, it does so by immediately turning its focus on the activities of the sixth day of creation. The planting of the garden of Eden should not be confused with the general creation of vegetation and plants on earth. The garden of Eden was specifically prepared for the human being, whom God created. However, as I highlighted in the previous chapter, Genesis 1:1–3:24 as a whole should be treated as a creation narrative not simply Genesis 2:4b–25.[5] The central argument in this chapter is that the final refrain in Genesis 1:31 does not connote "perfection"; rather, inasmuchas creation is evaluated as good, the so-called "fall of humanity" narration forms an intricate part of the creation process.

Humanity Pronounced "Good" or Not

The final refrain in Genesis 1:31, "God saw everything he made, and behold, it was very good," is usually understood as referring to the whole creation process, and yes, it may be properly understood in this fashion. If the final refrain is regarded as encompassing all the creation activities, as Ramantswana argues elsewhere, then there is an anomaly on the sixth day of creation as this would imply that humanity is not singled out as good but simply good in so far as humanity is part of God's overall "very good" creation.[6] If such a reading is pursued, the logical question that follow is: Why is humanity not singled out as "good"?[7] While it is possible and meaningful to explore this line of analysis, however, in this study, I explore an alternative reading. The final refrain, as I will highlight, may just as well be understood as referring

---

4. Fretheim, *God and World*, 41.

5. For more on the interlinks between Genesis 2 and 3, which necessisate that the whole unit be considered to be creation narrative, see Ramantswana, "Humanity Not Pronounced Good," 804–18.

6. Ramantswana, "Humanity Not Pronounced Good: A Re-reading," 425–31.

7. Ramantswana in his anaylsis explored the various options that the author could have used, if the aim was to single out humanity as good. Ramantswana, 426–21.

specifically to the creative activities that took place within the sixth day particularly relating to the human and food provisions cycle (Gen 1:26–30) and not so much the overall creation:

וַיַּרְא אֱלֹהִים אֶת־כָּל־אֲשֶׁר עָשָׂה וְהִנֵּה־טוֹב מְאֹד וַיְהִי־עֶרֶב וַיְהִי־בֹקֶר יוֹם הַשִּׁשִּׁי

("God saw all that he had made, and it was very good. *And there was evening, and there was morning – the sixth day*") (Gen 1:31, NIV)).

The final refrain, like all other previous refrains, falls within a particular day. If the author intended to express the overall goodness of creation, the plausible option that the author followed could be to shift the evaluation formula after the announcement of day. As such the text would likely have been as follows:

וַיְהִי־עֶרֶב וַיְהִי־בֹקֶר יוֹם הַשִּׁשִּׁי וַיַּרְא אֱלֹהִים אֶת־כָּל־אֲשֶׁר עָשָׂה וְהִנֵּה־טוֹב מְאֹד

(And there was evening, and there was morning – the sixth day. *God saw all that he had made, and it was very good*. Emphasis added.)

The above sentence structure would have been befitting if the author intended to make an overall evaluation pronouncement over the creation activities over the six days. However, following the biblical text, the final refrain is contained within the sixth day of creation as it is bracketed by the end of day formula. In so doing, the uniformity with other creation cycles in Genesis 1 is maintained, with the exception of creation of raqia' cycle (Gen 1:5–8) within day two in which the evaluation formula is absent.

There is nothing unusual in finding two refrains on the same day; in actual fact, the third day and the sixth day basically follow the same structure.

Genesis 1:24–2:4a in Dialogue with Genesis 3:1–24 (Fall Creation Story)

Genesis 1:9–13 (NIV)	**Genesis 1:24–31**
God said, "Let the water under the sky be gathered into one place, and let the dry ground appear"... And it was so... *And God saw that it was good.*	And God said, "Let the land produce living creatures according to their kinds... And it was so... *And God saw that it was good.*
Then God said, "let the land produce vegetation: seed-bearing plants and trees on the land that bear fruit with seed in it, according to their various kinds." And it was so.... *And God saw that it was good. And there was evening, and there was morning, the third day.*	Then God said, "Let us make mankind in our image, in our likeness, and let them rule over the fish of the sea and the birds of the air, over the livestock, over all the earth, and over all the creatures that move along the ground"... God blessed them and said to them... Then God said... And it was so. *God saw all that he had made, and it was very good.* And there was evening, and there was morning, the sixth day.

Regarding the final refrain, וַיַּרְא אֱלֹהִים אֶת־כָּל־אֲשֶׁר עָשָׂה וְהִנֵּה־טוֹב מְאֹד ("and God saw all that he made and behold it was very good"), the question is: what is the reference of the כָּל ("all")? Is it all the creation activities from day one to day six? Or is it with all the creation activities relating the human cycle in Genesis 1:25–30? While both questions may be answered positively; however, considering narrative patterns and the seven-days framework, the final refrain is focused on the human and food provisions cycle (Gen 1:26–30) and not on the overall creation activities. This is clear if we consider the the parallels between day three and day six of creation:

Day Three	Day Six
Section A: Gen 1:9–10 Dry land appears and it is called "earth" (אֶרֶץ) Evaluation formula	Section A: Gen 1:24 The earth (הָאָרֶץ) produces living creatures Evaluation formula
Section B: Gen 1:11–13	Section B: Gen 1:26–30 Human beings created and given dominion over living creatures (sea creatures, flying creatures, livestock, creeping creatures) and over all the earth (כָּל־הָאָרֶץ).
The earth (הָאָרֶץ) produces vegetation (דֶּשֶׁא and עֵשֶׂב)	Human beings and living creatures are instructed to eat vegetation (עֵשֶׂב).
Evaluation formula	Evaluation formula

In Genesis 1:26–30 two cycles are fused together: the human cycle (Gen 1:26–28) and the food provisions cycle (Gen 1:29–30). As Westermann also notes, "The provision of food is an element often found in stories of creation of humanity" as it is also evident from the Hymn of Amon Re, Sumerian Creation myth, and Gilgamesh Epic.[8] Considering the use of the evaluation formula and also the "and it was so" formula (וַיְהִי־כֵן formula), in all the other previous usages of the two formulas, they are not used together; it is only in Genesis 1:30–31, where the two formulas are used together following each other. The author by shifting the וַיְהִי־כֵן formula to the end of the creation activities within the human and food provisions cycle (Gen 1:26–30) signals the end of the creation activities. Therefore, the final refrain comes as a climactic refrain as it concludes the human and food provisions cycle.

Furthermore, while the final refrain may be regarded as climactic; yet it is not the final word nor the concluding statement. The concluding statement is to be found on the seventh day of creation:

> Thus the heavens and the earth were finished, and all their multitude. And on the seventh day God finished the work that he had done, and he rested on the seventh day from all the work that he had done. So God blessed the seventh day and hallowed it, because on it God rested from all the work that he had done

---

8. Westermann, *Genesis 1–11*, 162–63.

in creation. These are the generations of the heavens and the earth when they were created. (Gen 2:1–4, NRSV)

The concluding statement on the creation process does not include the evaluation refrain "God saw that the heavens and the earth and their multitude were good,"[9] or "God saw that it was good,"[10] or "God saw everything that he made, and behold it was very good."[11] It is only on day seven of creation where we find a reflection on the rest of the creation process unlike in any of the preceding days:

וַיְכֻלּוּ הַשָּׁמַיִם וְהָאָרֶץ וְכָל־צְבָאָם

("Thus the heavens and the earth were finished, and all their multitude," Gen 2:1a).

Thus, Genesis 2:1 is that point in the narrative where there is a reflection over all creation activities, and not in the כָּל ("all") in Genesis 1:31. Therefore, in my view, the כָּל ("all") in the final evaluation formula should be regarded as referring specifically to the creation activities with human and food provisions cycle, Genesis 1:26–30, and therefore, in this sense Genesis 1:26–31 follows the same pattern as in day three of creation. The sixth day of creation appears to have been the most eventful day of all the creation days. If we only consider Genesis 1:24–31, the following may be noted:

1. Compared to all the other days of creation, this is the day in which God speaks the most.
2. It is on this day that God invites others to participate in the creation work: "Let us" (Gen 1:26).
3. Like the fifth day, it is a day of blessings, a day of double blessing – blessings to animals and blessings to humanity.
4. It is a day of instructions – human beings (and other living creatures) are given the instruction regarding what they should eat.

---

9. If the pattern of the evaluation formula with regard to the light is followed in which a particular entity is specified.

10. If the general pattern of the evaluation is followed in which no particular entity is specified.

11. If the pattern of evaluation that is used with regard to the human cycle is followed.

However, more happened on the sixth day of creation, especially when we consider the dialogic relationship between two creation narratives. Below, we focus particularly on how Genesis 3 illuminates the sixth day of creation.

Genesis 1:24–31 in Dialogue with Genesis 3

In Genesis 1:1–3:24, we do not just have two creation narratives juxtaposed; as Anderson argues, there is awkwardness in the relationship between the two creation narratives.[12] Genesis 2:4b–3:24 as a whole functions as resumption of the sixth day of creation, not just Genesis 2:4b–25.

There is textual evidence, however, that the events described in Genesis 3:1–24 also fall within the sixth day of creation. First, if we choose to end the creation activities at Genesis 2:25, we have to contend with the fact that the first humans are yet to have names. So far in the narrative, human beings are called in three different ways: humankind (הָאָדָם), male and female (זָכָר וּנְקֵבָה), and the man and his wife (הָאָדָם וְאִשְׁתּוֹ) or man/husband and woman/wife (אִישׁ and אִשָּׁה). How can creation be completed with human beings who do not have names and are only referred to by generic terms? An argument may be made here that the woman is already named in Genesis 2:23, as man exclaims, "She shall be called woman [אִשָּׁה]." The answer is no, she is not named; rather, she is merely acknowledged. As Trible points out:

> ʾiššâ itself is not a name; it does not specify a person. Moreover, this word appears in the story before the earth creature "calls" it: the narrator reports that "Yahweh God built the rib which he took from the earth creature into a woman [ʾiššâ]" (2:22). Thus, the creature's poem does not determine who the woman is, but rather delights in what God has already done in creating sexuality.[13]

The only point in the narrative at which אָדָם starts to function as the proper name "Adam," is in Genesis 3:17, 21, where for the first time it loses the article (הָ). Notably, there is a hierarchy in the naming: God names the man, Adam, and the man in turn names his wife. In Genesis 3:20, "the man called

---

12. Anderson, *Genesis of Perfection*, 208.
13. Trible, *God and Rhetoric*, 100.

the name of his wife Eve" (own translation). The combination of separation and naming, as Westermann argues, belong together as important components of the creation process.[14] I disagree, however, with the argument that separation and naming are hallmarks of the Priestly source, Genesis 1:1–2:4b, not of the Yahwist source or non-P, Genesis 2:4b–3:24. The first human beings in Genesis 1 are not named except to note their gender difference. It is specifically the concern of Genesis 2:4b–3:24 to expand on how humanity came into being through the process of separation, the man from the dust of the ground and the woman from the rib of the man, and how they came to have their names Adam and Eve.

Second, the judgment pronouncements to humankind in Genesis 3:16–24 are organized around the blessings to humankind and instruction regarding man's livelihood from Genesis 1:28–29:[15] (a) In his pronouncement to the woman, God addresses specifically the blessing, the multiplication of humankind. The woman's fertility is not a divine penalty; rather, it is the blessing that humankind received in Genesis 1:28, affirmed in the divine judgment in Genesis 3:16.[16] What the fall altered was not the blessing but the condition of being a wife and a mother. There is now an increase of pain in childbearing and of domination in the husband-wife relationship.

(b) It was in the wake of the judgment that humankind came to acknowledge the creation mandate to multiply, be fruitful, and fill the earth. In naming his wife, Adam calls her Eve, meaning "the mother of all the living" (Gen 3:17). Even though humankind is threatened by death, the divine command to be fruitful and multiply is affirmed as Adam reclaims the creation blessing by naming his wife Eve.[17]

(c) The judgment on Adam affirms the creation mandate to subdue the earth by serving and cultivating it and gaining his survival from it; however, the conditions of the earth have now changed, requiring humans to engage in a painful and ceaseless toil to take care of the earth and produce food from

---

14. Westermann, *Genesis 1–11*, 122.

15. Walton, *Genesis*, 238.

16. In contrast to Williams's claim that we have two traditions regarding mankind's fertility: P's version – fertility as a divine mandate, and J's version – fertility as part of divine penalty. Williams, "Relationship of Genesis 3:20," 357–74.

17. See Westermann, *Creation*, 104; Von Rad, *Genesis*, 96; Hamilton, *Book of Genesis*, 206–7.

it. As Barr points out, "his [humankind's] death is not the punishment, but is only the mode in which the final stage of the punishment works out. He was going to die anyway, but *this* formulation of his death emphasized his failure to overcome the soil and his own belonging to it" (emphasis in original).[18] The blessings are not withdrawn in the judgment; rather, they are affirmed under new conditions.

Third, Genesis 1:26 and 3:22 form an *inclusio*. The fact that human beings are created "in the image of God in accordance to his likeness" finds its affirmation at the wake of the fall. I am not concerned here with trying to define or explicate in depth the meaning of "image of God" or "likeness" of God. I am only interested here with the tie between Genesis 1 and Genesis 3. In Genesis 1:24–31, the sixth day of creation, animals are created first, then humanity (male and female) last, created in the image of God, as the climax of creation. In Genesis 2:7–2:25, the man is created first and put in the garden of Eden, animals are created second, and lastly the woman is created as the climax of creation; however, in this case nothing is said about humankind created in the "image" or "likeness" of God. In Genesis 3, the issue of humankind's "likeness" to God is at the central issue. Humankind is tempted to be like God, knowing good and bad (v. 5) and does indeed become like the divine, "the man has become like one of us, knowing good and bad" (v. 22). Also notable is that the motif of likeness is accompanied with a divine dialogue – "Let us make man in our image, in our likeness" (Gen 1:26) and "the man has become like one of us" (Gen 3:22, NRSV). There is, however, a contrastive element to these divine dialogues. In Genesis 1, the *making* of humankind in the image and likeness of God is coupled with exaltation – to rule – whereas in Genesis 3, the *becoming* of humankind like God results in demotion – expulsion from the royal garden temple. In Genesis 3 there is no withdrawal of the creation mandate of Genesis 1:28; there is, however, a loss of privilege. The *making* is good, whereas the *becoming* is bad.

Considering the second creation narrative in *toto*, Genesis 3:22 presents a negative which is not undone unlike all the other negatives within.[19] The prohibition of humankind to eat from the tree of life following their disobedience of God's command implied a loss of a chance to immortality as the

---

18. Barr, *Garden of Eden*, 9.
19. Ramantswana, "Humanity Not Pronounced Good," 804–18.

human couple was expelled from the garden. The Genesis 2:4b–3:24 creation narrative, as Schmid notes, does not highlight a loss of the original immortality; rather, it was a loss of a chance to immortality. As Ramantswana notes, "a loss for humanity was a gain for creation, as human beings are returned to the ground outside to work it; thereby solving the initial deficiency of creation (see Gen 2:5 and 3:23)."[20] Furthermore, as Ramantswana argues, "From outside the garden, the return to the garden and the eating from the tree of life becomes the goal for humanity. The hope for humanity lies in the undoing of the final negative in Gen 3:22."[21]

It may be concluded that the Genesis 2:4b–3:24 narrative is interested in establishing the immediacy of human disobedience.[22] It seems probable to me that Genesis 3 falls within the sixth day of God's creation week. This implies that the second creation narrative finds its proper conclusion not in Genesis 2:25, but in Genesis 3:24. This implies that the fall happened on the same day that humankind was created, meaning that Adam and Eve spent no more than a day in paradise. Below, we explore two things which contributed toward the so-called fall of humanity: the presence of the serpent in the garden of Eden, and the distinction between clean and unclean food.

The Presence of a Deceptive Serpent in the Garden, a Sacred Space

Within the Genesis 2:4b–3:24 creation narrative, the first dialogic encounter is found in 3:1–5. One of God's creatures, called "the serpent" (הַנָּחָשׁ), engages in a dialogue with the human couple. It should be recalled, however, that in Genesis 1:25, God created all kinds of animals and pronounced them "good." So the serpent, like all the other animals is, "good," but is it really that "good"?[23]

---

20. Ramantswana, 813.

21. Ramantswana, 813.

22. I am indebted here to Anderson, *Genesis of Perfection*, 205–8; and Kearney, "Creation and Liturgy," 375–87.

23. Elsewhere in Scripture, the serpent is regarded as an opponent of God (Isa 27:1; cf. Job 26:12–14) and also as hostile to mankind (Gen 49:17; Exod 4:3; Isa 14:29; 27:1; Jer 8:17; Amos 9:3); however, there is one exceptional case, Moses's bronze serpent, which was later destroyed by Hezekiah, as it had become an object of idolatry (Num 21:8; 2 Kgs 18:4).

In the ancient Near East, the serpent was associated with things that may be potentially good or bad: wisdom, magic, health, fertility, life and recurring youth, immortality, and chaos; it was also worshiped as a god. For detailed discussions of the serpent symbolism in the ancient Near East, see Sarna, *Genesis*, 24; Scullion, *Genesis*, 47; Joines, *Serpent Symbolism*,

In Genesis 3 the serpent has at least one quality that sets it apart and above all the other beasts of the field – it is "more crafty [עָרוּם] than any other beast of the field that the LORD God had made" (Gen 3:1, own translation). Though this creature is clearly differentiated from the first human couple, it has human capabilities – it is a rational creature, and it can speak. But in the end it is not human; it is a beast like any other beast of the field. The only other creature that speaks in the Old Testament is Balaam's ass, which miraculously speaks as a mouthpiece of God: "The LORD opened the mouth of the ass" (Num 22:28, RSV).

Apparently, as beastly as the serpent was, it knows both the limitations of human beings in the garden and their desires and cravings, and it is willing to manipulate the human couple. The command regarding the tree of the knowledge of good and bad provides the serpent with the loophole it needs to seduce human beings into disobeying God and eating of this forbidden tree. He says to the woman, "Did God really say: You shall not eat of any tree of the garden?" (Gen 3:1b, own translation). The serpent does not raise the issue of the forbidden tree directly; neither does he mention the tree by its name.

The narrator, however, already anticipates the thought process of his human characters. The trees in the garden are "desirable [נֶחְמָד] for seeing" and "good [טוֹב] for eating" (Gen 2:8–9). As White argues,

> by linking human sight to desire, and presenting the value of the trees of the garden in terms of their power to evoke these human sensory and subjective responses, the author conveys the human condition as one of lack, deficiency, or emptiness which can be filled by obtaining and consuming these sensorially stimulating objects.[24]

The trees in the middle of the garden – the tree of life and the tree of the knowledge of good and bad – represent a crucial lack in humankind, the lack of immortality.[25]

In response to the snake, the woman says, "We may eat fruit from the trees in the garden, but God did say, 'You must not eat fruit from the tree

---

19–24; Joines, "Serpent in Gen. 3," 1–11; Walton, *Genesis*, 202–3; Jacobsen, "Mesopotamian Gods and Pantheons," 24.

24. White, *Narration and Discourse*, 118.

25. More on this in chapter 5.

that is in the middle of the garden, and you must not touch it, or you will die'" (Gen 3:2–3, NIV). The woman speaks in the first person plural; thus she speaks not only for herself but for her husband as well, "we may eat." In addition, the woman also refers back to God's commandment invoking both the prohibition(s) and the danger of transgression.[26]

The serpent, on the other hand, responds to the woman by negating God's words: God has stated, "you shall surely die" (מוֹת תָּמוּת; Gen 2:17), whereas in 3:4 the serpent states, "you will not surely die" (לֹא־מוֹת תְּמֻתוּן; Gen 3:4). From the serpent's perspective, human beings had nothing to fear from eating any of the trees in the garden, including the prohibited tree. Furthermore, "For God knows that when you eat of it your eyes will be opened, and you will be like God, knowing good and bad" (Gen 3:5, own translation).[27]

The serpent does not simply invalidate God's word; rather, it suggests to humankind an alternative. Instead of dying, by eating, humankind will have their eyes opened and they will be like God, knowing good and bad. The issue of God likeness is one already encountered in the first creation story. In Genesis 1:26–28, humanity is said to be created in *the image of God*, and *in his likeness*. What the narrator has revealed to the reader in Genesis 1:26–28 is unknown to his human characters in the second creation narrative. The reader comes to Genesis 3 in a privileged position, thus already having an answer to the serpent's temptation: we are created in the image of God, and in his [God's] likeness. However, the first human couple is not in this privileged position; this information was apparently not known to humankind because it was intradivine dialogue or perhaps part of an exchange in the divine assembly. The serpent capitalized on humankind's lack of knowledge, and so tempted humankind to pursue it – to be like God. However, how the serpent knew about the issue of *likeness* remains veiled. The serpent presents God as one who has not revealed his true motives or rather the whole truth behind his prohibiting the first human couple to eat from the tree of the knowledge of good and bad.[28] In this process, the serpent offered humankind an alternative to God's command.

---

26. More on this in chapter 5.

27. The author's own translation.

28. It is possible that the book of Job was written as a counterexample to the primordial example of the first human couple. In both stories, the reader has a surplus vision. The reader is taken into the divine realm and overhears a divine dialogue that is unknown to the human

The serpent by offering an alternative provoked humankind to start paying attention to the prohibited tree. In this sense, the serpent functioned as an eye opener of the human couple: the narrator tells us that "the woman *saw* that the fruit of the tree was *good* for food and *pleasing* to the eye, and also *desirable* for gaining wisdom" (Gen 3:6a, NIV, emphasis added).[29] The desires and cravings of humankind were aroused, and the prohibited tree was now like other trees, "pleasing to the eye and good for food" (cf. Gen 2:9, NIV), but now, with a new and distorted potentiality, not death and not life, but "desirable for gaining wisdom [לְהַשְׂכִּיל]." As White argues,

> the inadmissible desire for god-likeness is carefully concealed behind more acceptable desire for "wisdom." Thus a division is established in her consciousness between what she can articulate to herself as her desires and what she cannot. The serpent says: "You will be like God," but she thinks it is "desirable for wisdom." But beneath this is the unspeakable, possible thought: "I desire to be like God."[30]

The serpent did not give the human couple the mandate to transgress, but it contradicted the threat of punishment and provided the verbal basis for them to make their own transgressive decision.[31] Humankind possessed a sense of autonomy. There was a certain degree of distance between the creator and humankind that made room for humankind to freely respond to the temptation by either trusting God and voluntarily coming to him or by trusting the serpent and being alienated from God. The Eden narrative, as we will observe subsequently, is one which culminates in alienation.

It may be concluded that the particular serpent of Genesis 3 is good only in so far as it is part of God's good creation; however, it is bad in that it seduces humankind to disobey God. In contrast to Fretheim, who suggests that the

---

characters. In the case of the first human couple, they lose their possession as a result of their disobedience, whereas in the case of Job, he loses everything due to his obedience only to gain it all back and even more. In both narratives, the divine motives made known to the reader have no bearing on how human characters respond to their testing.

29. The author makes a word-play on the human couple's "nakedness" (עֲרוּמִּים) and the serpent's "craftiness" (עָרוּם). The word-play here links the serpent with the human couple's deception, which resulted in a realization of their nakedness; compare Gen 2:24; 3:1, 7.

30. White, *Narration and Discourse*, 134.

31. White, 134.

serpent is presented as a neutral figure simply mediating options in God's creation,[32] the serpent is presented as an antagonist of Yahweh and as a threat to humankind. The serpent negates God's words and presents itself as worthy of human beings' trust. I do agree with Fretheim that at the "deepest level the issue of knowledge becomes an issue of trust."[33] Whose word is to be trusted, God's word or the serpent's word, the creator's word or a creature's word? But is it right to paint the serpent as an antagonist and a threat to humankind, when he does appear to be truthful?

The answer should be yes. Though, as the serpent says, humans do not die immediately, their eyes were indeed opened as the serpent had said (Gen 3:7), and God acknowledges, by eating of the forbidden fruit that "human being has become like one of us," and humankind does come to know good and bad (Gen 3:22). The issue is not so much whether the serpent was telling the truth or lies; it is rather the motive behind the truth that the serpent told.[34] As Barr suggests, the serpent spoke the truth in order to commit evil.[35] The serpent's motive was to bring disorder in God's creation by inciting humankind to disobey God.

The presence of the serpent should also be understood as a violation of the sacred space. Important for the author is not simply to let the readers know of the dialogue between the serpent and humankind. Where the dialogue happened is just as important for the author. Genesis 2:15–3:24 narrates the chain of events from the placement of humankind in the garden to his expulsion from the garden. The garden of Eden, as already noted, was an earthly dwelling of Yahweh, the holy of holies, so to speak. The presence of the serpent in the garden symbolizes something that was not supposed to be in the garden being in the garden and being entertained by humankind who were supposed to keep guard (*šamar*) over the garden. Walton rightly observes, "the creation account in Genesis 1 contained no serpentine sea monster to threaten God's establishment of cosmic order, but here we find

---

32. Fretheim, "Is Genesis 3?", 150–51. Fretheim writes, "the serpent is a living metaphor, representing anything in God's good creation that is able to facilitate options for human will and action." Fretheim, Is Genesis 3?", 149.

33. Fretheim, 151.

34. Barr, "Is God a Liar?", 13. For alternate positions on this issue, see Moberly, "Did the Serpent Get?", 1–27; LaCocque, "Cracks in the Wall," 3–29.

35. Barr, "Is God a Liar?", 13.

a serpent who begins to work against the order that existed in the human realm."[36] The presence of the serpent in the garden suggests that something "bad" had already made its way into God's good creation even prior to humankind's disobedience – the spirit of deception, disguised in craftiness, was attacking God and his priest in the sacred space.

Clean and Unclean Food

In Genesis 1:29–30, God gives humankind and other earthly creatures instructions regarding food. The instructions are given in positive terms, and no prohibitions are spelled out.

> God said, "See, I have given you every plant yielding seed that is upon the face of all the earth, and every tree with seed in its fruit; you shall have them for food. And to every beast of the earth, and to every bird of the air, and to everything that creeps on the earth, everything that has the breath of life, I have given every green plant for food." And it was so. (Gen 1:29–30, NRSV)

The provision of food to humanity within the creation stories was common in the ancient Near Eastern cosmogonies. While Genesis 1:29 highlights no restrictions regarding what humankind may eat within those things that are prescribed as food, the Genesis 2:4b–3:24, highlights an important restriction – humankind is not supposed to eat from the tree of the knowledge of good and bad. Thus, from the perspective of Genesis 2:4b–3:24, the freedom to eat from any or all vegetations is not without limitations.

There is, however, one more perspective from which the tree of the knowledge of good and bad is viewed; this may be regarded as the woman's perspective or perhaps more accurately the priestly perspective. In the dialogue exchange between the serpent and the woman, the woman, quoting God, states: "God did say, '*You must not eat* from the tree that is in the middle of the garden, and *you must not touch* it, or you will die'" (Gen 3:3, NIV, emphasis added). The woman's words have been understood in many different ways, particularly in consideration of the addition to the prohibition as originally stated in 2:17. The woman's words have been understood as a

---

36. Walton, *Genesis*, 203. I discuss the issue of the sea serpent and specifically the issue of the serpent of Genesis 3 in chapter 5.

restatement of God's will,[37] a presentation of what her husband told her,[38] an attempt to build a protective fence around the prohibitive command (Torah) to ensure obedience,[39] and distortion, exaggeration, or misrepresentation of God's words through emendation.[40]

The woman's words, as Townsend argues, anticipate the later unclean-clean code in the subsequent books of the Pentateuch.[41] The woman's words have as their parallel Leviticus 11:8 and Deuteronomy 14:8:

Gen 3:3	Lev 11:8	Deut 14:8, NIV
Regarding the tree that is in the middle of the garden, God said, "you shall not eat from it and you shall not touch it, lest you die."	Of their flesh you shall not eat, and their carcasses you shall not touch; they are unclean.	The swine . . . is unclean for you; their flesh you shall not eat, and their carcasses you shall not touch.
וּמִפְּרִי הָעֵץ אֲשֶׁר בְּתוֹךְ־הַגָּן אָמַר אֱלֹהִים לֹא תֹאכְלוּ מִמֶּנּוּ וְלֹא תִגְּעוּ בּוֹ פֶּן־תְּמֻתוּן׃	מִבְּשָׂרָם לֹא תֹאכֵלוּ וּבְנִבְלָתָם לֹא תִגָּעוּ טְמֵאִים הֵם לָכֶם	אֶת־הַחֲזִיר . . . טָמֵא הוּא לָכֶם מִבְּשָׂרָם לֹא תֹאכֵלוּ וּבְנִבְלָתָם לֹא תִגָּעוּ

In these three texts, not only do we have a parallel in the vocabulary and structure of the prohibition, even more so, in all cases the prohibition is against eating and touching forbidden or unclean food.[42]

This is especially significant, because this combined prohibition against eating and touching is repeated throughout Leviticus 11, which is especially focused on prescribing what the Israelites may or may not eat, the food laws (vv. 8, 11, 13, 24b, 26b, 27b–28a). Touching and eating of prohibited food required immediate cleansing and made one temporarily unclean, until evening (Lev 11:24–28, 31 –32, 39–40; 17:15). In addition, touching of unclean

---

37. See Bonhoeffer, *Creation and Fall*, 69; Cassuto, *Commentary on Genesis*, 1:145.
38. Sarna, *Genesis*, 24.
39. Scullion, *Genesis*, 38; Trible, "Feminist Hermeneutics," 117.
40. See Von Rad, *Genesis*, 88; Westermann, *Genesis 1–11*, 239–40; Leupold, *Exposition of Genesis*, 148; MacIntosh, *Genesis to Deuteronomy*, 28; Morris, *The Genesis Record*, 111; Vawter, *On Genesis*, 78; Stigers, *Commentary on Genesis*, 74; Knight, *Theology in Pictures*, 36; Boice, *Genesis*, 135; Vos, *Genesis*, 26; Candlish, *Commentary on Genesis*, 62.
41. Townsend, "Eve's Answer," 399–420.
42. Townsend, 406.

food required the perpetrator to make a sin offering like that of any other temporary uncleanness (Lev 5:2, 5–6).

Furthermore, the consequences of temporary uncleanness were severe, the perpetrator was held responsible (Lev 17:16) with the threat of being cut off from the community (Lev 7:21). Even more so, the whole Israelite community was threatened with the loss of land if they failed to keep the decrees and laws prescribed (Lev 20:22–24), which is a clear parallel to the punishment of the first human couple.[43] Also notable in Leviticus 20:22–24 is that the threat of the loss of land is immediately followed by a reinforcement to distinguish between clean and unclean food: "You must therefore make a distinction between clean and unclean animals and between unclean and clean birds. Do not defile yourselves by any animal or bird or anything that moves along the ground, those which I have set apart as unclean for you" (Lev 11:25).

The difference between the first human couple and the later Israelite community is simply that the former were vegetarian, whereas the latter were also allowed to eat meat. The Adamic generation was only allowed to eat of plants (Gen 1:29); it was only with the re-creation of the earth during the time of Noah that humankind was permitted to eat animals: "Everything that lives and moves will be food for you. Just as I gave you green plants, I now give you everything" (Gen 9:3). Townsend rightly concludes that in light of the parallels, "the original readers of Eve's words would have understood that story in the context of God's commands concerning unclean foods, and would have understood that the fruit of the Tree of knowledge of Good and Evil was unclean food."[44] This, as Townsend argues, should have significance on how Genesis 3 and the original sin is to be perceived.[45]

Significant for us at this point is to note that the distinction between clean and unclean was already functional within creation in its original state of goodness. It may even be stated that the tree of the knowledge of good and bad was unclean whereas the tree of life and the rest of the trees in the garden were clean. The tree of the knowledge of good and bad was good in so far as it was part of God's good creation; however, that it was unclean food that humankind was not supposed to eat or touch implies that eating and

---

43. Townsend, 407, 412.
44. Townsend, 407.
45. Townsend, 407.

touching it would have rendered the human couple unclean. Furthermore, if the garden of Eden is viewed as a temple or a holy of holies, then, it follows from the presence of the tree of the knowledge of good and bad that there was an unclean thing in the sanctuary that posed a threat to the priests who served therein.

Fallen but Functional Creation

The two creation narratives, Genesis 1:1–2:4a and Genesis 2:4b–3:24, stand in a dialogic relationship in which they mutually enrich each other. I suggest that the sequence of events on the creation week be visualized as follows:

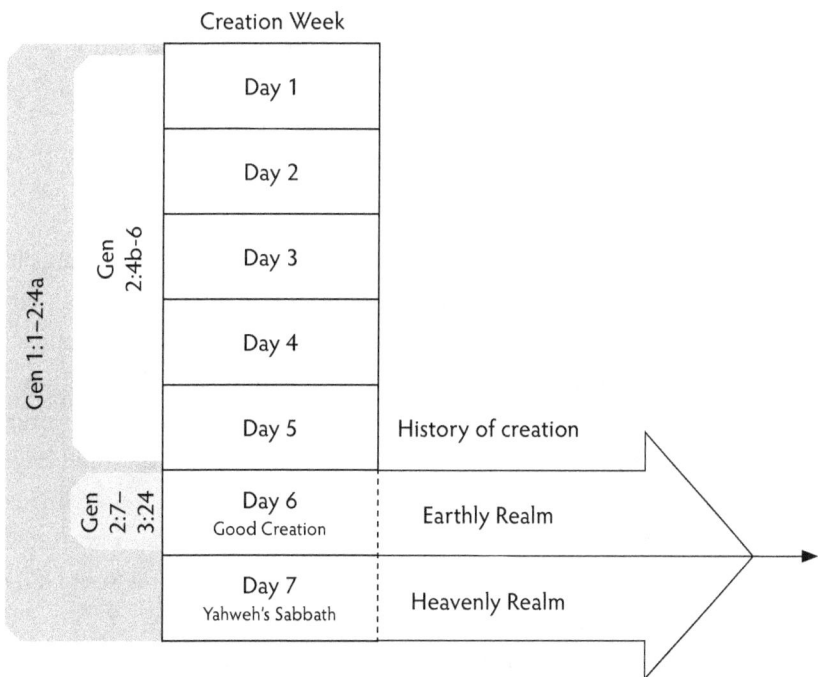

Figure 2: The Good Creation within the Seven-Day Framework

The structuring suggested in figure 2 above does not allow us to leave Genesis 1:1–2:4a behind; rather Genesis 2:4b–3:24, puts us right back within it, thereby forcing us to understand these two narratives as standing in a dialogic relationship with each other. The one cannot do without the other.

An objection may be raised that placing the events in Genesis 3 within the sixth day would make God the author of evil. On the contrary, placing the events in Genesis 3 within the sixth day of creation does not make God the author of evil or sin. As Bavinck argues,

> What is important is that, according to Scripture, the fall is essentially distinct from the creation itself. Sin is a phenomenon whose possibility was indeed given in the creation of finite, mutable beings, but whose reality could only be called into being by the will of the creature, a power that originally did not exist, but that came by way of disobedience and transgression, that is, entered the creation unlawfully, and did not belong there. It is there and its existence is not an accident. With a view to the counsel of God that incorporated it and assigned a place to it, it may up to a point and in a sense even be said that it had to be there. But then certainly it always *had to* be there as something that *ought not* to be and has no right to exist.[46]

God is no author of evil or sin; however, as Bavinck's words captures it, it does not follow that evil or sin is outside the scope of God's counsel. For the author of Genesis, sin or disobedience of God's command has cosmic effects for the worse: the earth cursed on account of humankind, humankind unclean, and paradise lost for the rest of humankind. By contrast, however, obedience to God's command, it may be reasonably inferred, would have had cosmic effects for the better – the earth would have been blessed on account of humankind, humankind would have remained clean and paradise possessed would have remained in humankind's possession and would have improved radically and expanded geographically.

In Genesis 1:1–2:4a, there is a smooth progression in the creation narrative, reaching its climax in the creation of humankind and finding its conclusion in God taking his seat to rest. In Genesis 2:4b–3:24, things turn sour very quickly. The human being is placed in paradise, and he is immediately given the commandment regarding the trees in the middle of the garden, but

---

46. Bavinck, *Reformed Dogmatics*, 74.

the human being hardly enjoys the garden alone. In response God creates animals, but a helper is not found; immediately, God makes another attempt: the woman is created, and the problem is resolved. However, the man and his wife hardly enjoy any leisure before the serpent approaches them. If Adam and Eve ever enjoyed the paradisiacal environment, the narrator does not let us enjoy it with them.[47] The serpent wastes no time; it immediately seduces the human couple to disobey the commandment, and so the fall was disobedience to "the first and only command given to them."[48] God immediately appears back in the scene, and the human couple runs away and hides, but they are found. Immediately, judgment is administered, and the story concludes with the human couple expelled from paradise. I therefore suggest that the sequence of events in Genesis 2:4b–3:24 be mapped out as follows: garden of Eden and placement creation of the human couple (Gen 2:4b–25), temptation and the fall (Gen 3:1–7), judgment and restoration (Gen 3:8–21), and expulsion (Gen 3:22–24). This sense of immediacy is evidenced by the parallels this narrative has within the larger story of Israel.

I have already alluded in a number of instances to the parallels between Genesis 1:1–3:24 and the Sinai event – the erection of the tabernacle (Exod 24:15–40:38). The tabernacle creation mirrors the sevenfold creation pattern in Genesis 1:1–2:4a,[49] but there is also a parallel with Genesis 2:4b–3:24 in the narrative sequence: creation (Exod 25–31), the fall (Exod 32–33), and restoration (Exod 34–40).[50] I am more interested here in the latter parallels. Exodus 32–34 has functions for Israel similar to those of Genesis 3 for humankind in general.[51] Hafemann observes, "Like the original creation narrative, the re-creation of a people to enjoy God's presence at Sinai is followed

---

47. Bavinck, 3:74.

48. Bavinck, 3:74.

49. Anderson notes the following patterns: "The sevenfold activity begins immediately after Moses ascends to Mt. Sinai. He waits for six days and then on the seventh God draws to him near to his very presence (Exod. 24:15b–18). The initial plans for the tabernacle are given to Moses in a set of seven addresses that conclude with the command to observe the Sabbath rest of the seventh day (Exod. 25:1; 30:11, 17, 22, 34; 31:1, 12). The fashioning of priestly vestments is marked by the sevenfold refrain 'he did as the LORD commanded him,' (Exod. 39:1, 5, 7, 21, 22, 27, 30) as is the erection of the tabernacle itself (Exod. 40:19, 21, 23, 25, 27, 29, 32)." Anderson, *Genesis of Perfection*, 200–201.

50. Kearney, "Creation and Liturgy," 384.

51. Abasciano, *Paul's Use*, 46; see also Hafemann, *Paul, Moses*, 228–31; Fretheim, *Exodus*, 279; Houtman, *Exodus*, 3:608.

by a 'fall' which separates them from the glory of God both determinative and paradigmatic for Israel's future as God's people."[52] As Moberly argues, the golden calf incident is, so to speak, Israel's "first sin," which immediately follows their creation as a people.[53]

The Sinai event takes place within the context of the making of the covenant, the giving of the Torah, and the erection of the tabernacle. It is the Sinai context in which Israel immediately lapses into disobedience. Israel, the people of God, who had just heard the verbal Torah proceeding from God, did not have the patience to wait to receive the written Torah; their speedy fall from grace is evidenced by their erection and worship of the golden calf. Thus, God's covenant with Israel is immediately shattered by the disobedience of Israel. The immediacy of the fall of Israel can also be viewed from a creational perspective in relation to the building of the tabernacle. In Exodus 25:1–31:18, Moses receives the blueprint of the tabernacle; the work is suddenly interrupted by the rebellion of the people (Exod 32–33); however, God in his graciousness restores Israel and allows the work of the tabernacle to continue and be finished (Exod 34–40).

The rebellion of Israel did not frustrate God's plan to make his dwelling among them, and furthermore, the work still found positive evaluation: "And Moses saw all the work, and behold they had done it; as the LORD had commanded, so had they done it" (Exod 39:43, RSV; cf. Gen 1:31). It should also be added that God's purpose and plan in creation were not frustrated by humanity's rebellion; God continued with his creation activities and brought his work to its proper conclusion. Even with the fractured relationship between God and humanity and the new conditions on earth as a consequence of the fall, God could still look back at his creation activity and find satisfaction in his deeds: "God saw all that he made, and it was very good" (Gen 1:31).

The final refrain assures the reader ahead of time of the functionality of creation. The cosmic effects of humankind's disobedience did not render creation nonfunctional or nonexistent. God did not reverse creation to its nonfunctional state as a result of humankind's disobedience. Creation remained functional, what had changed were conditions under which it was to

---

52. Hafemann, *Paul*, 229–30. See similar comments from Moberly, *At the Mountain*, 46; Childs, *Book of Exodus*, 564–65.

53. Moberly, 46, 89.

continue to function. Readers of all generations beginning with the original audience or reader are, in the final refrain of Genesis 1, assured that creation is functioning well in accordance to God's purpose and direction. Creation is not aimlessly and purposelessly created.

The refrains of Genesis 1 and specifically the final refrain are no claim for the perfection of creation. I am convinced that if the author of Genesis had wanted to express the idea of "perfection," he would have possibly gone with a different terminology than טוֹב. There are two Hebrew words which carry the notion of perfection or are translatable as "perfect." First is the adjective תָּמִים or the short form תָּם, which expresses the idea of wholeness, soundness, completeness, entirety, fullness (Deut 34:2; Josh 10:13; 2 Sam 22:31, 33; Job 1:1, 8; 2:3; 8:20; 9:20, 21–22; 36:4; 37:16; Pss 18:30, 32; 19:7; 25:21; 37:37; 64:5; Prov 2:7; 13:6; 29:10); it is most often used for human morality carrying the idea of "blameless" or following the Lord wholeheartedly (Gen 6:9; 17:1; Deut 18:13; 2 Sam 22:24, 26; Job 1:1, 8; 2:3; 8:20; 9:20–22; Pss 1:1; 25:21; 37:37; 64:5; Prov 2:7; 13:6; 29:10; Ezek 28:15); sacrificial animals were to be presented "without blemish" (Exod 12:5; Lev 1:3, 10; 3:1, 6; 4:3, 23; 5:15, 18, 25; 22:19, 21; 23:12; Num 6:14; 28:3, 9, 11, 19, 31; 29:2, 8, 13, 17, 20, 23, 26, 29, 32, 36; Ps 37:18; Ezek 43:22–23; 45:18, 23; 46:4, 6, 13); it is also used to describe the ways of God or his works (Deut 34:2; 2 Sam 22:31, 33; Job 12:4). Second is שָׁלֵם, when used adjectivally, also carries the idea of wholeness, completeness, soundness, peace (1 Kgs 8:61; 11:4; 15:3, 14; 2 Kgs 20:3; 2 Chr 8:16; 15:17; 16:9; 19:9; 25:2; Isa 26:3; 38:3). As LaRondelle argues, "the word 'perfect' is neither applied to the empirical world nor to the static metaphysical world, but to the dynamic world of God's actions and the concrete revelation of His will."[54] In the Old Testament, God is the norm of "perfection": "He is the Rock, his work is perfect" (Deut 32:4, NIV); "As for God, his way is perfect" (2 Sam 22:31, 33, NIV); "The law of the LORD is perfect" (Ps 19:7, NIV).

Some of the early church fathers, especially Irenaeus, argued for an ontological imperfection of creation. It is this imperfection of creation that makes the fall possible, but not inevitable.[55] Irenaeus states regarding the creation of man,

---

54. LaRondelle, *Perfection and Perfectionism*, 40.
55. See Brown, "On the Necessary Imperfection," 17–25; Farrow, "St. Irenaeus of Lyons," 333–55, esp. 348.

God had power at the beginning to grant perfection to man; but as the latter was only recently created, he could not possibly have received it, or even if he had received it, could he have contained it, or containing it could he have retained it. . . . There was nothing, therefore, impossible to and deficient in God [implied in the fact] that man was not an uncreated being; but this merely applied to him who was lately created, [namely] man.[56]

As Brown points out, the necessary imperfection is that of the creature by nature, as "all creatures lack the perfection possessed by their Creator."[57] Important for Irenaeus is not only the creator-creature distinction, but also that creation is geared toward a goal. Humanity, although created imperfect, had to mature to attain the perfection destined for them.[58] As Williams points out, in the Irenaean scheme "the actualization and fulfillment of human perfection are located not in the beginning but in the end. The temporal orientation is not towards the past but the future."[59]

Creation at the end of the sixth day was "finished" or "completed" (כָּלָה): וַיְכֻלּוּ הַשָּׁמַיִם וְהָאָרֶץ וְכָל־צְבָאָם (Gen 2:1). As is clear in Exodus 20:11; 31:17, כִּי שֵׁשֶׁת־יָמִים עָשָׂה יְהוָה אֶת־הַשָּׁמַיִם וְאֶת־הָאָרֶץ. In six days creation was עָשָׂה and כָּלָה, the operational system was in place, fully functional, thereby inagurating the history of creation. The good creation is neither an end nor the goal of the creation activities; rather, it is very good because it is goal-oriented (*teleological*) – moving toward its Sabbath. The creation process finds its *telos* on the seventh day of creation. The good creation is transcended. God's creation week is not the first of subsequent weeks to follow; rather, it is one vertical full and complete week; it finds its culmination on the seventh day. As Westermann argues,

---

56. Irenaeus, *Against Heresies*, 4.38.2.

57. Brown, "On the Necessary Imperfection," 22.

58. Irenaeus describes the maturity process as follows: "Man, a created and organized being, is rendered after the image and the likeness of the uncreated God . . . making progress day by day, and ascending towards the perfect, that is, approximating to the uncreated One. For the Uncreated is perfect, that is, God. Now it is necessary that man should in the first instance be created; and having been created, should receive growth; and having received growth, should be strengthened, should abound and having abounded, should recover [from the disease of sin]; and having recovered, should be glorified; and being glorified, should see his Lord. For God is he who is yet to be seen, and the beholding of God is productive of immortality, but immortality renders one nigh unto God." Irenaeus, *Against Heresies*. 4.38.3.

59. Williams, "Sin and Evil," 194–221, esp. 217.

Creation is good for that which God intends. What that is has not yet been stated. The Creation story with its goal as the rest on the seventh day shows that Creation introduces a self-contained history – history in the broadest sense that can be given to the word – a history of the cosmos and in the midst of it history of the human race which, as it has grown out of God's Creation, will also have a goal, which has been set for it by God. Looking then at the history of the cosmos and of humankind, "all is very good."[60]

God's creation week culminates on the seventh day in blessedness, holiness, and rest. The holiness of the Sabbath pertains to two things, among others: sacred time and sacred space. Thus, the first creation culminates in separation, "God blessed the seventh day *and made it holy* [וַיְקַדֵּשׁ אֹתוֹ "set it apart"]" (Gen 2:3a). Before we turn to these two things, it should be noted that the seventh day does not have an inherent holiness apart from God's declaration. Unlike the previous six days in which creation is deemed good or very good, the seventh day is the day that God separates for himself, for his rest. God is able to declare things holy because he himself is "holy" – he is the source of holiness (Isa 6:3; 57:15). Milgrom's definition of holiness summarizes well these ideas: "Holiness is the extension of [God's] nature; it is the agency of his will. If certain things are termed holy – such as the land (Canaan), person (priest), place (sanctuary), or time (holy day) – they are so by virtue of divine dispensation."[61]

Now, with regard to sacred time, by declaring the seventh day holy, God had divided time, to use Westermann's words, into "time and holy time, time for work and time for rest." However, before any of the analogy between weekly Sabbaths and the seventh day of creation can be drawn, it cannot be emphasized enough that the seventh day of creation is God's day, not human's day.

The seventh day is God's holy period of time, which has no end – a day without evening and morning. In God's creation week, creation has in time progressed from darkness to light. God's time of creation work, six days of creation, is something of the past, which cannot be repeated; whereas his holy

---

60. Westermann, *Creation*, 61.
61. Milgrom, *Leviticus 1–16*, 730.

time of rest is the fullness of time with perpetual significance. The perpetual significance of the Sabbath is shown by God's command for Israel to observe the Sabbath throughout their generation as an everlasting covenant as a sign of God's work and rest at creation, and as mark of Israel's holiness:

> The LORD said to Moses: You yourself are to speak to the Israelites: "You shall keep my sabbaths, for this is a sign between me and you throughout your generations, given in order that you may know that I, the LORD, sanctify you. You shall keep the sabbath, because it is holy for you; everyone who profanes it shall be put to death; whoever does any work on it shall be cut off from among the people. Six days shall work be done, but the seventh day is a sabbath of solemn rest, holy to the LORD; whoever does any work on the sabbath day shall be put to death. Therefore the Israelites shall keep the sabbath, observing the sabbath throughout their generations, as a perpetual covenant. *It is a sign forever between me and the people of Israel that in six days the LORD made heaven and earth, and on the seventh day he rested, and was refreshed.*" (Exod 31:12–17, NRSV)[62]

The seventh day of creation not only stands as an archetype for the weekly Sabbath, it is also a transcendent day, a heavenly reality of perpetual significance. The seventh day of God's creation week, as already observed, is a day without end – a day without evening and morning; however, its continuation is not on the vertical axis but on the horizontal axis. The heavenly Sabbatical reality now continues concurrently with world history at the center of which stands humankind, the "image of God." Thus, the weekly Sabbaths stand as continual shadows of the heavenly reality – heavenly blessedness, holiness, and resting. As Westermann argues, "to give the holy a special place in the stream of events is to indicate the goal of creation, a goal which corresponds to that which God set for himself. This goal is not part of the six ordinary days, but a holy day set apart."[63]

Regarding sacred space, the rest (שָׁבַת) of God does not take place in vacuum; rather it takes place in space. The state of the seventh day is referred

---

62. Emphasis added.
63. Westermann, *Genesis 1–11*, 172.

to in Exodus 20:11 by the verb נוּחַ ("rest"). Walton notes that the verb שָׁבַת describes a transition to a state of נוּחַ, that is a state of stability (Deut 12:10; cf. Josh 21:44; 23:1).[64] The verb נוּחַ is also associated with the noun מְנוּחָה ("resting place"), which is used elsewhere in the Old Testament for the resting place of God, that is, the tabernacle and temple, and particularly the holy of holies, that is, the throne room of Yahweh (Ps 132:7–8, 13–14; cf. 1 Chr 28:2; Ps 95:11; Isa 66:1), wherein he sits enthroned on the cherubim (2 Sam 6:2).

In Israel, the earthly sanctuary, the tabernacle or temple, is the primary place of holiness. During the wilderness period, the sanctuary was located at the center of the camp; it is called "a holy place" (Exod 29:31; Lev 6:16, 26–27 [MT 6:9, 19–20]; 10:13). It was a sacred spot because it mediated the presence of the holy God. In the tabernacle or temple structure there is the demarcation of the sacred space into "grades of sanctity" – the outer camp outside, the holy place, and the most holy place or the holy of holies.[65] Only the high priest could enter the holy of holies, and that also only once a year on the Day of Atonement.

The dwelling of God, the tabernacle or later the temple, and particularly the most holy place is that realm of the clean, the unmarred and the unblemished.[66] The priests who served in the sanctuary were supposed to be טָהוֹר and תָּמִים or תָּם, particulary the high priest, who entered the holy of holies (Lev 21:10–23).[67] The prophet Isaiah, when he found himself in the presence of God, cried out, "Woe is me! I am lost, for I am a man of unclean lips, and I live among a people of unclean lips; yet my eyes have seen the King, the LORD of hosts!" (Isa 6:5; NRSV). In other words, earthly sanctuaries of God were supposed to be a holy realm of God by replicating God's heavenly "holy dwelling (Exod 15:13; Deut 26:15; 2 Chr 30:27; Ps 68:5; Jer 25:30; Zech 2:13). Such holiness, however, could only be relatively attained in a fallen creation.

God's Sabbath day transcends the good creation. This in turn implies that the Sabbath institution is no pre-fall creation mandate. As Sarna argues, the seventh day derives its special character from God; its holiness "is a reality

---

64. Walton, *Lost World of Genesis*, 73.
65. For further discussion on "graded holiness," see Jenson, *Graded Holiness*, 89–114.
66. See also Milgrom, *Leviticus 1–16*, 732.
67. Alexander, *From Eden*, 151–55.

irrespective of human activity."[68] The creation week, it should be recalled, is God's week – a vertical week. Humankind's week begins within God's creation week; however, it does not continue on a vertical axis; rather, it proceeds on the horizontal axis. God's creation week should not be defined by merely referring to the creation of humankind and humankind's activity within it; God rested "from all the work of creating that he had done."[69] Humankind did not enter into God's rest; man's week had just begun on the sixth day of creation, but it does not merge with God's seventh day. God's week, however, is, in one sense, an archetype of humankind's week.[70] Yet from another perspective, at creation, Yahweh did not make his rest with humankind. By the end of the sixth day of creation, humankind was expelled from the royal garden-temple.

Israel's weekly Sabbath, as Gaffin argues, gave man a sense of purpose and hope for the future (goal). The daily labors were not to be viewed as a meaningless and ceaseless repetition of days; "rather, at the beginning of each week he [humankind] could look forward to the rest of the seventh day. That weekly cycle impressed on him that he, together with the created order as a whole, was moving toward a goal."[71] This goal should have been realized at creation, but it was not, because of humankind's uncleanness by eating from an unclean tree or the forbidden tree that defiled the land – "cursed is the ground [הָאֲדָמָה] because of you [Adam]" (Gen 3:17, ESV). Consequntly, the holy God could not share a space and time with humankind and so humankind was expelled from paradise.

---

68. Sarna, *Understanding Genesis*, 21.

69. As Robinson observes, "the word *klh*, is repeated here [Gen 2:1–3] twice and it is no accident. P intends to stress the fact that nothing is left out for anyone else to make a claim on creatorship." Robinson, *Origin and Development*, 299.

70. Israel is in many instances called to work for six days or six years (Exod 16:4–5, 22–30; 20:9; 31:15; 35:2; Lev 23:3; 25:1–8) and thus prohibited to work on the seventh day and seventh year (Exod 16:26, 29b; 20:10; 23:12; 31:15; 34:21; 35:2; Lev 23:3; 25:4b, 5; cf. Neh 13:15–22; Jer 17:19–27). For Israel to observe the Sabbath is to imitate God: just as God worked for six days and rested on the seventh day, so should God's people imitate him by working six days and desisting from all their work on the seventh day. In this sense, the Sabbath is both for God and man. For more discussion on the Sabbath in the Old Testament, see Stolz, "Sabbath, Schöpfungswoche," 159–79; Jenni, "Die theologische Begründung," 3–40; Sarna, "Psalm for Sabbath Day," 155–68.

71. Gaffin, *Calvin and the Sabbath*, 155.

Conclusion

If Genesis 3 is considered as describing events within the creation process, it then dialogically illuminates the Genesis 1:1–2:4b narrative in a number of ways: First, the events described in Genesis 3:1–24 have to be understood as part of the resumption of creation activities of the sixth day of creation considering the following: a) If naming is considered a creation activity, it is only in Genesis 3 that naming of human being occurs – it is only in Genesis 3:17 and 21 where the concept אָדָם functions as a proper name, and the woman is named חַוָּה; b) Genesis 1:28–29 and Genesis 3:16–19 form an *inclusio* as the blessing for multiplication finds its affirmation in the divine judgment in Genesis 3:16–17, the creation mandate to subdue the earth in Genesis 1:28 is affirmed, be it under different conditions, and the creation of humanity in the likeness of God is also affirmed (cf. Gen 1:26 and 3:22).

Second, the presence of the deceptive serpent in the garden of Eden should be understood as the presence of an antagonist to God within the sacred space and paradisaical situation.

Third, the presence of the tree of the knowledge of good and bad in the sacred space should be understood as pointing to the presence of clean and unclean food in that space. The instructions of what to eat and what not to eat (Genesis 1:29; 2:16–17), and the woman's response to the temptation to eat of the tree of the knowledge of good and bad evoke the priestly laws regarding clean and unclean food (cf. Gen 3:3; Lev 11:8; Deut 14:8). Therefore, the failure of the first human beings to uphold the distinction point to their failure to fulfill their priestly function to guard and keep the garden.

When Genesis 1:24–31 is read in dialogue with Genesis 3:1–24, then the two creation stories do not project an ideal creation but a creation of potentialities considering the possibilty that was there for human beings to either obey or disobey God, and the possility to attain life or to die. Therefore, as part of the creation process human beings do die.

Therefore, the final refrain in Genesis 1:31, even if understood as referring specifically to the creation activities within the sixth day and not all creation activities from day one as it is commonly viewed, does not have to be understood as implying perfection of the overall creation. Rather, creation at the end of the sixth day is very good because it is functional, that is, moving toward its goal.

CHAPTER 5

Conflicts at Creation[1]

Introduction

In chapters 2–4, I argued that creation in its original state of goodness was in no ideal state of perfection. The goodness of creation simply relates to its functionality in accordance to God's purpose. Methodologically, our focus in the previous chapters was on the internal dialogue within Genesis 1–3. From this point onward, we will be widening the scope to include other canonical voices. Genesis 1–3 is part of a growing canon: Genesis, Genesis–Deuteronomy, Genesis–2 Kings, the rest of the Old Testament. The Old Testament or the Hebrew Bible, to use Bakhtin's words, is a "polyphonic" text which contains a plurality of voices, which implies that the Old Testament contains a plurality of ideas and worldviews which are in a dialogic relationship with each other. Genesis 1–3 is no isolated Scriptural utterance; rather, it is an utterance that interacts with other voices past and future. In Bakhtin's terms, Genesis 1–3 may be described as double voiced – on the one hand, it interacts with previous discourse to which it reacts and responds, and, on the other hand, it foresees and anticipates the reaction of future discourse.[2]

In this chapter, we explore the dialogic relationship between Genesis 1–3 with voices from the Psalter, particularly Psalms 74 and 89, and Job 26:12–13, which to some extent deal with the creation theme. As Todorov

---

1. A revised version of this chapter has been published as follows: Ramantswana, "Conflicts at Creation," 553–78.
2. See Bakhtin, *Dialogic Imagination*, 324.

puts it, "intentionally or not, all discourse is in dialogue with prior discourses on the same subject, as well as discourses yet to come."[3] Reading Genesis 1–3 in dialogue with other texts enriches both this text and the other texts. The focus of this chapter will be on the following theme: creation conflict. I will argue that creation in its state of goodness is one in which multiple rebellions had happened – rebellion in the sea by the sea serpent and rebellion on land by the serpent, a beast of the field, and by humankind.

Creation with or without Conflict, or Conflicts at Creation

In the previous chapters, we alluded to Gunkel's *Chaoskampf*, or "battle against chaos." Gunkel argued that in the ancient Near East, creation was generally thought to have emerged from primordial chaos – conflict between the creator god and another god or the sea or a dragon or monster representing the forces of chaos.[4] In the *Enuma Elish*, which is a Babylonian myth, the origin of the universe is traced to a fierce battle between Marduk and Tiamat. For Gunkel, Genesis 1 is not a free construction by the author of Genesis, or, more precisely, not of the Priestly source; rather, it is a borrowing of Babylonian creation myth. By the turn of the nineteenth century, it was generally agreed among critical scholars that Genesis 1 was dependent on the Babylonian creation myth. Gunkel regarded the *tĕhôm* in Genesis 1 as a demythologized proper name for a mythical figure, which is reminiscent of the Babylonian form of Tiamat.[5] Gunkel further associates the *tĕhôm* with other Hebrew monsters – Rahab,[6] Leviathan,[7] Behemoth,[8] the dragon,[9] and the serpent,[10] which he regarded as variants of Marduk's battle with Tiamat.

---

3. Todorov, *Mikhail Bakhtin*, x.
4. Gunkel, *Creation and Chaos*. This work was originally published in German as Gunkel, *Schöpfung*. See also the condensed version, Gunkel, "Influence of Babylonian Mythology," 25–52.
5. Gunkel, *Creation and Chaos*, 75–76.
6. Job 9:13; 26:12–14; Pss 40:5; 87:4; 89:10–14; Isa 30:7; 51:9–16.
7. Job 3:8; 40:25–41:26; Ps 74:12–19; Isa 27:1.
8. Job 40:19–24; Ps 68:31; Isa 30:6–33.
9. Job 7:12; Ps 44:20; Jer 51:34, 36, 42; Ezek 29:3–6a; 33:2–7.
10. Amos 9:2–3.

Since the discovery of the Ugaritic Baal Cycle myth, many regard the combat or battle motif to have been mediated through this Canaanite mythology.[11] In the Baal Cycle, Baal, the god of storm and fertility, battles with Yamm ("Sea"), the god of chaos, and also battles with Mot, death, and comes out as victor in both battles. The Baal-Yamm conflict came to be regarded as a parallel of the Babylonian Marduk's victory over Tiamat. As Green observes, "the primary reason to interpret the Baal-Yam conflict as another example of a mythical portrayal of the battle between order and chaos is the fact that the name of Baal's antagonist, *Yam* 'Sea,' recalls Tiamat of Babylon."[12]

Furthermore, Yamm is also associated with the sea monster, variously called Lotan, the dragon, and the crooked serpent; the various names are regarded as different ways of referring to Yamm, "Sea."[13] Day claims that the Canaanites associated Baal's victory over the sea and the dragon with the creation of the universe.[14] Fisher and Clifford, on the other hand, argue that the Baal Cycle, although not necessarily concerned with the origination of the world is nonetheless a true cosmogony concerned with the establishment of human society and its continuation.[15] The Baal Cycle, however, does not appear to have creation overtones. First, it does not deal with the creation in the cosmic sense but with the maintenance of the created order in the face of threats of chaos. Second, in Canaanite mythology El is the creator god; Baal is not. As Tsumura observes, "it is probably wise to limit the meaning of 'creation' to El's activities in the ancient Ugaritic and to distinguish *Chaoskampf* myths with a creation motif, such as *Enuma Elish*, from *Chaoskampf* myths without a creation motif, such as the Baal Cycle."[16] Third, in the Baal Cycle

---

11. Herdner, *Corpus des tablettes*, no. 3.3.33–44; 5.1.1–5; Kaiser, *Die mythische Bedeutung*, 74–75; Kaufmann, *Religion of Israel*, 62; Kraus, *Psalmen*, 518; Day, *God's Conflict*; see also his summary in Day, *Yahweh and the Gods*, 98–107.

12. Green, *Storm-God*, 186.

13. Wakeman, *God's Battle*, 163.

14. Day, *God's Conflict*, 17–18. Note also Grønback, "Baal's Battle with Yam," 27–44; Wakeman, *God's Battle*, 149–64.

15. Fisher, "Creation at Ugarit," 313–24; Clifford, "Cosmogonies," 183–201. According to *Pace* Fisher and Clifford, the Baal Cycle does not appear to have any concern with the ordering of human society. The main focus of the Baal Cycle, unlike that of Enuma Elish and Atrahasis, which do have a concern with the ordering of society, is on the activities of the gods. Smith, *Ugaritic Baal Cycle*, 82. As Smith argues, in the Baal Cycle, "the accent falls entirely on Baal's conflict with his enemies Yamm and Mot, and his kingship in the cosmos." Smith, 1:84.

16. Tsumura, *Creation and Destruction*, 145. See also Kloos, *YHWH's Combat*, 67–74.

the existence of the earth is assumed prior to Baal's battle with Yamm.[17] Fourth, the existence of humankind is assumed prior to Baal's battle with Mot.[18] Therefore, Saggs's conclusion that the theme of divine combat has no essential connection with creation seems to hold water.[19]

There are two other combat myths that evince no linkage between combat and creation: the myth of Ninurta and Asag, and the myth of Anzu. The link between creation and the combat motif, as Watson points out, "resulted in an approach whereby divine conflict with the sea is often assumed in [Old Testament] passages where the presence of such allusions could hardly be supposed on the basis of the biblical text itself."[20] Further-more, following Gunkel, the names of the biblical sea monster – Leviathan, Rahab, the dragon, the crooked serpent – came to be regarded as various ways of referring to the sea or *tĕhôm*, "deep," the primordial opponent of Yahweh.[21]

In chapter 2, I argued that creation as described in Genesis 1:1–2:4a already contains both the good and the bad; the bad – the darkness and the *tĕhôm* – posed no threat to God at all. God also created the "great sea

---

17. Prior to the battle, it is proclaimed: "*To the earth the noble will fall*, And *to the dust the mighty.*" And again, when Yamm is struck by Baal, it is said: Kothar fashions the weapons/ And he proclaims their names: 'Your name, yours, is Ayyarmarri: Ayyarmarri, expel Yamm/ Expel Yamm from his throne, Nahar from the seat of his dominion/May you leap from Baal's hand, Like a raptor from his fingers/Strike the head of Prince Yamm, Between the eyes of Judge River/May *Yamm sink and fall to the earth*.' The weapon leaps from Baal's hand, [Like] a raptor from his fingers, It strikes the head of Prince [Yamm], Between the eyes of Judge River/*Yamm collapses and falls to the earth*, His joints shake, And his form sinks." Translation taken from Smith, *Ugaritic Baal Cycle*, 323, emphasis added.

18. See Batto, *Slaying the Dragon*, 78; Batto, "Covenant of Peace," 198–99.

19. Saggs, *Encounter with the Divine*, 59.

20. Watson, *Chaos Uncreated*, 2.

21. Saggs, *Encounter with the Divine*, 59. Saggs further argues against the supposition on the basis of Mesopotamian parallels that monsters are primordial or pre-existent. As he points out, there are many examples of monsters "which are neither primordial nor pre-existent, and not necessarily opposed to the gods. In *Enūma Eliš* itself there are monsters which are neither primordial nor pre-existent; such as those created by Tiamat ad hoc for the coming fight with Marduk. There are many mythical monsters of the deep mentioned as though still existing in historical times, fully analogous with Leviathan whom Yahweh created to sport in the sea: 'Shamash, your rays read down to the abyss, so that the Lahmu of the ocean behold your light.' Elsewhere '50 monsters of the sea' are said to praise Ea, suggesting that they are Ea's creatures and not his adversaries. Therefore there is no reason, on the basis of Mesopotamian evidence, to seek to resist the clear indication of several biblical passages (Isa. 27:1; Job 3:8; Ps. 104:26; 148:7 [RSV]; Amos 9:3) that the sea monsters referred to in connection with Yahweh's power were monsters regarded as existing in historical and not merely mythic time, and that, far from being pre-existent rivals of Yahweh, according to some passages the monsters had been created by Yahweh, and were his agents." Saggs, 60–61.

monsters" (אֶת־הַתַּנִּינִם הַגְּדֹלִים), sea creatures which do not challenge God or pose any threat to his creation; they are perhaps simply larger sea creatures (Gen 1:21). In Genesis 1, God creates without encountering any opposition or conflict at all. According to Levenson, the theology underlying this text may be properly summarized as "creation without opposition."[22] This, however, should be understood as a relative claim; it works well only if Genesis 1 is treated in isolation as a polemic against other ancient Near East mythologies. Some regard Genesis 1 as a demythologization of other ancient Near Eastern myths of creation.[23] Some follow Von Rad in claiming that Genesis 1 "breathes a strong anti-mythical pathos."[24] According to Smith, "the first creation story in Genesis 1:1–2:4a points to a vision of a holy universe, which adds to the older model of the universe as a site of conflict. . . . With but a word, without conflict, God effects the opening of creation. In omitting the divine conflict, Genesis 1 marks a paradigm shift in the presentation of creation."[25]

I am convinced that in dealing with creation narratives in the Old Testament, a proper distinction must be made between creation through conflict, that is, God's conflict with the forces of chaos that resulted in the world coming into being, and conflict in the creation process, God's conflict with his created order or creatures. The former, I am convinced, is totally absent in the Old Testament, whereas the latter is attested. Creation in the Old Testament is not a result of conflict between Yahweh and the sea or some primeval monsters; however, the Old Testament does attest to conflicts arising within the creation process. The conflicts within the creation process are evidenced by two rebellions, rebellion in the sea and rebellion on land. This argument, as will be observed, does not amount to a dualistic worldview that would render creation as intrinsically and irredeemably evil. Furthermore, the hope in the Old Testament is that creation can be purged from rebellion through uncreation, the penultimate answer to the problem,

---

22. Levenson states it thus: "In Genesis there is no active opposition to God's creative labor. He works on inert matter. In fact, rather than *creation ex nihilo*, "creation without opposition" is the more accurate nutshell statement of the theology underlying our passage." Levenson, *Creation and Persistence of Evil*, 122.

23. In this argument, what particularly differentiates Genesis from other ancient Near East myths is its view of God. See Childs, *Myth and Reality*, 42–43; Barr, "Meaning of 'Mythology,'" 7; McKenzie, *Two-Edged Sword*, 101–2.

24. Von Rad, *Genesis*, 53.

25. Smith, *Origins of Biblical Monotheism*, 168.

and through re-creation, the ultimate eschatological answer to the cyclical pattern of rebellion.

Rebellion in the Sea

In this study, we do not presume that the *těhôm* or the sea is a divine opponent that God had to conquer in order to effect creation; rather, the sea is understood as God's creature on which God continually exercises his majestic controlling power. The *těhôm*, unlike Tiamat in *Enuma Elish*, or Yamm or Mot in the Baal Cycle, is nowhere in the Old Testament presented as a primordial "god" who stands on the same par with God (or Yahweh) as his opponent. In the combat myths, the opponents are fairly matched; for example, Marduk versus Tiamat in the Babylonian myth, and in the Baal cycle, Baal versus Yamm, and again Baal versus Mot.[26] In the Baal-Yamm battle and the Baal-Mot battle, both Yamm and and Mot are actually killed, and their bodies are dismembered and scattered. Nothing new is created from the bodies of either Yamm or Mot.

The sea, however, as we will observe, is associated with a rebellious sea creature variously called Leviathan, the dragon, the serpent, and Rahab. Though Yahweh's conflict with this foe does not have any connection with the originating act of creation, it does, however, point to a rebellion in the sea in the creation process – a rebellion from the sea creatures that probably precedes the rebellion of the earthly creatures, which we will attend to subsequently. I will focus primarily on Psalm 74:12–17 (Own translation), which narrates Yahweh's conflict with Leviathan at creation:

וֵאלֹהִים מַלְכִּי מִקֶּדֶם פֹּעֵל יְשׁוּעוֹת בְּקֶרֶב הָאָרֶץ׃	But God, my king of old, bringer of salvation upon the earth;
אַתָּה פוֹרַרְתָּ בְעָזְּךָ יָם	You divided the sea by your power;
שִׁבַּרְתָּ רָאשֵׁי תַנִּינִים עַל־הַמָּיִם׃	You smashed the heads of the dragon in the waters.
אַתָּה רִצַּצְתָּ רָאשֵׁי לִוְיָתָן	You crushed the heads of Leviathan;
תִּתְּנֶנּוּ מַאֲכָל לְעָם לְצִיִּים׃	You gave him as food to fellow beasts;
אַתָּה בָקַעְתָּ מַעְיָן וָנָחַל	You opened up a spring and a brook;

---

26. See Watson, *Chaos Uncreated*, 25–26.

אַתָּה הוֹבַשְׁתָּ נַהֲרוֹת אֵיתָן׃	You dried up the ever-flowing river.
לְךָ יוֹם אַף־לְךָ לָיְלָה	To you belongs day, also to you belongs night;
אַתָּה הֲכִינוֹתָ מָאוֹר וָשָׁמֶשׁ׃	You established the moon and the sun.
אַתָּה הִצַּבְתָּ כָּל־גְּבוּלוֹת אָרֶץ	You set up all earth boundaries;
קַיִץ וָחֹרֶף אַתָּה יְצַרְתָּם׃	You made both summer and winter.

In the Psalter, especially in the lament psalms, Yahweh's ancient deeds are often recalled by the psalmist as they entreat him to act again in the present (Pss 44:2–9; 74:12–17; 77:12–21; 80:9–12; 83:10–13; 89:2–38).[27] The allusion in Psalm 74 to Yahweh's act of dividing the sea and slaying the dragon, if only the immediate context be considered, refers to his redemptive act at the Red Sea;[28] however, it may potentially be taken as referring to God's act at creation[29] or perhaps as alluding to both these acts.[30] I consider this psalm as referring to both these acts. The shepherd motif in verse 1 is used in several other psalms in relation to the exodus event and wilderness wanderings (Pss 77:21; 78:52–53a; 79:13; 80:2; 95:7–11; 100:1–5). Reference in verse 2 to "the assembly, which you [God] acquired of old" culminating with his bringing the tribe of his possession to Mount Zion is the same pattern that we find in the Song of the Sea in Exodus 15, especially verses 16–18 (cf. Deut 32:6). The language of deliverance or redemption (גָּאַל) in verse 2 alludes to the Red Sea event, which is Yahweh's first great redemptive act in Israel's history. Furthermore, Yahweh's act of deliverance at the Red Sea is one aspect that gives the psalmist confidence that he will intervene in the current crisis.

The turning point in Psalm 74 is verse 12: the psalmist does not stop at the Red Sea; rather, he looks back via the exodus to creation. The event at the Red Sea and wilderness experiences may, on the one hand, be described as that point in Israel's history where Yahweh divided the sea and smashed the heads of the Egyptian Leviathan, provided Israel with water, and dried up the Jordan River.[31] At the same time, however, the language in verses 13–17 also

---

27. See Clifford, "Creation in the Psalms," 57–69; Clifford, *Creation Accounts*, 151–62; Clifford, "Hebrew Scriptures," 507–23.

28. Watson, *Chaos Uncreated*, 152–68; Seybold, *Die Psalmen*, 289.

29. Gunkel, *Creation and Chaos*, 27–30; Emerton, "'Spring and Torrent,'" 122–23, 130–31; Smick, "Mythopoetic Language," 90.

30. Kraus, *Psalms: A Commentary*, 303–4, 310; Goldingay, *Psalms*, 420–37; Tate, *Psalms 51–100*, 239–55; Mays, *Psalms*, 245.

31. See Goldingay, *Psalms*, 431; Mays, *Psalms*, 245.

becomes more and more creation language. At the Red Sea, just as at creation, Yahweh divided and separated the sea so that dry land would appear. The issue of interest for us, however, is the smashing of the Leviathan and its relation to creation, which I will return to subsequently. Verses 15–17 generally refer to God's authorship over everything: In creation Yahweh separated the waters so that dry land might appear; day and light belong to him; the heavenly luminaries; and the seasons – winter and summer. The language here clearly recalls Genesis 1. This passage's use of merisms (day and night, moon and sun, winter and summer) reflects a common notion found elsewhere in the Hebrew Bible (Gen 1; 8:22; Isa 45:7) of the binary structure of the cosmos.

Now, we turn our attention back to verses 13–14. If we do accept that the language in verses 12–17 is also creation language, then the conflict between Yahweh and Leviathan may be understood not simply within the context of the deliverance at the Red Sea but also within the context of creation. As Tate observes, the conflict between Yahweh and the dragon in verses 12–14 does not have creational meaning as it does in the Babylonian creation account, *Enuma Elish*; rather, it is a "struggle for cosmic power and divine kingship."[32] The conflict between Yahweh and Leviathan is not the basis of creation. Creation activity, as observed in the previous chapter, is not a process that begins with the separation of the waters, but one that begins with the creation of heaven and earth, with the earth covered by the sea as a garment and darkness (Gen 1). The separation of the waters into the waters above and the waters below is an event that took place only on the second day of creation, and the gathering of the waters below into one place for dry land to appear is an event that happened on the third day of creation. Genesis 1 says nothing about Yahweh's struggle with the dragon on day two or day three because the dragons were yet to be created. The "great sea monsters" or "dragons" were created along with other sea creatures on the fourth day of creation.

Psalms 74:13–14; 89:10–14; and Job 26:12–13 all evince a conflict between Yahweh and the sea dragon at creation. According to Psalm 74:13b–14a, "You [i.e., God] smashed the heads of the dragon in the waters. You crushed the heads of Leviathan." The dragon in the water and Leviathan stand in a synonymous parallelism; thus, the name of the many-headed dragon (לִוְיָתָן) is Leviathan. Leviathan is also described here as many-headed, as evidenced by

---

32. Tate, *Psalms 51–100*, 251.

reference to "heads," although without the number of heads specified. There are various descriptions of Leviathan. In Isaiah 27:1, it is described as follows:

> On that day Yahweh, with his hard, great and strong sword,
> [he] will punish Leviathan the fleeing serpent (בָּרִחַ נָחָשׁ),
> Leviathan the twisting serpent;
> He will slay the dragon that is in the sea.

In Job 41:1–8 and 18–21, Leviathan is described as a terrifying, powerful, fearless crocodile-like creature with an astonishing nose snorting out flashes of light and breathing out firebrands through its mouth. In Psalm 89:9–14 and Job 26:12–13, Yahweh is depicted as battling another creature at creation, Rahab, or perhaps the same creature under a different name:

Psalm 89:9–14	Job 26:12–13
You rule the raging of the sea; when its waves rise, you still them. You crushed Rahab like one of the slain; with your strong arm you scattered your enemies. The heavens are yours, and yours also the earth; you founded the world and all that is in it. You created the north and the south; Tabor and Hermon sing for joy at your name. Your arm is endued with power; your hand is strong, your right hand exalted. (NIV)	By his power he stilled the sea; by his understanding he struck down Rahab. By his wind the heavens were made fair; his hand pierced the fleeing serpent [בָּרִיחַ נָחָשׁ]. (NRSV)

Rahab is depicted with descriptions similar to those of Leviathan. Rahab, like Leviathan is slain, "the fleeing serpent" (נָחָשׁ בָּרִיחַ), a dragon תַּנִּין, Isa 51:9), and a sea creature. Rahab appears to have had accomplices in his rebellious act that invited Yahweh's action against him (Job 9:3). The mythic descriptions of Leviathan and Rahab make them indistinguishable.[33] In the book wherein both these names are found, Rahab and Leviathan do not appear together; the two names appear in separate texts and contexts.[34] Watson further argues that "the motifs of the slaying of Rahab and Leviathan were [probably] not regarded as concerning independent events which might be presented sequentially, but rather . . . they existed as separate traditions which

---

33. Watson, *Chaos Uncreated*, 304.
34. Watson, 304.

had, at least in part, acquired the same content and which were regarded as alternative of the presentations of the same event."[35] Leviathan and Rahab are equated in the Old Testament and should, therefore, be viewed as one and the same creature under different names.

The descriptions of Leviathan that we find in Psalm 74:13 and Isaiah 27:1 have parallels in the Ugaritic Baal Cycle. In the Baal Cycle, it appears as if both Anat and Baal are credited with destroying "Lotan" (OT Leviathan):

Anat takes credit:	Baal is credited:
What enemy has risen against Bal u (what) adversary against Cloud-Rider? I have smitten Illu's beloved, Yammu, Have finished off the great god Naharu. I have bound the dragon's [*tnn* (cf. Heb. *tannîn*)] jaws, have destroyed it, have smitten the twisting serpent, the close-coiled one with seven heads.[36]	When you smite Lotan, the crooked serpent, and make an end to the twisting serpent, The tyrant with seven heads, The heavens will grow hot and droop, I will crush you to pieces and I will eat you. You will descend into the throat of Mot the Son of El.[37]

The dragon (*tnn*) in the Baal cyle is also a watery enemy; it is once described as being "in the sea."[38] Leviathan, as already observed is also a many-headed creature, presumably seven-headed, as is Lotan in the Baal Cycle. According to Dahood, the seven heads of Leviathan/Lotan presumably correspond with the sevenfold "you are the one who. . . ." in Psalm 74.[39] However, as Green points out,

> there is no indication . . . that either Lotan, the "Crooked Serpent," or Yam is of the same form, nor do the names Yam and Lotan ever appear in parallelism. In the one recorded instance

---

35. Watson, 304–5.
36. Pardee, "BaÁlu Myth," in COS, vol. 1, 1.86.92, 252; CTA 3.iii.32–iv.51.
37. Translation of CTA 5, taken from Green, *The Storm-God*, 197, compare with COS, 265.
38. Pardee, "BaÁlu Myth," in COS, 1.86. Compare with *The Cuneiform Alphabetic Texts* (CTA) 6 vi.50 in Green, *The Storm-God*, 273.
39. Dahood, *Psalms II, 51–100*, 205.

in which they do appear together in the Anat text above, they represent two creatures, each of which is successively conquered by the goddess.[40]

Psalms 74 and 89, and Job 26 all seem to agree that the conflict between Yahweh and Leviathan or Rahab or the dragon or the serpent happened within the creation process; however, this conflict had no creational effect. These passages, unlike Genesis 1, which has a time framework, do not tell us exactly at what point the conflict between Yahweh and the dragon happened; they do, however, seem to point to a time after the separation of the sea and the appearance of dry land. If we consider Leviathan to be a sea creature (Ps 104:26) and follow the Genesis 1 framework, then it is most likely that this rebellion happened on the fifth day of creation, the day the sea creatures were created. This would imply that there was a rebellion in the sea, a rebellion from the sea creatures that preceded the creation of land creatures, including humankind.

Why did Yahweh feel compelled to smash the heads of Leviathan? What did this creature do to incite such actions against himself and perhaps also against his accomplices? None of these passages tells us of the motive behind the conflict between Yahweh and the dragon, though they do highlight the fact that God's kingship is made manifest in his conquest of the primordial enemy (Pss 74:12–14; 89:9–11).[41] In Psalm 74, Yahweh's defeat of the primordial opponent is viewed as an act that had a salvific function and provided ground for the hope that Yahweh will again defeat the contemporary political and military enemies to restore stability.[42] The defeat of the primordial enemy may

---

40. Green, *The Storm-God*, 184.

41. In Psalms 74 and 89, as Clifford argues, "The selection of details from the 'days of old' differs according to what is being lamented. Psalm 89, lamenting the defeat of the Davidic king by his enemies, recites Yahweh's sharing of the fruits of his cosmogonic victory with David in the past and his naming David *'elyon* ("Most High") among the kings of the earth by an unconditional oath. This recital poses a specific question to God: if you unconditionally promised worldwide sovereignty to the Davidic line when you created the world, why does your king now suffer defeat? Psalm 74 retells Yahweh's ordering of the paired elements of the universe (springs and torrents, lands and waters, day and night, moon and sun). These elements are now threatened by the destruction of the Temple, which commemorates that creation. The question: will you let your enemies destroy the symbol of your creation?" Clifford, *Creation Accounts*, 154–55; see also Clifford, "Psalm 89," 35–47.

42. Middleton notes, "Particularly interesting, although only implicit in the psalm [Ps 74], is the connection between the combat myth and temple-building. Just as the conclusion of Baal's battles with his opponents (in the Ugaritic myth) results in the construction of his

thus be viewed as God's redemptive act, a display of his royal power over the anti-creational force to guarantee the functionality of the cosmos. Particularly interesting in Psalm 89 is that the defeat of Rahab, the primordial enemy, is regarded as part of an exercise of Yahweh's royal function. In this psalm, the creation process is viewed from a royal perspective, as an exercise of rule and might (Ps 89:8–10, 13). It is Yahweh's exercise of his rule and might that guarantees the stability and functionality of creation. Furthermore, this psalm through the conflict theme elevates the Davidic king. As Levenson points out, "It is now the Davidic throne that guarantees cosmic stability, the continuation of order established through primeval combat. In Psalm 89, as in the Enuma Elish, the bond between the exaltation of the deity and the imperial politics of his earthly seat of power is patent."[43]

The creation conflict motif or "cosmic mastery" motif, as Levenson calls it, is the predominant way, in the Hebrew Bible, of expressing God's sovereignty.[44] The restoration of order during the creation process, as Levenson argues, "is intrinsically an act of creation";[45] however, this is not an act that initiated the creation process; rather, it is an act that brought order to that creation to ensure its stability and functionality.

In *Atrahasis*, *Enuma Elish*, and the Baal Cycle, rebellion forms part of the fabric of the heavenly pantheon. In *Atrahasis*, the rebellion of the junior gods leads to the creation of humans, whereas in *Enuma Elish* the conflict between Marduk and Tiamat forms the basis of creation of the cosmos.[46] In the Baal Cycle, the focus is on the cyclical events of nature: Baal's kingship is not forever intact. Baal is in a continuous struggle with the two primordial antagonists, Yamm and Mot. "The Canaanites could explain the change from one season to another and the differences between good and bad years only

---

temple/palace, presumably if YHWH once more defeated the forces of Chaos, thus enacting the primordial battle in history, the culmination of the victory would be God's coming to rest in his royal sanctuary Zion. The implied outcome of the new battle would be a new temple. Israel's sacred historical cosmos would once again be secure." Middleton, *The Liberating Image*, 247.

43. Levenson, *Creation and Persistence of Evil*, 22–23.

44. Levenson, 6–7. Similarly, Mettinger writes, "The conception of the Lord as King has many dimensions, but the question is whether the notion of God's battle with the hostile Powers is not itself the central idea." Mettinger, "Fighting Powers of Chaos," 26.

45. Levenson, 12.

46. Goldingay, *Old Testament Theology*, 65.

by believing that sometimes Baal was weak, sick, or even dead."[47] The Old Testament, with its monotheism, unlike ancient Near Eastern mythologies, does not entertain the idea of gods rebelling against Yahweh at creation; rather, the focus turns out to be on rebellion from Yahweh's sea creatures. The battle between Yahweh and the dragon is depicted as an earthly one, not a heavenly one. Yahweh's defeat of the dragon at creation is regarded as the basis for the belief that Yahweh will defeat the current enemies.

Levenson argues that these texts do not speak in an unqualified way of an absolute, unconditional victory in primordial times.[48] The Old Testament sometimes presents Leviathan or Rahab or the dragon, or the serpent, as still being on the loose, and perhaps more specifically, Yahweh's conflict with the dragon is often historicized or reenacted in Israel's own history.[49] It is most logical that in the Old Testament the control and defeat of the sea dragon at creation is extended to other enemies of God and his people in creation.[50] Pharaoh or Egypt is regarded as a *tannîn* (Ezek 29:1–5; 32:2–8), as Rahab (Isa 30:7; 51:9–11; Ps 87:4);[51] the Babylonian king is regarded as the *tannîn* (Jer 51:34); it is unclear who Leviathan in Isaiah 27:1 represents – Egypt, Babylon, or Persia,[52] – and for Job, Leviathan is the dreadful creature that, if roused, can cause great destruction for humanity (Job 3:8; 41:1–34). The dragon had become for Israel a symbol for those powers that threaten God's people.

There is also a sense in which Yahweh's victory over this rebellious creature is eschatologized.[53] An example of this eschatologizing of the combat myth motif is Isaiah 27:1. This passage is part of an Isaianic apocalypse (Isa 24–27),

---

47. Mulder, "Baal," 2:200. As Gibson points out, "The battle is not once for all (as in the cases of Marduk and Yahweh and perhaps El Elyon of Jerusalem and for all we know, at one time, El of Ugarit) in order to make creation possible, but has to be fought anew every year in order to guarantee the continuance of life and fertility on earth. The kingship which Baal wins and has to keep winning that the dangers of the flood and drought might be kept at bay is therefore a delegated kingship, the victor being called King because he is in effect El's regent or executive – the god who does and acts while El from his central office, as it were, thinks and plans." Gibson, "Kingship of Yahweh," 105.

48. Levenson, *Creation and Persistence of Evil*, 14–50, esp. 16–18, 26–31.

49. See Day, *God's Conflict*, 88–140.

50. Ryken et al., *Dictionary of Biblical Imagery*, 564.

51. Psalm 87:4, as Day points out, mentions Rahab alongside Babylon, Philistia, Tyre, and Ethiopia, probably having Egypt in view, as Egypt is also called by this name elsewhere (cf. Isa 30:7; 51:9). Day, *God's Conflict*, 90.

52. Day, 112–13.

53. See Levenson, *Creation and Persistence of Evil*, 48.

and, as Johnson points out, it fits well with the theme of this whole section, which is repeated throughout, that "Yahweh will defeat the enemy."[54] However, it should also be noted that Leviathan in Isaiah 27:1 probably served to represent some imminent historical enemy.[55] The point the passage appears to be making is that God's creation is still threatened by the anti-creational force, which was crushed at creation but keeps on reinventing itself again and again.[56] The recurring call upon Yahweh to act against the primordial enemy as in the "days of old" is indicative and acknowledges that "those adversarial forces were not annihilated in perpetuity in primordial times" (Ps 74:12; Isa 51:9).[57]

Other Old Testament voices that are in tension with Genesis 1:1–2:4a – with the latter evincing no combat conflict within the creation process – suggest that there was a conflict within the creation process between God and a dragon, a sea creature known as Leviathan, Rahab, or serpent, and its accomplices. In conquering this creature, God was exercising his royal power over his creation and restoring order to ensure the functionality of the cosmos.

Rebellion on Land

In the first creation story in Genesis 1:1–2:4a, as already noted, God creates without opposition. This claim is true, but for the author of Genesis, the first creation story in Genesis 1:1–2:4a is not the absolute, normative, quintessential, or the final word; it is just one perspective from which he wished to describe the creation process. The creation conflict motif as already noted is predominant in the Old Testament and is considered by scholars to be earlier than the motif of creation without conflict in Genesis 1.[58] The author of Genesis, as though perceiving a potential for misunderstanding, retold his story, this time incorporating the conflict motif in Genesis 2:4b–3:24. In this

---

54. Johnson, *From Chaos to Restoration*, 84.

55. Johnson, 84.

56. See Levenson, *Creation and Persistence of Evil*, 28.

57. Levenson, 12.

58. See Levenson, 6–7; Smith, *Origins of Biblical Monotheism*, 168. Smith elsewhere writes, "The presentation in Genesis 1 carries an especially powerful force for an audience that knows and presumes the traditional stories of its warrior-god's victories over the ancient cosmic enemies. Such a presentation assumes that the audience knows how such stories convey God's mastery over the universe. Genesis 1 plays on this knowledge and thereby extends the picture of divine mastery." Smith, *Memoirs of God*, 98.

case, however, the conflict is not with the sea serpent, but rather with the land creatures, namely, the serpent, which is a beast of the field, and humankind.

In the previous chapter, I argued that Genesis 3 should be regarded as falling within the sixth day of creation. I do not intend to rehearse those arguments here, but I will draw out their implications.

Genesis 3 may also be understood as a reflection on a conflict between Yahweh and his earthly creatures that occurred within the creation week. As observed in the previous chapter, man's rebellion against God was incited by the "serpent" (הַנָּחָשׁ), one of the beasts of the field. The only background information given concerning this creature is that it was "more crafty than any other beast of the field that the LORD God had made" (3:1). The craftiness of this creature is not good. Its intention is to oppose and to contend with God. It aims at reversing and invalidating God's word in three crucial areas.

Concerning the trees in the garden, God said, "You may freely eat from all the trees in the garden" (Gen 2:16, RSV), but the serpent says, "Did God say, 'You shall not eat from any tree in the garden?'" (Gen 3:1b, RSV). Concerning what would happen if man were to eat from the exceptional tree, the tree of the knowledge of good and bad, God said, "You will surely die" (Gen 2:17, RSV), but the serpent says, "You will not surely die" (Gen 3:4, RSV). And concerning man created in the image of God in accordance to his likeness, God said, "Let us make man in our image according to our likeness ... So God created man in his own image, in the image of God he created him, male and female he created them" (Gen 1:26–27, RSV), but the serpent says, "God knows that when you eat of it your eyes will be opened, and you will be like God, knowing good and evil" (Gen 3:5, RSV).

As it stands, the serpent has taken an offensive stance not just by attacking God's image on earth, but also by attacking God himself by attacking his words. The serpent seizes on the command of God to man to launch its attack, twisting God's command by which he gave man freedom to eat of every tree in the garden, and making it into a command of bondage that leaves man without freedom. He turned the good command into something bad for man. Furthermore, he turned the curse "you will surely die" into a blessing "you will not surely die." The motivation that this antagonist offers to man is that man "will become like God, knowing good and bad" (וִהְיִיתֶם כֵּאלֹהִים יֹדְעֵי טוֹב וָרָע) by eating of the tree of the knowledge of good and bad.

Not only is the serpent represented as rebellious toward God, but it also seduces humankind to rebel against God. Humankind succumbs to the serpent's seduction by considering becoming "like God" as something to be grasped: "When the woman *saw* that the tree was good for food, and that it was a delight to the eye, and that the tree was desirable to make one wise, she *took* from its fruit and *ate*; and she also *gave* to her husband, and he *ate*" (Gen 3:6, NIV).[59] Humankind rebelled against God by eating from the tree of the knowledge of good and bad, which God commanded them not to eat. As a result of this duo's rebellion, both the serpent and humankind are judged.

Thus, in Genesis 3 we find earthly creatures teamed up in their attempt, so to speak, to overthrow God. The Genesis narrative does not clarify the motives of the serpent in challenging God and seducing humans to rebel against God; thus, for reasons unknown, the serpent, one of God's earthly creatures, has turned out to be Yahweh's antagonist. Apparently, it is nothing unusual in the Old Testament creation fragments for the motives behind conflicts in creation to remain veiled. In the conflict between Yahweh and the dragon, the motives for that conflict are veiled. As already observed, we are not told why the many-headed serpent deserved to be smashed. What did he do, and why did God find it necessary to smash the sea serpent? However, when it comes to the rebellion on land, there is at least one question that is clarified: Why did humanity rebel against God? It is because humans wanted to become like God; humankind desired wisdom.

For the author of Genesis 1–3, the first human couple were themselves kings created in the image of the creator-king and set as guards over the garden of Eden. As Middleton states it, "the cumulative evidence suggests that the biblical *imago Dei* refers to status or office of the human race as God's authorized stewards, charged with the royal-priestly vocation of representing God's rule on earth by their exercise of cultural power."[60] The first human couple was unique not just because they were physically the first human

---

59. Note particularly the progression in the action verbs: at first humankind *saw*, but the action climaxes when they *took* and *ate*. As the man and the woman were in the process of seeing, their desires were aroused and new significances were attached to the tree – good for food, delightful, desirable to make wise. White argues, "Now the individual desire, rather than the illocutionary power of the word of Yahweh Elohim, has become the force behind Issah's action.... She desires the attribute of God-likeness to be attached to her." White, *Narration and Discourse*, 134–35.

60. Middleton, *Liberating Image*, 235.

beings on earth created by God himself but also because the Father-son/daughter relationship was also understood at a different level. The first human couple was created to be viceregent, raised from the dust and given dominion over the earthly realm (Gen 2:7; cf. 1:28).[61] As viceregent, the first human couple was "children of God," so to speak; they had a divine heritage; their kingship was derived from Yahweh himself, and they had to function as his representatives on earth (cf. 2 Sam 7:12–14; 1 Chr 17:11–13; 22:9–10; Pss 2:7; 110:1). The father-son relationship between the deity and the king was in the ancient Near East part of the royal entitlement. In the ancient world, the king's function as a representative of the divine on earth was to mediate the will of the deity and maintain order in his kingdom and beyond.[62]

As I noted earlier, the defeat of the primordial sea serpent was an exercise of Yahweh's royal power. Similarly, humankind's encounter with the serpent was an opportunity for the human couple to exercise their royal function by crushing the serpent. Apparently, swords to do the job were available in paradise: the cherubim, who were set to "guard" (*šamar*) the way to the tree of life following humankind's expulsion, were armed with swords (Gen 3:24). The verb *šamar* used to describe the role of the cherubim is the same verb used to describe the role of humankind in the garden: humankind was set in the garden to *'ābad* it and *šamar* it (2:15). It is possible that like the cherubim, the first human couple were armed guards of the garden. However, instead of drawing their swords when they suspected foul play, the first human couple entertained the enemy and were defeated; they thereby failed to fulfill their royal or redemptive function. The first human couple, I am convinced, were not ill-equipped guards of the royal garden-temple. They were supposed to have been the first to spill the blood of another earthly creature by slaughtering the serpent; the first victim was not to be their son Abel who offered God fat portions of the firstborn of his flock, a deed for which his blood was spilled (Gen 4:4).

The opportunity missed at the beginning was deferred to the future: "And I will put enmity between you [the serpent] and the woman [Eve], and between

---

61. See Brueggemann, "From Dust to Kingship," 1–18.
62. For detailed discussion on this subject, see Walton, *Ancient Near Eastern Thought*, 278–86; Baines, "Ancient Egyptian Kingship," 16–53; Hallo, "Texts, Statues and Cult," 54–66; Curtis, *Man as Image of God*; Curtis, "Image of God (OT)," 3.389–91.

your offspring [the serpent's] and hers [Eve's]; he [her seed] will crush your head [the serpent's], and you will strike his heel [that of the woman's seed]" (Gen 3:15, NIV).[63] It should be noted that the battle is not between the serpent's seed and the woman's seed, but between the serpent and the woman's seed. It seems to me that there is a sense of particularity when it comes to the serpent. Reference is not to any serpent; rather, this particular cursed serpent would be crushed.

Boyd rightly concludes that "if we take the Old Testament's combat motif seriously, we must acknowledge that, at the very foundation of creation and in the cosmic environment of the earth, something rebelled against God and threatened the world."[64] This rebellious something is regarded in the Old Testament as serpentine (הַנָּחָשׁ), the rebellious sea serpent, לִוְיָתָן נָחָשׁ בָּרִחַ וְעַל לִוְיָתָן נָחָשׁ עֲקַלָּתוֹן ("Leviathan the fleeing serpent, Leviathan the twisting serpent" [Isa 27:1]), and the land serpent, הַנָּחָשׁ . . . חַיַּת הַשָּׂדֶה; ("the serpent . . . beast of the field"). The sea serpent is presented as a rebellious creature slaughtered by God at creation. The land serpent, on the other hand, is cursed but not slaughtered; one may perhaps say that the serpent was weakened, but still given room to continue to operate within the created order. Thus, it is probable that the serpentine language is metaphorical, representing the enemy of God who by default was also humankind's enemy, whom humankind, as guards of the garden of Eden, initially failed to recognize and counter. God's enemy is humankind's enemy as well.

One thing binds the sea serpent and the land serpent – they are both rebellious. What differentiates these two is their sphere of operation; one operates in the sea, whereas the other operates on land. The Old Testament does not seem to equate these two creatures. LaCocque, however, is of the opinion that the later symbolists and apocalyptists do equate them – Job 26:18 and Isaiah 27:1.[65] This would imply that the rebellious sea serpent, Leviathan, was given room to reinvent itself among the land creatures. This position,

---

63. Fuller, *Unity of the Bible*, 223. Genesis 3:15 has come to be regarded as the *protoevangelium* – the first proclamation of the gospel.

64. Boyd, *God at War*, 99.

65. LaCocque, "Cracks in the Wall," 14. LaCocque argues that "the serpent has the distinct advantage of moving on the ground while coming from the sea (under the form of Leviathan). It is at any rate an infernal creature that ends up eating dust, a symbol of sterility and lifelessness, there where Adam returns after death (Genesis 3:14)." LaCocque, 14.

however, seems highly unlikely, as the symbolists and apocalyptists that LaCocque refers to appear to be drawing their imagery from the Baal Cycle myth. Therefore, it is better to conclude that in the Old Testament, the sea serpent and the land serpent are kept as separate entities who rebelled against God at creation. The equation of the sea serpent and the land serpent is rather found in subsequent literature (*Apoc. Abr.* 23:7; *3 Bar.* 4:8; *Odes Sol.* 22:5; *T. Ash.* 7:3; Rev 12:9).[66]

The rebellious serpentine creatures should be viewed as "anti-creational forces" that are opposed to Yahweh, unlike the cherubim, warrior guards, whom Yahweh set to guard the "tree of life" in the garden of Eden so that man would not stretch out his hand and eat from it. The cherubim in Genesis 3:24 are said to have "flaming swords," which clearly alludes to a battle motif. If humankind were to try to approach the tree of life, they would, like Rahab/Leviathan the sea dragon, be cut to pieces. The cherubim are envisioned in the Old Testament as flying winged creatures. On the mercy seat covering the ark of the covenant were carvings of two cherubim at the two ends with their wings spread upward, overshadowing the mercy seat covering (Exod 25:18–22; 37:9). Yahweh rides on these creatures, which soar on the wings of the wind (Ps 18:10). Ezekiel describes the cherubim as four-faced creatures: "One face was that of a cherub, the second the face of a man, the third the face of a lion, and the fourth the face of an eagle" (Ezek 1:4–28; 10:1–22). The origin of these mysterious cherubim is not explained; however, there is no reason to doubt that they are also God's creatures. Whether they were created as earthly or heavenly creatures, we cannot tell, but their present sphere of operation is heaven. Just as there is no reason to demythologize these creatures, there is also no reason to demythologize the existence of the many-headed Leviathan slain by God at some point in the creation week, just as humankind could have been slain had they attempted to eat from the tree of life following their rebellion. It may be perhaps that creatures such as the many-headed Leviathan should be classified with the many-faced cherubim. The only other beasts in the Old Testament that may be classified with these creatures are the four beasts in Daniel's apocalypse (Dan 7).

---

66. *Apoc. Ab.* 23:7; *3 Bar.* 4:8; *Odes Sol.* 22:5; *T. Ash.* 7:3; Rev 12:9. Similarly, the equation of the serpent in Genesis 3 with Satan also comes from subsequent literature: *L.A.E.* 16, *Vit. Pro.* 12.

Modern scholars have particularly noted the close affinities between Daniel 7:2–14 and Genesis 1–3 along with the other creation fragments considered above, which heightens the correspondence between Daniel's monsters and the creation monsters.[67] In his vision Daniel uses creation language to speak about future things, as the language follows the cosmological pattern: battle/victory/kingship/judgment/re-creation.[68] However, a significant thing that sets Daniel's vision apart from other creation fragments is that his vision is not merely eschatological but also historicized through the interpretations provided.

Daniel's vision, like Genesis 1, opens with the "great sea" (יַמָּא רַבָּא) and the four winds of heaven churning over the waters. The four beasts – the lion-eaglelike beast, the bearlike beast, the leopard-birdlike beast, and the-one-of-a-kind, ten-horned beast, like the rebellious sea dragon, all come up from the sea. The-one-of-a-kind, ten-horned beast, like the sea dragon, is slain; however, the other three monster beasts, like the land serpent, are allowed to live for a period of time, presumably until such time when they will also be crushed. The One like the Son of Man in Daniel's vision – unlike Adam, who fails in his kingship role by conspiring with the beast, the land serpent (Gen 1–3) – is a human representative and "his kingship is on the model of Adam's kingship: non-political, it is a universal, cosmic, humanization process, whose ultimate aim is communication with the Creator (the Ancient of Days, the One who was before the beginning) and with the created, which in the process is transformed (transfigured) into a 'people of the saints,' that is, a 'double nature' people, both human and angelic."[69] Furthermore, the judgment scene in Daniel 7 also recalls the judgment scene in Genesis 3. Whereas the-one-of-a-kind, ten-horned beast is slain, like Leviathan, the other three beasts, like the land serpent, are given some time before they are crushed, and unlike Adam, who failed to counter the serpent, the One like the Son of Man, the second Adam, so to speak, brings about the new age through

---

67. See Wilson, "Creation and New Creation, 190–203; LaCocque, "Allusions to Creation," 114–31; Doukhan, "Allusions à la création," 285–92; Day, *God's Conflict*, 151–78.

68. LaCocque, "Allusions to Creation," 118. I disagree, however, with LaCocque and others who suggest that the pattern followed in Daniel 7 is an Ugaritic cosmological pattern. As already argued, the Ugaritic Baal Cycle myth is not necessarily a cosmogony. This is not to deny that Daniel 7 may also be interacting and drawing from the Baal Cycle and other ancient Near Eastern cosmogonies; however, Daniel 7, as will be observed, evokes Genesis 1–3 in many ways.

69. LaCocque, "Allusions to Creation," 124.

perseverance against the ultimate monster. Just as God killed Leviathan, the sea serpent, and condemned the land serpent to be crushed, also at the end (or new creation), God will kill the ultimate beast and his accomplices through the "Adamic" figure, thereby bringing about a new world order.

Thus, Daniel 7 agrees with Genesis 1–3: humankind is God's ultimate designated king, who at the first creation failed to exercise his authority, glory, and sovereign power given to him, in contrast to the second Adam. Thus, if the first Adam had exercised his authority, glory, and sovereign power, he would probably have been honored with the right to enter Yahweh's rest.[70]

The reality of monsterial/draconic rebellious serpentine creatures and of the monsterial/draconic cherubim, birdlike creatures, at creation does not compromise Old Testament monotheism nor does monsterial language imply that such creatures are by nature evil. First, regarding monsterial language, it is possible, based on what we have observed, to make a distinction between bad monsters, such as Leviathan, and good monsters, such as the cherubim. Monsterial language is not necessarily language for evil; this language is sometimes even used for God: In Psalm 18:8–9, Yahweh is described in monsterial language and as riding on the monsterial creatures,

---

70. We should recall here the argument made in the previous chapter that God's creation week is a vertical week, unlike mankind's weeks, which are horizontal, which implies the possibility that if mankind had successfully defeated the serpent through obedience to the probationary command, they would have been graciously rewarded with the right to enter Yahweh's rest. Thus, mankind would have proceeded from the sixth day, mankind's first day, into the seventh day. Another way of looking at it is through Yahweh's justice. Genesis 3 is not only a scene of rebellion but also a scene of judgment, which implies that the sixth day of creation, mankind's first day, was also judgment day. The sixth day was going to be the day of judgment even if mankind could have successfully fought against the serpent and been found obedient; in that case, God's justice would be served in the favor of mankind but to the detriment of the serpent.

the cherubim.[71] The language used here for Yahweh closely resembles the description of Leviathan in Job 41:18–19.[72] Thus, monsterial language is used in both these contexts to present on the one hand Yahweh as a terrifying and powerful God against whom the psalmist's enemies cannot stand, and, on the other, in Job to describe Leviathan as a terrifying and most powerful creature who leaves destruction in his wake.

Second, regarding monotheism, the serpentine creatures are not some primordial entities that Yahweh did not create; rather, they are God's creatures, whose rebellion resides in their own will. As Boyd observes,

> the understanding manifested in this *Chaoskampf* material is that the forces opposing Yahweh had a beginning, which is precisely why the Old Testament authors can be confident that, sometimes despite their appearances, they shall also certainly have an end. In contrast to everything their neighbors were saying about the matter, the Old Testament assumes, even in its earliest combat material, that Yahweh is the sole Creator of all that is.[73]

These creatures "freely rebelled against their Creator, and thus ought not to be as they now are."[74] The difference between the serpents' rebellions and humankind's rebellion appears to reside in the effects their rebellions had on their relationships with God. The Old Testament appears to envision the

---

71. Ps 18:8–10 (NIV):
    Smoke rose from his nostrils;
      consuming fire came from his mouth,
      burning coals blazed out of it.
    He parted the heavens and came down;
      dark clouds were under his feet.
    He mounted the cherubim and flew;
      he soared on the wings of the wind.
72. Job 41:18–19 (NIV):
    His snorting throws out flashes of light;
      his eyes are like the rays of dawn.
    Firebrands stream from his mouth;
      sparks of fire shoot out.
    Smoke pours from his nostrils
      as from a boiling pot over a fire of reeds.
    His breath sets coals ablaze,
      and flames dart from his mouth.
73. Boyd, *God at War*, 99.
74. Boyd, 99.

relationship of the serpents with Yahweh as irredeemable. The end of the land serpent would be the same as the end of the sea serpent; he too will be slain (Gen 3:15).

Third, God's conflicts with the sea serpent and the land serpent and with humankind are part of the creation process. The rebellion by the serpents and by humankind required the activation of God's royal power over creation. At stake in these rebellions was the functionality of creation. To reimpose order on creation, God crushed the sea serpent, and he pronounced judgment upon the land serpent and upon humankind.

Conclusion

In this chapter, I have shown first of all that creation in its state of goodness is one in which multiple rebellions happened: (a) rebellion by the sea serpent, variously called Leviathan, or Rahab, or the dragon or the monster; (b) rebellion by the land serpent, who challenged God by invalidating God's command and luring humankind into disobeying God; (c) rebellion by humankind, who rebelled by eating from the tree of the knowledge of good and bad, from which God commanded them not to eat. The creation process may also be properly described as the era of conflicts; however, not conflicts permanently resolved. Rather, creation is functionally "very good," because it is moving toward the resolution of the primordial yet ongoing conflict between Yahweh and the anti-creational forces, and toward the resolution of the conflict between humankind and their primordial enemy.

CHAPTER 6

Creatio in Extremis: First Creation as Paradigm for Eschatological Uncreation and Re-Creation

Introduction

The Old Testament as observed in chapter 5 evinces that the problem of rebellion by the serpentine creatures can be resolved; the sea serpent, no matter how many times it keeps on reinventing itself, will always be crushed; and the land serpent also awaits the same fate as the sea serpent at the hands of the seed of the woman.

In chapter 4, I argued that the disobedience of the first human couple did not render creation nonfunctional; rather, the disobedience of the first human couple altered the condition under which creation continued to function. Following the rebellion of the first human couple, human wickedness continued to escalate inviting what Brueggemann terms, *creatio in extremis*, implying God's extreme measures of judgment and hope with regard to creation.[1] As Brueggemann notes, "Creation itself is a sign and measure of Yahweh's capacity to do beyond what the world thinks is possible."[2]

In this chapter, I will argue that God's deliberate and extreme measures against human wickedness involved, on the one hand, a reversal of creation

---

1. Brueggemann, "Jeremiah," 152–70.
2. Brueggemann, 165.

to its nonfunctional state and, on the other hand, a re-creation of the cosmos by a restoration of creation to its functional state. In the Old Testament, as we will observe, there is a pattern of new creation preceded by reversal of creation to its nonfunctional state; both extremes, as we will observe, follow the pattern established in Genesis 1–3. Gunkel captured some dimensions of this dilemma in his *Schöpfung und Chaos*, which argues for the correspondence between the *Urzeit* and the *Endzeit* (beginning time and end time or primeval era and eschaton).[3]

The cyclical pattern of uncreation and re-creation, which is our main focus in chapter, culminates with the ultimate or ideal eschatological new creation. The ideal new creation, as envisioned in the Old Testament, is not a mere return to the beginning and a continuance thereof, but an inauguration of a new reality whose conditions supersede the conditions of the first creation in its original state of goodness.[4] The first creation, as we will observe, is superseded not because it was not good, but rather because its conditions were non-ideal – the conditions required radical improvement.

Genesis 1–11: Creation – Uncreation – Re-creation Pattern

The theme of Genesis 1–11, the primeval history, as Clines argues, may be viewed as "creation – uncreation – re-creation."[5] There are several indicators that do support this structuring of Genesis 1–11. Genesis 1–3, as argued in

---

3. Gunkel, *Schöpfung*; (English Translation) *Creation and Chaos*. For an abridged translation of this work, see Gunkel, "Influence of Babylonian Mythology," 25–52. Gunkel's focus, however, was specifically on the *chaoskampft* motif: "In the end time what had happened in primal time will be repeated. The new world order will be preceded by a new chaos. The monsters of primal time will appear on the earth a second time." Gunkel, *Creation and Chaos*, 233.

4. As Childs states it, "according to the Biblical scheme the new can be described as a return and a continuance of the old while bringing, at the same time, a totally different element into being." Childs, *Myth and Reality*, 80. Similarly, Pannenberg argues, "the eschatological texts of Jewish . . . literature express the idea that the final age and the primal age correspond. There is not simply a 'linear' understanding of the historical process, but neither is there an identity, a return to the beginning. Rather, there is a correspondence of the kind which has long been discussed under the heading of 'typology.'" Pannenberg, *Basic Question in Theology*, 1–79, 58–59.

5. Clines, "Theme of Genesis 1–11," 483–507; Clines, *Theme of Pentateuch*, 66–86. The pattern suggested by Clines is not the only meaningful pattern for understanding these chapters; there are various other structural indicators that do allow for one to view these chapters as a unity.

the previous chapter, may be viewed as a description of God's creation week. Throughout the creation activities, God continually evaluated his creation as "good." However, creation in its state of goodness is one in which man rebelled against God, thereby introducing various levels of separation or alienation. The first is alienation in the God-human relationship: human beings rebel by the eating of the forbidden tree (3:6), they hide away from God (3:8–10), and they are judged (3:16–20) and expelled from the garden of Eden (3:24). The second is alienation in human-animal relationship: enmity between the serpent and the woman's seed (3:15). The last is alienation in interpersonal relationships: the man blames the woman and ultimately God (3:12).[6] In the midst of such alienations, there was hope: hope in the seed of the woman to crush the serpent and fulfill the creation mandate. God's confidence in humankind continued even after the creation week, after humankind's expulsion from the garden of Eden. This is evidenced by God's dialogue with Cain following the rejection of his sacrifice. There was hope that Cain could do what is right – he could conquer sin and master it (Gen 4:6–7). However, with the exception of those who started calling upon the name of God (Gen 4:26) and men like Enoch and Noah, who walked with God (Gen 5:24; 6:9), the disintegration continued to escalate, leading up to the ultimate refrain:

> The LORD saw how great man's wickedness on the earth had become, and that every inclination of the thought of his heart was only evil all the time. The LORD was grieved that he had made man on the earth, and his heart was filled with pain. (Gen 6:5, cf. 6:11–12, NIV)

Both inside the garden of Eden and outside of it, humankind failed to live up to God's expectations. From inside the garden of Eden, humankind's rebellion brought a curse upon creation (Gen 3:17). From outside the garden, humankind destroyed the goodness of creation by his wickedness – as the narrator tells us "now the earth was corrupt in God's sight and was full of violence" (Gen 6:11) – and brought an ultimate judgment upon creation: uncreation, a reversal of all life, or, more generally, the destruction of the earth. Just as in the garden of Eden, human actions have cosmic effect. As Harland argues, "there is a clear connection between right human behavior

---

6. See Hauser, "Genesis 2–3," 20–36.

and the functioning of creation."[7] In Fretheim's words, "human sin and its judgmental effects ripple out and adversely affect the entire created order."[8] Through wicked human behavior, creation progressively degenerated from "good" to "bad." As Clines argues, Genesis chapters 3–6 "are not simply the story of human sin matched by divine grace, but the story of undoing of creation. The flood is only the final stage in the process of cosmic disintegration that began in Eden."[9] As Harland notes, "as the world has destroyed (שחת) itself through sin, God sees that it is destroyed (שחת). What God destroys has already set itself on the road to destruction and by its corruption has virtually destroyed itself."[10] The degeneration of the Adamic generation had finally reached its peak, which required that God take the most extreme measure:

> So the LORD said, "I will wipe humankind, whom I have created, from the face of the earth – men and animals, and creatures that move along the ground, and birds of the air – for I am grieved that I have made them." (Gen 6:7, NIV)

> So God said to Noah, "I am going to put an end to all people, for the earth is filled with violence because of them. I am surely going to destroy both them and the earth." (Gen 6:13, NIV)

> I am going to bring floodwaters on the earth to destroy all life under the heavens, every creature that has breath of life in it. Everything on earth will perish. (Gen 6:17, NIV)

The underlying message in the texts above is that God is about to uncreate what he created. The list of entities to be uncreated in Genesis 6:7 reverses the order of creation that is in Genesis 1:20, 24, and 26. The reversal of creation is the reversal of all life, which may be generally be described as a destruction of the earth. The Noahic flood brings about a reversal of creation by removing the boundaries set at creation. God opened the springs of the great deep and the floodgates of heaven, allowing the waters above the firmament and the waters below to reunite, returning the earth to its initial state of lifelessness, or its nonfunctional state (Gen 7:11–12). The flood waters swallowed up the

---

7. Harland, *Value of Human Life*, 106.
8. Fretheim, *God and World*, 160.
9. Clines, *Theme of Pentateuch*, 81.
10. Harland, *Value of Human Life*, 106.

earth and sucked all life out of it (Gen 7:17–23). The reversal, however, was not a complete annihilation, as God chose to preserve humanity and other living creatures from the Adamic generation.

The act of remembrance in Genesis 8:1 brings the uncreation process to a halt, inaugurating the process of re-creation. The similarities between Genesis 1–2 and Genesis 8–9 signal a new beginning of creation: (a) God sends his *rûaḥ* (wind) over the flooded earth (Gen 8:1; cf. 1:2); (b) the boundaries of the *tĕhôm* (deep) are re-established – the springs of the deep are shut and floodgates of heaven are closed (Gen 8:2; cf. 1:6–9); (c) dry land appears (Gen 8:13–14; cf. 1:9–10); (d) the land becomes productive again (Gen 8:11; cf. 1:11–12); (e) living creatures are restored on earth (Gen 8:15–19); (f) days and seasons are restored (Gen 8:22; cf. 1:14–19); (g) God's blessing to humankind is restored – "Be fruitful and increase in number and fill the earth" (Gen 9:1, 7; cf. 1:28); (h) humankind again receives dominion over the earth (Gen 9:2); (i) food is provided for humankind (Gen 9:3; cf. 1:29–30); (j) the image of God in man reaffirmed (Gen 9:4–6; cf. 1:26–27).[11] Baldwin writes, "The flood is an eschatological step-by-step 'uncreation' of the world and humanity followed by a step-by-step 're-creation' of the new world."[12] The uncreation of the ancient world ushered in the new world of the patriarchs and, later, Israel.

The re-created world, however, is a relative return to the first creation. The paradise lost by the first Adam is not regained by Noah, a type of Adam. There is also a significant difference between Adam as originally created and Noah – "Every inclination of his [humankind's] heart is evil from childhood" (Gen 8:22).[13] Thus, the re-creation process did not restore creation to its pre-fall condition. Instead, the re-created world stands in continuity with the fallen creation. The effects of the fall of the first Adam and the tendency of the human heart of the Adamic generation continue in the re-created world. The fall of the first Adam is also reenacted in Noah's sin.[14] There are a number of parallels between the two: (a) Adam's transgression happens in a garden (Gen 3:1), whereas Noah's happens in a vineyard (Gen 9:20); (b) Adam eats

---

11. Davidson argues that "the overarching literary structure of 're-creation' in the Flood narrative underscores its universal dimension by parallels with the cosmic Creation account in Genesis 1–2"Davidson, "Biblical Evidence," 89.

12. Davidson, 89–90.

13. Smith, "Structure and Purpose," 311; Fretheim, *Creation, Fall, and Flood*, 113.

14. See Cassuto, *Commentary on Genesis*, 2:158–70; Cage, *Gospel of Genesis*.

the fruit, which results in shame over his nakedness (Gen 3:7), whereas Noah drinks wine resulting in his nakedness; (c) Adam's realization of his nakedness brings a curse upon himself and his descendants (Gen 3:16–19, 23–24), whereas Ham's seeing his father's nakedness brought a curse on Canaan (Gen 9:25–27); (d) God covers Adam's nakedness with garments of skin (Gen 3:21), whereas Shem and Japheth cover Noah's nakedness with a garment. The world of the patriarchs and later Israel may thus be called a new creation, yet a fallen one, which stands in continuity with the old.

There are many parallels that connect this section of Scripture with the rest of the Pentateuch and the rest of the Old Testament.[15] Important for us to note at this point are the following: First, what happens in the end (eschatology) corresponds with what happened in the beginning (protology), as evidenced by the parallels between Genesis 1–3 and Genesis 6–9. There is an interdependence between the *Urzeit und Endzeit* (the beginning and the ending), with the ending being an inauguration of a new beginning. Second, the Noahic generation is a continuance of the Adamic generation. The continuation of un-re-created humanity signals a continuance of the old that brought corruption to creation; therefore, creation is still threatened by humanity. Third, there is interconnectedness between human behavior and creation at large – "the interconnectedness of life."[16] God's creation is at stake in human behavior, not simply the more specific relation between human beings and God.[17] Fourth, Genesis 1–11 as an introduction to the Old Testament is important because it makes a diagnosis of the problem of creation: How did creation that was initially good turn out to be corrupt and full of violence? The answer is that the problem lies within the human heart. Genesis 1–11 shows that the resolution of creation's corruption would require more than just a reversal and re-creation of the physical world; the problem is deeply engraved in the human heart: "Every inclination of the thoughts of his [humankind's] heart was only evil all the time. . . . Every inclination of his [humankind's] heart is evil from childhood" (Gen 6:5; 8:21, NIV).

---

15. See Stanton, "Asking Questions," 156–65; Smith, "Structure and Purpose," 318–19; Clines, *Theme of Pentateuch*, 84–86; Cage, *Gospel of Genesis*, 66–69.

16. See Fretheim, *God and World*, 160.

17. See Fretheim, 165.

Genesis 1–11 stands as an introduction of the entire Primary History (Gen–2 Kgs). The story of Israel is set diachronically as a follow-up to two creations (macrocosms) that both culminate in disaster: the Adamic generation is wiped out as a result of human wickedness, and the Noahic generation continues the wickedness of the previous generation and is ultimately scattered over the surface of the earth. Israel's story (microcosm) is essentially the same or "a long drawn replay of it": it is a story of creation–uncreation–re-creation.[18] The Primary History, as Clines points out, is a story in a downhill direction concluding in a disastrous mode with Israel in exile.[19] Israel subsequently becomes a two-kingdom state, the kingdom of Israel and the kingdom of Judah – and both kingdoms end in disaster. The history of the kingdom of Israel ends in a tragic climax, with the ten tribes of Israel exiled and dissolved – uncreated with no hope of re-creation (2 Kgs 17:7–23).[20] The kingdom of Israel, like the Adamic generation, "did wicked things that provoked the LORD to anger" (2 Kgs 17:11b; cf. Gen 6:5), which resulted in their removal from God's presence (2 Kgs 17:18, 20, 23). However, not all was lost: the kingdom of Judah was left, but like the Noahic generation, they too followed in the evil of the kingdom of Israel:

> So the LORD was very angry with Israel and removed them from his presence. Only the tribe of Judah was left, and even Judah did not keep the commands of the LORD their God. They followed the practices Israel had introduced. (2 Kgs 17:18–19; cf. Gen 8:21).

The history of the kingdom of Judah, like that of the kingdom of Israel, also comes to a tragic end; they too are exiled, this time in Babylon (2 Kgs 24:15–17; 25:21) and scattered throughout the surface of the earth (2 Kgs 25:25–27). This came upon the kingdom of Judah because they and their kings followed in the footsteps of their fathers by doing evil, but perhaps even more so because they broke the Noahic covenant:

---

18. See Clines, *What Does Eve Do?*, 97. Conversely, within Israel's story there are other micro stories which basically follow the same pattern, for example, Exod 19–40; Lev 8–10.

19. Clines, *What Does Eve Do?*, 93–98.

20. "The kingdom of Israel became the Ten Lost Tribes, not that they were lost in the sense of being misplaced and forgotten; they merged into the life of other races and lost their identity. They dissolved like salt in water." Bailey and Kent, *History of Hebrew Commonwealth*, 198.

> Surely these things happened to Judah according to the LORD's command, in order to remove them from his presence because of the sins of Manasseh and all he had done, including the *shedding of innocent blood. For he had filled Jerusalem with innocent blood*, and the LORD was not willing to forgive. (2 Kgs 24:3–4; cf. Gen 9:5b–6, NIV)[21]

Genesis 1–11 may, thus, be viewed as a pre-told Israelite story or, as Cage frames it, "the history of Israel (microcosm) is synthetically parallel to the history of the world (macrocosm), that is, the history of Israel from the exodus to the exile constitutes an elaborate reconstruction of the record of prediluvian history (Genesis 1–7)."[22] However, the biblical story does not find closure with Judah uncreated and dissolved. The author(s) of the Secondary History (1–2 Chronicles; Ezra–Nehemiah, Esther, and Daniel) offer a glimmer of hope: Judah did not dissolve, but continued to exist in exile (Esther and Daniel) and was restored (Ezra–Nehemiah). Through Judah, Israel's story does not end in uncreation; rather, its proper conclusion should be found in re-creation; however, old patterns die hard. The relapse of humankind into wickedness continues in the postexilic community (Ezra 9–10). Furthermore, the postexilic community realized that their restoration was far from ideal: the rebuilding of the land was a work in progress; worship was restored, but the temple was not restored to its former glory; the seed of David had returned, but the monarchy was not restored (Ezra 3:12–13; Neh 9:5–37). However, the disappointment did not quench the ever-increasing anticipation for Israel's visionaries.

Israel's Prophets: Eschatological Uncreation and New Creation

The creation–uncreation–re-creation pattern also provides a helpful framework for understanding some aspects of the message of the prophets regarding Israel's exile and return. The prophets resorted to the most extreme cases imaginable to express the message of judgment and hope.[23] There is an organic unity between judgment and hope. We will also observe that for

---

21. Emphasis added.
22. Cage, *Gospel of Genesis*, 66–67.
23. Brueggemann, "Jeremiah," 152–70.

Israel's prophets the actions of Israel do not merely affect Israel's relationship with its God; rather, Israel's actions have a cosmic effect. For the prophets, Israel's exile is expressed as a reversal of creation; whereas the return from exile is presented as cosmic re-creation or new creation.

The Day of Judgment as a Day of Uncreation

Israel's prophets, among others, used creation rhetoric to warn both the kingdom of Israel and the kingdom of Judah of the catastrophe that would befall them as a result of their continual disobedience of Yahweh. For the prophets, the Lord is fully capable of obliterating creation's operational system. Yahweh will reverse his creation to its nonfunctional state by bringing a complete destruction of humanity and other living creatures, and to make the land unproductive by terminating vegetation.

First, we observe the warnings of the eighth-century prophets Amos and Hosea against the kingdom of Israel. The prophet Amos in 5:18–27 pronounces woe on those "who long for the day of the LORD." The woe pronouncements in this section stand in contrast to the series of pronouncements to "seek me [the Lord] and live" or "seek good, not evil, that you may live" (5:4, 6, 14). The origin of the concept of "the day of the Lord" is much debated. The day of the Lord, for the prophet Amos, has come to refer to the day of judgment: "That day will be darkness, not light. . . . Will not the day of the LORD be darkness, not light – pitch-dark, without a ray of brightness?" (5:18c, 20). The contrast between darkness and light recalls the creation order; however, for Amos, the Lord, "who formed the mountains [and] creates the wind" is capable of turning off the light and plunging his people into complete darkness; it is "he who turns dawn to darkness" (4:13). Further on, the prophet states,

> "In that day," declares the sovereign Lord,
> "I will make the sun go down at noon,
> 　　and darken the earth in broad daylight. . . .
> In that day, the lovely young women and strong young men
> 　　will faint because of thirst.
> They who swear by the shame of Samaria, or say,
> 　　'As surely as your god lives, Dan,'
> 　　or, 'as surely as the god of Beersheba lives,'
> they will fall,
> 　　never to rise again" (Amos 8:9–14, NIV).

For Amos, Yahweh is the Lord of creation, and he has complete control over darkness and light; he is capable of turning light into darkness. In the creation process, darkness preceded the light – it was light that was turned on in darkness. Israel's sins, on the other hand, bring about the reversal of the creation order; it is now the light that will again be turned into darkness. The description of the eclipse of the sun puts emphasis on the catastrophic event that is to befall Israel, an event that will bring an end to Israel. However, not only is Israel affected by the judgment, but the rest of the cosmos is affected as well.[24]

The prophet Hosea, in a similar fashion, draws a connection between Israel's action and the cosmos:

> Hear the word of the LORD, you Israelites,
>   because the LORD has a charge to bring
> against you who live in the land:
> "There is no faithfulness, no love,
>   no acknowledgment of God in the land.
> There is only cursing, lying and murder,
>   stealing and adultery;
> they break all bounds,
>   and bloodshed follows bloodshed.
> Because of this the land mourns,
>   and all who live in it waste away;
> the beasts of the field and the birds of the air
>   and the fish of the sea are dying." (Hosea 4:1–3, NIV)

The "complaint" or "charge" (רִיב) motif in Hosea 4:1 is generally regarded as indicative of a covenant lawsuit (cf. Jer 2:4–13; Mic 4:1–8). In this covenantal lawsuit, the Lord lays the charge against Israel – the covenant people lack covenantal virtues: faithfulness, love (חֶסֶד), and acknowledgement of the Lord; instead they have violated the covenant by transgressing the Law through cursing or swearing (cf. Exod 20:7), lying (Exod 20:16; 23:1, 7; Deut 25:13–16), killing (Exod 20;13), stealing (Exod 20:15), adultery (Exod 20:14), and bloodshed after bloodshed;[25] as a result judgment is pronounced

---

24. Wolff, *Joel and Amos*, 329.

25. "These five crimes are not simply breaches of general morality; they are acts prohibited by the normative tradition of Israel which summarizes the will of Yahweh under the covenant

(Hos 3:3). The force of this covenantal lawsuit, as Deroche argues, can be fully appreciated if one takes into consideration the relationship between covenant and creation.[26] In the judgment pronouncement, "Hosea is not merely employing imagery of a drought to illustrate Israel's punishment; he is announcing a reversal of creation."[27] The judgment pictured is a reversal of the creation order in Genesis 1: fish (1:20a), birds (1:20b), and beasts (1:24). In Genesis 1:28, humankind is given dominion "over the fish of the sea and the birds of the air and over every living creature that moves on the ground." A similar list of animals is found in Hosea 2:20, which states that the Lord will in the future establish a covenant between Israel and the beasts if Israel is faithful to the covenant. As Deroche argues, the list that we find in Genesis 1, Hosea 2:20, and Hosea 3:3 is representative of all animal life.[28] Thus, the judgment announcement in Hosea 3:3 brings about a complete reversal of animal life on earth and in the sea. For Hosea, Israel like Adam has broken the covenant with the Lord, and likewise human sin has a cosmic effect (cf. Hos 6:7). Thus, Hosea presents Israel with two possible scenarios: Israel can remain true to the covenant and open up the possibility of a harmonious life on earth, harmony between humanity and living creatures, and harmony between living creatures and land (Hos 2:20–23), or Israel can continue to remain unfaithful to the covenant and bring about a complete reversal of creation. As Wolf observes, there is an "organic structure of order" – the interconnectedness of life that Yahweh has set in place.[29]

The prophecies of Amos and Hosea were not merely cosmic hyperbole. The prophets were warning Israel of complete discontinuity in the case of continuity of wickedness and covenant unfaithfulness. In keeping with the warnings sounded by these prophets, the kingdom of Israel was brought to an end by the Assyrians, and as already noted, they dissolved among the nations. The book of Amos and the book of Hosea were both preserved in the

---

[the Decalogue]. The last three are literally equivalent to prohibitions of the Decalogue (Exod 20:2–17; Deut 5:16–21)." Mays, *Hosea: A Commentary*, 64. It is a debated issue, however, as to whether the Decalogue had already attained its current form in the time of Hosea. See Nielsen, *Ten Commandments in Recent Perspectives*, 12; Stamm and Andrew, *Ten Commandments in Recent Research*, 22–69; Mayes, *Deuteronomy*, 162–65.

26. Deroche, "Reversal of Creation in Hosea," 400–409.
27. Deroche, 403.
28. Deroche, 403.
29. Wolff, *Hosea: A Commentary*, 68.

kingdom of Judah following the demise of the kingdom of Israel, and thus these prophecies also served as warnings to Judah.

Similar warnings were also sounded by southern prophets of the kingdom of Judah in the pre-exilic period. We note here particularly two prophetic voices, Zephaniah and Jeremiah, specifically Zephaniah 1:2–3 and Jeremiah 4:23–28. Both these prophets prophesied during the reign of Josiah, although Jeremiah's ministry extended to the time of the destruction of Jerusalem and exile by the Babylonians. The historical setting of Jeremiah 1:1–25:3 is "twenty-three years, from the thirteenth year of Josiah son of Amon king of Judah until this very day" (25:3); thus, it is reasonable to conclude these prophets sounded their warnings around the same time, one affirming the other.

> ² "I will sweep away everything
>   from the face of the earth,"
> declares the Lord.
> ³ "I will sweep away both *man and beast*,
> I will sweep away the birds in the sky,
>   and the fish in the sea.
> And the idols that cause the wicked to stumble."
>   "When I destroy all mankind
> on the face of the earth,"
>   declares the Lord. (Zeph 1:2–3, NIV)[30]

This prophecy makes significant allusions to the creation narrative, Genesis 1:1–3:24 and the flood narrative, Genesis 6–9, creation and uncreation. The following parallels between Zephaniah 1:2–3 and Genesis 1:1–3:24 may be observed: First, the list of the living creatures in Zephaniah 1:2–3 appear in a reverse order from the creation order in Genesis 1, thereby suggesting a reversal of creation.[31] Second, the pun between man (הָאָדָם) and the earth or land (הָאֲדָמָה) in Zephaniah 1:3 alludes to the creation narrative in Genesis 2:4b–3:24.[32] This word play is encountered in Genesis 2:5, 7; 3:17–19, 23, wherein the emphasis is on the close tie between man and the earth: man is created from the earth, to serve the earth; the earth is cursed on humankind's

---

30. Emphasis added.
31. Deroche, "Zephaniah 1:2–3," 107.
32. Deroche, 106.

account; humankind is dependent upon the earth for existence; and humankind returns to the earth when he/she dies. However, for Zephaniah the emphasis in the use of the pun points to the flood narrative.

The following parallels are notable between Zephaniah 1:2–3 and Genesis 6–9: First, in Zephaniah 1:2–3 and Genesis 6:7; 13; 7:4, divine action is intended to bring termination of life on earth. In Genesis 6:7, 13, the Lord threatens to "wipe out' (מָחָה) or "to put to an end" (קֵץ לְנֹחַ) or "destroy" (שָׁחַת), and he actually does so by opening the floodgates. In Zephaniah divine action is just as swift, although different action verbs are employed: in this case the Lord will "sweep away" (אָסַף) or "cut off" (כָּרַת) life from the earth (1:2, 3). The termination of life, in Zephaniah, is still in the future. Second, the phrase "from the face of the earth" occurs three times in the flood narrative, Genesis 6:7; 7:4; 8:8, and in two of these cases, there is a close parallel with Zephaniah 1:2–3:

Gen 6:7	Gen 7:4	Gen 8:8 (NIV)
So the LORD said, "I will wipe mankind, whom I have created, from the face of the earth – man and animals, and creatures that move along the ground, and the birds of the air, for I am grieved that I made them."	"Seven days from now I will send rain on the earth for forty days and forty nights, and I will wipe from the face of the earth every living creature I have made."	Then he sent out a dove to see if the water had receded from the face of the earth.

As Deroche points out, "the significance is that man is going to be cut off from the very substance he was created from and is dependent upon for his existence (Gen ii 7, iii 17–19)."[33] Third, the lists of representative creatures in both Zephaniah 1:2 and Genesis 6:7 reverse the creation order in Genesis 1. Fourth, both Zephaniah 1:2 and Genesis 7:4 proclaim a universal judgment on creation: "everything" (כֹּל) is affected by human wickedness. This judgment oracle, however, also retains a certain particularity, as the prophet was invoking creation language to warn Judah of the coming judgment. Fifth, in both Zephaniah 1:2–3 and Genesis 6–9, it is human sin that activates divine wrath against creation, resulting in the termination of humanity on

---

33. Deroche, 106.

earth. The Hebrew verb כָּרַת used by Zephaniah is also used for covenant-making between God and the people (Gen 15:18; Jer 31:31; 32:40); however, in Zephaniah's case the Lord is not making a covenant with the people; rather, he is cutting the people off for violating the covenant (cf. Gen 17:14). Zephaniah's announcement of the reversal of creation, as Deroche observes, in a sense nullifies the promise God made to Noah: "Never again will I curse the ground because of man, even though every inclination of his heart is evil from childhood. And never again will I destroy all living creatures, as I have done" (Gen 8:21, NIV).[34]

The prophet Jeremiah also announced the judgment of Judah using similar extreme creation language. Jeremiah, like Amos, Hosea, and Zephaniah, also envisioned God's coming judgment as a cosmic catastrophe.

> I looked on the earth, and lo, it was desolate and empty;
>   and to the heavens, and they had no light.
> I looked on the mountains, and lo, they were quaking,
>   and all the hills moved to and fro.
> I looked, and lo, there was no man,
>   and all the birds of the air had fled.
> I looked, and lo, the fruitful land was a desert,
>   and all its cities were laid in ruins before the LORD,
>   before his fierce anger. (Jer 4:23–26, NRSV)[35]

This passage, as Fishbane argues, serves as a counterpart of Genesis 1; its poetic structure reduces the essential order of the acts of God in creation.[36] Jeremiah uses language reminiscent of Genesis 1 and perhaps more broadly of Genesis 1–3; however, the prophet, as many have observed, is not merely quoting the creation narrative but actually reversing the creation order: The

---

34. Deroche, 106.

35. The authorship of Jeremiah for this prophecy has been questioned by some scholars. For example, Anderson argues that this prophecy was "composed toward the end of Jeremiah's career, around the fateful turn from the seventh to the sixth centuries B.C., when the nation of Judah stood on the eve of destruction." Anderson, *Creation versus Chaos*, 12. I see, however, no reason to doubt that this vision formed part of Jeremiah's early collection of prophecies instead of a late or redactional piece. The cosmic language used by Jeremiah in this vision is no different from what we have observed from Amos, Hosea, and Zephaniah. Some suggest that Jer 4:23–26 be viewed as apocalyptic due to the cosmic depiction of the destruction. see Childs, "Enemy from the North," 187–98; Eppstein, "Day of Yahweh," 93–97; Olson, "Jeremiah 4:5–31," 81–107.

36. Fishbane, "Jeremiah IV 23–26," 151–53.

earth has returned to its nonfunctional state of *tōhû wābōhû*. Futhermore, there is no more light in the heavens, this language probably implying that not only the heavenly luminaries – sun, moon, and stars of the fourth day – but also the cosmogonic light of the first day has departed, leaving creation to its state of darkness. The mountains and hills, which emerged with the gathering of the waters below to one place, are now quaking. And life is sucked out of the earth – "there was no man," referring to humankind created on the sixth day and probably to Genesis 2:5 ("there was no man to till the ground").[37] The birds have fled – the creatures that flew above the earth across the sky. The earth has become unproductive – the vegetation of the fourth day is all gone, and animals are not even mentioned. The absence of the primeval waters and the allusion to the desert also set this prophecy in close affinity with the second creation narrative (Gen 2:4b–3:24).[38] Carroll observes, "Out of the primordial chaos Yahweh created order and the world. . . . but in the conflict of nations and the forces of nature lay the return of that order to chaos. Israel's theologizing of this cosmic drama made Yahweh the creator and destroyer of order and life."[39] In Brueggemann's words, "Jeremiah 4:23–26 is a step-by-step subtraction from the 'very good' creation upon which Israel has counted and in which its own life is lived."[40]

The kingdom of Judah, like the kingdom of Israel, in keeping with the prophecies of Zephaniah and Jeremiah, also collapsed. The decline of the kingdom of Judah was completed with the destruction of the temple, the collapse of the monarchy, and exile at the hands of the Babylonians. Such a collapse was expressed by these prophets as a collapse of creation – "the most unimaginable discontinuity that could be uttered."[41] The temple, the divinely appointed order that established correspondence between heaven and earth, was reduced to rubble. The Davidic dynasty was reduced to nothing, powerless and without authority. The king, the Lord's representative on earth was deported to Babylon blinded and in chains. The land flowing with milk and

---

37. As Van Ruiten argues, "Gen 2:4b–6 describes in its own way the situation of chaos before the creation of man. Not only is there no man to till the ground. There is also a rainless land without vegetation, in short, a desert." Van Ruiten, "Back to Chaos," 29.

38. Craigie, Kelley, and Drinkard, *Jeremiah 1–25*, 81; Weippert, *Schöpfer des Himmels*, 51.

39. Carroll, *Jeremiah: A Commentary*, 168.

40. Brueggemann, *Jeremiah: Creatio in Extremis*, 156.

41. Brueggemann, 156.

honey was reduced to a desert and without inhabitants, as the people were taken to exile except for the poorest of the poor who were left. The author of Lamentations discerned that this could just as well be a point of total rejection, termination, and discontinuity of Judah, and he thus concludes, "Restore us to yourself, O LORD, that we may return; renew our days as of old unless you have utterly rejected us and are angry with us beyond measure" (Lam 5:21–22, NIV).

The creation rhetoric we have observed counters Brueggemann's claim that creation faith "is more inclined toward social stability than toward social transformation and liberation";[42] or, as he frames it elsewhere, "Creation faith tended to give questions of order priority over questions of justice."[43] As Fretheim argues, "God has created the world in such a way that deeds (whether good or evil) will have consequences."[44] The consequences of deeds, whether good or evil, have cosmic effects. Creation faith is not merely concerned with issues of order; the issue of justice is an intrinsic element of creation. The crushing of the rebellious sea monster at creation, the judgment upon the rebellious land serpent, and judgment on humanity in the garden of Eden are all concerns of justice. The consequences of the administering of justice at creation also had a cosmic effect – the natural order was affected as well, but not as a consequence of its own wrongdoing. In the same way, Israel's actions have a cosmic effect.

The threat of a cosmic reversal of creation has among others the following theological implications: First, God's creation is at stake in human (or Israel's) behavior. The whole of creation is affected by divine judgment; at stake in human (or Israel's) behavior are the nations and the world of nature. Second, creation rhetoric as used by the prophets does not legitimize the status quo in the society; rather, it calls for radical transformation of human behavior in the here and now in light of the cosmic disaster that human wickedness can effect. Third, the created order in the past serves as no guarantee for the status quo; what was created in the past can and might just as easily be uncreated. God, as revealed in the Old Testament, is capable of both creating and uncreating. Fourth, creation in its nonfunctional state has come to serve as a

---

42. Brueggemann, "Shape for Old Testament," 41–42.
43. Brueggemann, *Prophetic Imagination*, 33.
44. Fretheim, *God and the World*, 163.

paradigm of judgment. We have here an analogical relationship between the beginning and the end. Just as Yahweh created the cosmos, moving it from its nonfunctional state to a functional state, and furthermore, just as Yahweh was capable of reversing creation to its nonfunctional state in the time of Noah and re-creating it again, he is capable of reverting it to that state again and leave it there indefinitely as exemplified in the dissolution of the Northern Kingdom of Israel. The Old Testament, however, does not consider uncreation the last word. The future from the Old Testament perspective contains in a sense judgment and salvation, uncreation and re-creation. It is this latter aspect that will be the focus of our attention in the subsequent section.

Thus, creation in its functional state is far from ideal; it is continually in danger of being corrupted and being reversed back to its nonfunctional state. The reversal of creation to its nonfunctional state is the most extreme measure of judgment against creation imaginable; nothing can be worse.

Eschatological New Creation

Israel's prophets not only announced an eschatological return of creation to its primordial state but they also announced a possibility of re-creation; a re-creation of humanity, specifically Israel, which in turn leads to a cosmic new heaven and new earth. We will particularly focus on the prophecies of Isaiah, Jeremiah, and Ezekiel. The prophet Isaiah lived in the eighth century; however, in critical scholarship, only Isaiah 1–39 is attributed to this prophet; Isaiah 40–55, also known as Deutero-Isaiah (or Second Isaiah), from the exilic period, and Isaiah 55–65, also known as Trito-Isaiah (or Third Isaiah) from the post-exilic period, are regarded as later additions to the original core. I am, however, more inclined to view Isaiah 1–66 as a literary unit, but at the same time I accept the notion that there is a progressive development in the message of the book encompassing the pre-exilic, exilic, and post-exilic periods.[45] Isaiah 40–55, as some have observed, has the highest concentration of creation language in the whole of the Old Testament.[46] In this section, the

---

45. As Sweeney argues, "although Isaiah contains blocks of material that were composed, at least in part, in relation to distinct socio-historical settings, the present form of Isaiah constitutes a discreet literary entity in and of itself, rather than a collection of two, three, or more originally independent prophetic compositions." Sweeney, *Form and Intertextuality*, 28.

46. See Stuhlmueller, *Creative Redemption*, 209–29; Anderson, *Creation versus Chaos*, 124–26.

core message of this prophet is the re-creation of Israel. In Trito-Isaiah, the scope of re-creation is broadened to include the entire cosmos – the new heavens and the new earth. On the other hand, the prophet Jeremiah and Ezekiel all lived to witness and experience Israel's uncreation; yet in the midst of that process, they both undergirded the prophecy of Isaiah of a new Israel by announcing an inward re-creation.

Isaiah 40–55: Israel's Re-Creation

The doctrine of creation in Isaiah has been a subject of great debate since the publication of von Rad's influential essay in 1936.[47] Von Rad regarded creation faith as peripheral in the Old Testament, as evidenced on the one hand by its omission in Israel's creedal statement and its never having functioned as an independent doctrine in Israel until much later.[48] For von Rad, early Israel had an exclusive commitment to the history of salvation. Consequently, von Rad regarded creation faith as having had a subsidiary role to that of soteriology in Deutero-Isaiah, so subsidiary that it is never mentioned for its own sake: "The doctrine of creation has been fully absorbed into the complex of soteriological belief."[49] Von Rad's thesis regarding Isaiah has attracted both support and opposition.[50] In contrast to von Rad, Harner concludes that the doctrine of creation had a relative independence of its own and it functioned as a bridge between the exodus tradition and the expectation of the imminent restoration.[51] As Anderson argues, "the belief in creation is not an adornment

---

47. Von Rad, "Das theologische Problem," 138–47; English Translation of this edition: "Theological Problem of Old Testament."

48. Von Rad was not the first to relegate the doctrine creation to a peripheral statement of faith. Herman Schultz's Old Testament Theology, which appeared at the second half of the century, states that the primitive Semitic tribes had no idea of creation. Schultz, *Alttestamentliche Theologie*; English Translation of the 4th edition: *Old Testament Theology*. During Schultz's time, the ancient Near Eastern mythologies had not yet been brought to the attention of Old Testament scholars. However, during Von Rad's time, although Old Testament scholars were familiar with ancient Near Eastern material, the track that was followed was influenced by "dialectic theology," which privileged God's salvific interventions in Israel's history. See Rendtorff, "Some Reflections on Creation,", 204–5.

49. Von Rad, "Theological Problem," 58.

50. For further development of Von Rad's thesis, see Foerster, "Ktizo," 3:999–1015; Stuhlmueller, *Creative Redemption*; Brongers, *De Scheppingstradities*; Reumann, *Creation and New Creation*. For counterreactions to Von Rad's thesis, see Rendtorff, "Die theologische," 3–13; Rendtorff, "Some Reflections on Creation," 205–12; Harner, "Creation Faith," 298–306.

51. Harner, 304.

of this [Isaiah's] prophetic message rather its very substance. The salvation of Israel and of mankind is . . . firmly anchored in the purpose of the Eternal God, the Creator, who has made known the end from the beginning."[52]

Isaiah utilizes creation verbs, *bārā'* (create), *'āśāh* (make), and *yāṣar* (form), which appear prominently in Genesis 1–3. These three verbs appear in basically three categories: primordial deeds, historical deeds, and eschatological deeds.[53] In the eschatological deeds, as we will observe subsequently, something entirely new is envisioned, yet at the same time primordial deeds and historical deeds return.

For Isaiah, Yahweh's primordial deeds provide grounding for Israel and Judah's redemption from the Babylonian exile. In the previous section, we observed that the prophets used extreme creation language to announce the fall and collapse of both the kingdom of Israel and the kingdom of Judah. For Isaiah, Yahweh is the creator God; it is he who created the ends of the earth (Isa 40:26), who created the heavens and spread them out, who spread out the earth and all that comes out of it (Isa 42:5), who made the earth and created humankind upon it, who stretched out the heavens and marshaled their starry hosts (Isa 45:12), and who created the heavens and formed and made the earth (Isa 45:18). These claims by Isaiah not only served as a polemic against the gods of other nations, and particularly the gods of the Babylonian nation, who might have been with Judah's uncreation, but even more so served to declare Yahweh as an incomparable God; he alone is the cosmic creator and cosmic king from the beginning (Isa 40:25–26; cf. 42:5–9; 12–13, 18; 48:12–13).[54] I would like, however, to draw our attention to Isaiah 45:18, which is a statement of the purpose of creation:

---

52. Anderson, *Creation versus Chaos*, 123.

53. Anderson, 124–26.

54. Mann rightly argues that the position of Isa 40:12–31 "suggests that whatever actions in history may be attributed to Yahweh, they are grounded in a theology of Yahweh as 'creator of the earth.' In this sense, a theology of creation is prior to and foundational for a theology of history. This fundamental importance of God as creator in SI's theology is unprecedented within the prophetic corpus of ancient Israel." Mann, "Stars, Sprouts, and Streams," 142. *Pace* Stuhlmueller, claims that "the idea of creation must be accepted as a secondary motif, thoroughly subservient to that of redemption and quite inexplicable without it." Stuhlmueller, *Creative Redemption*, vii, 5. Isaiah 40:12–31; 42:5–9, 12–13, 18; 43:1; 45:9–13; 48:12–17; 51:9–16, as Harner observes, are distinct creation traditions in which creation faith alone serves as the basis for the proclamation that Yahweh is about to redeem Israel, without mention of the exodus tradition. Harner, "Creation Faith," 300–302.

> For thus says Yahweh,
>   who creates (בְּרָא) the heavens,
> he is God;
>   who formed (יָצַר) the earth and made (עָשָׂה) it;
> he founded it;
>   he did not create (בְּרָא) it to be empty (תֹהוּ).
>   but he formed (יָצַר) it for inhabitation. (Own translation.)

This passage alludes in a number of ways to Genesis 1–3: first, Isaiah uses creation verbs that are all found in the Genesis account; second, the purpose of the creation work by Yahweh was so that the earth would be inhabited; he did not create it to be a *tōhû*, which compares with Genesis 1:2. The Genesis 1 account reaches its climax with creation, which was initially a *tōhû wābōhû*, transformed into a productive and inhabited creation. This is in contrast to Weinfeld, Stuhlmueller, and Sommer, who tend to see Isaiah 45:18 as a polemic against Genesis 1. For these scholars, Isaiah 45:18 is a denial of any association of creation with chaos at its outset.[55]

For Isaiah, it is against God's purpose of creation that the land should return to its initial state of *tōhû*, a deserted creation (cf. Gen 1:2). The exile of God's people is viewed as going against Yahweh's purpose for creation. Thus, the prophet Isaiah could be hopeful that the land of Israel would be restored by drawing on God's purpose for creation.[56] This prophecy, however, stands in contrast to Isaiah's earlier prophecy in 24:1–23, which envisions a cosmic reversal of creation into a state of utter desolation. In Isaiah 24:10, the prophet uses the term *tōhû* for a city that has been reduced to rubble to express its state of desolation. For Isaiah, the automatic consequence of transgression or breaking of the "eternal covenant" (בְּרִית עוֹלָם, 24:5, cf. Gen 9:16) is the reversal of creation.[57] When human beings defile and corrupt the

---

55. Weinfeld, "God the Creator," 105–32; Sommer, *A Prophet Reads Scriptures*, 142–43; Stuhlmueller, *Creative Redemption*, 156–57.

56. Baltzer, *Deutero-Isaiah*, 246.

57. Various covenants have been suggested as the backdrop of Isaiah 24:5: (a) the Adamic covenant. Dumbrell, *Covenant and Creation*, 74; Young, *Book of Isaiah*, 158; Oswalt, *Book of Isaiah*, 446. (b) The Noahic covenant. Kaiser, *Isaiah 13–39*, 183; Seitz, *Isaiah 1–39*, 180–84; Childs, *Isaiah*, 179; Blenkinsopp, *Isaiah 1–39*, 351–52; Loete, "Premature Hymn of Praise," 226–38; Anderson, *From Creation to New*, 203. (c) Mosaic covenant. Johnson, *From Chaos to Restoration*, 27–29; Clements, *Isaiah 1–39*, 201–202; Polaski, "Reflections on Mosaic Covenant," 55–73; Kissane, *Book of Isaiah*, 271–72; Ludwig, *Die Stadt*, 108–9; Rudman, "Midrash in Isaiah

earth through their actions, the consequences of such rebellion are cosmic. As Mason points out,

> Isaiah speaks of worldwide judgment in language and imagery that many relate to a flood-like catastrophe. The heavens and the earth are laid waste and desolate, utterly despoiled (vv. 1–4); the earth suffers from a curse (v. 6); the windows of heaven are open (v. 18); the earth staggers like a drunkard (v. 20); the LORD will punish the heavens and earth and its inhabitants (v. 21); and few will be left (v. 6), for "they have transgressed laws, violated statutes, broken the everlasting covenant" (v. 5). These are laws and statutes of the everlasting covenant established in Gen 9:1–7.[58]

Isaiah, like Amos, Hosea, and Jeremiah, also uses extreme creation language to express judgment; however, this prophet can also draw from the same creation language to express extreme hope, the hope for God's creation purpose to be fulfilled even in the midst of adversity, the hope for the restoration of the land with the transformation of wilderness into paradise (Isa 41:17–20; 43:19–21; 51:3),[59] and hope for the return of Israel from the Babylonian exile through Yahweh's servant, Cyrus (Isa 45:13).

For Isaiah, Israel's land will again be inhabited with a people Yahweh created, Israel. The prophet uses creation verbs to express the origin of Israel: "It is he who created [בָּרָא] you, O Jacob, he who formed [יָצַר] you, O Israel (43:1); "I am the LORD, your Holy One, Israel's creator [בּוֹרֵא, participle of the verb בָּרָא], your king" (43:15). Isaiah views the Babylonian exile as a threat

---

Apocalypse," 404–8, esp. 405. (d) a combination of covenants. Chisholm, "'The Everlasting Covenant,'" 237–53; Polaski, "Reflections on Mosaic Covenant," 55–73; Motyer, *Prophecy of Isaiah*, 199; Woudstra, "Everlasting Covenant," 22–48, esp. 32.

58. Mason, "Another Flood?," 94. Seitz observes, "In the poetic language of ch. 24, the author argues that the nations have returned to the violent ways of their forebears in the days of Noah. The world is not destroyed again by a forty-day flood, as God had promised, but rather by the centuries-long assaults of the nations." Seitz, *Isaiah 1–39*, 182.

59. Note particularly the language used in Isa 51:3,
> For the LORD will comfort Zion;
>   he will comfort all her *waste places*,
>   and will make her *wilderness* like Eden,
>   her *desert* like the garden of the LORD;
>   joy and gladness will be found in her,
>   thanksgiving and the voice of song.

to undo God's creation; for that reason he draws from the exodus motif to express God's redemptive act to reclaim his people to be what he created them to be. The exodus motif appears in a number of texts in Isaiah 40–55: 40:3–11; 41:17–20; 42:14–17; 43:1–7; 43:16–21; 44:1–5; 44:27; 48:20–21; 49:8–12; 50:2; 51:9–10; 52:11–12; 55:12–13.[60] In these texts, the event that is particularly in view is the Red Sea event, when Yahweh dried the sea for his people to pass and victoriously defeated the Egyptian army (Exod 15). The Red Sea event was not a creative event itself; rather, as Fretheim points out, "redemption is in the service of creation."[61] This is in contrast to Stuhlmueller and Anderson, who tend to equate creation with redemption by regarding the Red Sea event as a creational event and the new exodus announced by Isaiah as new creation.[62] The redemptive act of God is not the end by itself; rather, it is the means to an end – new creation.[63]

For Isaiah, there is a typological relationship between Egypt and Babylon. Just as Yahweh was victorious at the Red Sea, when "he made a way through the sea, a path through the mighty waters, who drew out the chariots and horses, the army and reinforcements together and they lay there, never to rise again, extinguished, snuffed out like a wick" (Isa 43:16b–17, NIV), he will again be victorious against Babylon. Furthermore, Babylon is considered in Isaiah as a "historical embodiment of cosmic forces of evil," just as Egypt was at the beginning of Israel's history. Isaiah uses the combat conflict motif to express Yahweh's victory over the Babylonians:

> Awake, awake! Clothe yourself with strength,
>   O arm of the LORD;
> awake, as in days gone by,
>   as in generations of old.
> Was it not you who cut Rahab to pieces,
>   who pierced that monster through?
> Was it not you who dried up the sea,
>   the waters of the great deep,

---

60. For a thorough working through these texts, see Stuhlmueller, *Creative Redemption*, 59–98.

61. Fretheim, *God and World*, 125.

62. See Stuhlmueller, *Creative Redemption*, 59–98; Anderson, *Creation versus Chaos*, 126, 129.

63. Fretheim, *God and World*, 126.

> who made a road in the depths of the sea
> so that the redeemed might cross over? (Isa 51:9-10, NIV)

The invocation for Yahweh to awake and crush Rahab, the rebellious and anti-creational monster, as in the days of old indicates that God's victory has a cosmic scope. In Fretheim's words, "given the anticreational forces ... no simple local or historical victory will do; God's victory must be and is cosmic in scope."[64] Simkins rightly notes, "God's activity in creation, as portrayed by the conflict myth, served as the paradigm of God's repeated acts of redemption for Israel; and God's victory at the sea was the preeminent example of this cosmogonic activity."[65] The conquering of the anti-creational force incarnate in Babylon opens up the way for God's people to be what he created them to be.

The restored Israel or new Israel is to be "a covenant and light of the Gentiles" and to bring restoration to the entire creation (Isa 42:6; 49:6). The new creation begins with Israel but is not limited to Israel. Yahweh the creator of Israel is not a local god who is merely concerned with the affairs of the microcosm; rather, he is "creator of the ends of the earth," whose salvation call extends to the entire cosmos – "turn to me and be saved, all you ends of the earth; for I am God, and there is no other" (Isa 45:22-23; 49:6; 51:5-6, 8; 52:10). The goal of the sole Creator God is to bring renewal to the entire human family (Isa 42:5).

Isaiah 55-66: New Heavens and New Earth

The scope of renewal not only encompasses Israel and the nations; in Isaiah 55-66, the scope of renewal is enlarged even further to encompass virtually the whole of creation – the heavens and the earth. In Isaiah 65:17-18 and 66:22-23, which is the *locus classicus* for the concept of the new heavens and a new earth, is stated,

> For I am about to create [בָּרָא] new heavens and a new earth;
> the former things shall not be remembered or come to mind.
> But be glad and rejoice forever in what I will create,
> for I will create Jerusalem to be a delight and its people a
> joy. (Isa 65:17-18, NRSV)

---

64. Fretheim, 124.
65. Simkins, *Creator and Creation*, 112.

> For as the new heavens and the new earth,
>   which I will make [עָשָׂה], shall remain before me, says the LORD;
> so shall your descendants and your name remain.
>   From new moon to new moon, and from sabbath to sabbath,
> all flesh shall come to worship before me, says the LORD.
> (Isa 66:22–23, NRSV)

As Russell argues, "the announcement of the new heavens and a new earth in Isaiah 65:17–25 represents in the most comprehensive terms the work of salvation embracing both the faithful servants and their world."[66] For Isaiah the era of salvation history initiated by the exodus event, particularly the Red Sea deliverance, came to an end with the destruction of Jerusalem and the exile to Babylon.[67] The prophet regarded the Red Sea event and the Sinai event as "old" or "former" things that will not be remembered or come to mind (Isa 65:11–65:25, esp. 65:17b; cf. Isa 43:18–19): the deliverance from Babylon and return to Jerusalem initiated a new chapter in salvation history that would climax with the new heavens and a new earth.[68] In so doing, the prophet continues the theme of Yahweh creating something new, which is dominant in Isaiah, bringing it to its proper climax – new heavens and a new earth (Isa 9:1; 43:9, 16–21; cf. 44:21; 46:8–9; 48:3).

---

66. Russell, *"New Heavens and New Earth,"* 75.

67. See Harner, "Creation Faith," 304.

68. This is particularly evident in Isa 63:11–65:25: first, the people remember the days of old – "the days of Moses and his people" when Yahweh brought them through the sea (63:11–14); second, the people implore Yahweh to "look down from heaven and see from your lofty throne, holy and glorious" their present predicament (63:15–19); third, the people implore Yahweh to "tear (קָרַעְתָּ) the heavens and come down" as in the ancient times, particularly recalling the Sinai event and calling upon Yahweh to remember his ancient deeds (64:1–5); fourth, the people realize that they are unclean, their sins sweep them away, and all that they treasured is now destroyed or uncreated: "Your [the Lord's] sacred cities have become a desert; even Zion is a desert, Jerusalem a desolation. Our holy and glorious temple, where our fathers praised you, has been burned with fire"; therefore, they call upon Yahweh to relent from his anger (64:6–12); fourth, Yahweh's response to the people's call is three dimensional: (a) The Lord demands full payment of the people's sins (65:1–8). (b) Yahweh will not completely destroy his people: "There is yet some good"; he will preserve some from Jacob and Judah, yet the rest will die (65:8–16). (c) Yahweh announces eschatological creation of the new heavens and a new earth, and a new Jerusalem transformed from a desert into a garden of delight and joy, the holy mountain of God (65:17–25).

Isaiah 65:17–66:24 stand in a dialogic relationship with Genesis 1–3, as there are several elements in the latter that alluded to the former.[69] First, we observe that there is an analogical relationship between the past and the eschatological, Genesis 1–3 and Isaiah 65:17–25: (a) For Isaiah the first creation is Yahweh's great act in the primordial times. Yahweh is the one "who has measured the waters in the hollow of his hand and marked off the heavens with a span, enclosed the dust of the earth in a measure, and weighed the mountains in scales and the hills in a balance" (Isa 40:12). In a similar fashion, "Thus says the LORD, your redeemer, who formed you from the womb: I am the LORD, who made all things, who alone stretched out the earth by myself" (Isa 44:24; cf. 45:12, 18; 48:13). The same God who created the heavens and the earth in the past will again create the new heavens and a new earth (Isa 65:17; 66:22). (b) Both Genesis 1–3 and Isaiah 65:17–25 speak of the creation of the new heavens and a new earth; however, the first creation is now old, a thing of the past, in light of the new.[70]

Second, there is a qualitative distinction between the past and the future. For Isaiah, the future creation of the heavens and the earth will not be a mere repetition of the past. The new heavens and a new earth will supersede the former, "the former things shall not be remembered, they shall never come to mind" (Isa 65:17). As Stuhlmueller observes regarding the contrast between the former and end things, the prophet was announcing not simply the fact that exile would come to an end "but rather the *exceptional* qualities about the end of time" (cf. 43:18–21; 48:6b–8a, emphasis in original).[71] Furthermore, the verbs used for the new creation are none other than *bārā'* and *'āśāh*. These verbs are used by Isaiah "to designate God's initial creation of the heavens and earth" and for its continual maintenance and preservation (42:5–6), and even more significantly for the new things (48:6, 18; 65:22). We note the following qualitative distinctions between Genesis 1–3 and Isaiah 65:17–25:

---

69. See Steck, "Der neue Himmel,", 350–65; Van Ruiten, "Eve's Pain in Childbearing?", 9–11.

70. See Van Ruiten, "Eve's Pain in Childbearing?", 10.

71. Stuhlmueller, *Creative Redemption*, 139. I disagree with Miscall's claim that Isaiah, by making a contrast between the primordial heavens and earth and the new heaven and earth and by calling upon his audience to forget the former things, intends for them to replace the earlier texts: "Read Isaiah and not these other books." Miscall, "Isaiah: New Heavens," 41–56.

First, the new creation will be a place of eternal delight and joy with no foreseeable judgment: "Never again shall be heard there the sounds of weeping and wailing" (Isa 65:18–19); this is comparable to the joy and delights in the garden of Eden which were short lived. When Eve and Adam ate from the tree that looked "good for eating and a delight to the eyes, and that tree was desirable as a source of wisdom," they brought judgment upon humanity and a curse upon the earth (Gen 3:6, own translation).

Second, for Isaiah, there will be no more premature death; instead there will be a long life-span on a new earth. The life span in the Adamic generation was extremely high compared to the life span of the Noahic generation and even more so to the Abrahamic generation. By the time of the flood, which brought about an end to the Adamic generation, the life span of humanity has been significantly reduced to "one hundred and twenty years" (Gen 6:3); and by the time of Moses the life span has been reduced to "seventy or eighty years" (Ps 90:10); however, in the new creation the downward trend is actually reversed, and life span of man is on the rise: "He who dies at a hundred will be thought a mere youth; the one who fails to reach a hundred will be considered accursed" (Isa 65:20, NIV).

Third, in the new creation, humankind shall build houses and dwell in them and at the same time enjoy the labor of their hands as they plant vineyards and enjoy their fruit without fear that someone else will dwell in their houses and eat what they have planted (Isa 65:21–22). The immediate reference point for the audience would have been their current experience in exile in Babylon, away from their homes and fields in Jerusalem; however, the story also points to the initial creation story, wherein humankind was expelled from his ultimate home prepared for him by Yahweh, a garden of delight, paradise, which humankind was supposed to serve and guard, but now lives outside of.

Fourth, the prophet concludes this vision of the new creation by citing from his earlier messianic vision (Isa 11); he does so not in toto, but invoking the vision as a whole. For this prophet, the eschatological new age is tied to the messianic age.[72] The messianic age will bring about harmony that supersedes by far the garden of Eden, wherein animosity was developed. In the new creation living beings shall live in harmony with each other – wild beasts

---

72. See Van Ruiten, "Intertextual Relationship," 31–42; Childs, *Isaiah*, 538–39.

and domestic animals shall be in harmony: "The wolf and the lamb shall feed together" (v. 25a); human beings and animals will also be in harmony: "The lion will eat straw like the ox" and "The serpent's food shall be dust"; the wild animals will not pose a threat at all "in all my holy mountain" (v. 25bcd).

In the initial creation, a serpent, a wild beast, appeared to represent the anti-creational force. The serpent opposed God's purpose for creation and deceived humankind to rebel against him; in contrast, this wild beast will pose no such threat in the new creation. Van Ruiten suggests that "the serpent that eats dust is explicitly used as an expression of comparison for the attitude of humility among nations, which were once violent and hostile."[73] A similar expression is used in Micah 7:17: "They will lick dust like a snake, like creatures that crawl on the ground. They will come trembling out of their dens; they will turn in fear to the LORD our God and will be afraid" (NIV). As van Ruiten observes, the expression "lick dust" is used in Micah for the nations that were once hostile but have now been deprived of their power and brought to shame so they show their humble submission to Yahweh by licking the dust like a crawling serpent.[74] In Isaiah 11:8, the serpent is depicted as completely harmless: "The infant will play near the cobra's den, the young child will put its hand into the viper's nest. They will neither harm nor destroy on all my holy mountain" (NIV).

Fifth, in the new creation, there will be full divine presence that encompasses the macrocosm, in contrast to the limited presence in microcosm, as in Eden, the tabernacle, and the temple. The new heavens and a new earth that Yahweh will create in Isaiah 65:17 appear to be equated with the Jerusalem that Yahweh will create in verse 18. In both cases, the same creation verb is used, *bārā'*. It is virtually impossible to speak in Isaiah 65:17–25 of the new heavens and a new earth as if they are separated from Jerusalem. The description of the new Jerusalem is the description of the new heavens and new earth. The name Jerusalem is in turn used synonymously as "holy mountain" (65:25); see particularly the reference to "Jerusalem my holy mountain" in Isaiah 66:20. As Levenson notes, the postexilic reconstruction of the temple-city was

---

73. Van Ruiten, "Intertextual Relationship," 40.
74. Van Ruiten, 40.

viewed as a reenthronement of Yahweh and even more so as a re-creation of the cosmos, of which the Jerusalem temple was a microcosm.[75]

The eschatological new heavens and new earth, the temple-city, as envisioned by the prophet, however, is no mere reconstruction of the microcosm; rather, it is Yahweh's overhaul of the macrocosm. The creation of the new heavens and a new earth is the erection of a macrocosm built not by human hands but by Yahweh himself. As Timmer notes, in Isaiah 66, "the localized modes of presence are not merely undone, but replaced and superseded. God's presence with his people in the new heaven and new earth will be more pervasive and more proximate than was possible with any of the prior arrangements, be it Eden, the tabernacle, or the temple."[76]

Third, whereas humankind was expelled from the garden of Eden, the eschatological Jerusalem, the holy mountain, is transformed into a place for the nations. Isaiah pictures all the nations moving from the peripheral toward the center of the earth, Yahweh's holy mountain, and there being presented as an offering to the Lord (66:18–21). As Childs notes,

> The most significant change in the rendering of Israel's hope for salvation is that the deliverance from Babylon – a major theme of Second Isaiah – has now been understood within the book as a whole as only one instance of God's unfolding eschatological purpose for his people. Third Isaiah has instead rendered the ultimate salvation of Israel into an eschatological picture of the new heavens and new earth.[77]

The new world order centered on Jerusalem is one which includes "all flesh" (Isa 66:23).

Yet, there is continuity between the first creation and the new creation. For Isaiah 65:17–25, there is continuity of the familiar: Jerusalem (v. 18), which has come to be understood as the center of the earth, is the "holy mountain" in verse 25; there is a continuity of death (v. 20); family life will continue, and with that labor (vv. 21–22); childbearing will continue (v. 23); the need for God will still be there (v. 24); and animals will still be there, including

---

75. Levenson, *Creation and Persistence of Evil*, 89–90.
76. Timmer, *Creation, Tabernacle, and Sabbath*, 149.
77. Childs, *Isaiah*, 545.

the serpent (v. 25). The curse on the snake is not reversed; it will continue to eat dust from the ground. Isaiah 66:23–24 particularly notes the continuity of years and Sabbaths – "and new moon after new moon, and sabbath after sabbath, all flesh shall come to worship me."

For the prophet Isaiah, what is required is not simply a restoration of Jerusalem, the temple-city, to its functionality; rather, it is a re-creation of the cosmos for which the temple was a microcosm. However, the re-creation of the cosmos as envisioned by this prophet is no mere return to the beginning, but a hope of something better. For Isaiah, human institutions have failed to embody the divine purposes of creation. Yahweh himself is capable of improving the conditions of the cosmos, and by his hand he will create a new thing. The "new things" of the eschaton are not mere renewal of the "old things"; the two are contrasted: "Do not remember the former things, or consider the things of old" (Isa 43:18; cf 48:6b). The new is not a mere renewal of the old, but the entrance of the better – the old is superseded.

Jeremiah and Ezekiel – New Heart

I argued in the previous chapter that humankind in their original state were capable of either obeying or disobeying God's command, and humankind disobeyed. We also observed earlier in this chapter that the problem of the Adamic generation was the continued deterioration of the human heart: "Every inclination of the thoughts of his heart was only filled with evil" (NIV) which consequently led to the reversal of creation (Gen 6:5). Humans, who were created morally righteous, had corrupted themselves to the point that evil had become a natural part of their heart composition from childhood or birth (Gen 8:22; cf. Ps 51:5). For Jeremiah and Ezekiel, who both lived to witness the uncreation of Judah by the flood of the Babylonian armies, Israel's problem is an inward one; it is the problem of the heart.[78]

Jeremiah described the condition of the heart in terms similar to those in Genesis 6:5 and 8:22. For this prophet, humankind's heart has become naturally corrupt: "Judah's sin is engraved with an iron tool, inscribed with a flint point, on the tablets of their hearts" (17:1); furthermore, "the heart is deceitful above all things, beyond cure" (17:9). The people of Judah followed "the

---

78. For the relationship between Jeremiah and Ezekiel regarding the message of inward renewal, see Leene, "Ezekiel and Jeremiah," 150–72.

stubbornness of their evil hearts" (3:17; 7:24; 9:13; 11:8; 13:10; 16:12; 18:12; 23:17), and as a result they had become so corrupt that they were incapable of doing good, "Can the Ethiopian change his skin, or the leopard its spots? Neither can you do good (יָטַב) who are accustomed to evil (רָעַע)" (13:23).

Ezekiel also uses strong language to describe the inward attitude of the people of Judah. The problem of the people was the inward idolatry that had corrupted them; they had set up "idols in their hearts" (גִּלּוּלֵיהֶם עַל־לִבָּם), to which they devoted themselves (14:3; cf. 11:21; 14:4, 7; 20:16). Not only were these people devoted to the inward idols, their hearts had also become hardened as stone so that the prophet speaks of the house of Israel as "hardened and obstinate" (3:7–9), having "a heart of stone" (11:19; 36:26). Ezekiel makes it clear that the exile was a deserved consequence in light of their inward disposition toward idolatry:

> Then in the nations where they have been carried captive, those who escape will remember me – *how I have been grieved* by their *adulterous hearts*, which have turned away from me, and by their eyes, which have lusted after their idols. They will loathe themselves for the evil they have done and for all their detestable practices. And they will know that I am the Lord; I did not threaten in vain to bring this calamity. (Ezek 6:9–10, NIV)[79]

The story of the Adamic generation was for Jeremiah and Ezekiel an archetype of Israel's story. Israel like the Adamic generation had become inwardly corrupted, and God had once again been grieved. The uncreation of Israel that we observed above is one that was well deserved; however, for these prophets, unlike Genesis 8:21, which offers no solution for such inward corruption, there is hope.

The hope for these prophets lies in the inward re-creation of the heart. Both Jeremiah and Ezekiel make the heart the focal point of the eschatological renewal. Ezekiel on his part announced an eschatological inward re-creation of the heart that goes hand in hand with a new spirit: "new heart and new spirit" (לֵב חָדָשׁ וְרוּחַ חֲדָשָׁה; Ezek 11:19–20; 36:26–27).[80] For Ezekiel, the "adulterous hearts" that are so devoted to idols (6:9) will be replaced with

---

79. Emphasis added.

80. Some scholars equate Ezekiel's "new heart and new spirit" with Jeremiah's "new covenant." See, for example, Leene, "Ezekiel and Jeremiah," 150–72; Gowan, *Eschatology in*

an "undivided heart" focused upon the Lord (11:19); their "hearts of stone" will be replaced with hearts of flesh (Ezek 11:19; 36:26). For Jeremiah, the eschatological inner renewal of the human heart would guarantee covenant loyalty, thereby making it possible to establish an arrangement that supersedes all previous covenant arrangements, arguably including the Adamic covenant.

> "The time is coming," declares the LORD, "when I will make a new covenant with the house of Israel and with the house of Judah. It will not be like the covenant I made with their forefathers when I took them by the hand to lead them out of Egypt, because they broke my covenant, though I was a husband to them," declares the LORD. "This is the covenant I will make with the house of Israel after that time," declares the LORD. "I will put my law in their minds and write it on their hearts. I will be their God, and they will be my people. No longer will a man teach his neighbor, or a man his brother, saying, 'know the LORD,' because they will all know me, from the least of them to the greatest," declares the LORD. "For I will forgive their wickedness and will remember their sins no more." (Jer 31:31–34, NIV)

The writing of the new covenant on the tablets of the people's hearts brings about a surpassing knowledge of the Lord, thereby reversing their old nature of sin "engraved in with an iron tool, inscribed with a flint point on the tablets of their hearts." The allusion to tablets unquestionably recalls the Mosaic covenant; however, the problem of the human heart goes back to the Adamic generation and ultimately to the first human couple and their probationary testing – the test of the human heart with the tree of the knowledge of good and bad. The re-creation of the human heart completely alters the inward disposition from evil to good, thereby reversing the Adamic inclination from evil to good.

For Jeremiah and Ezekiel, what is required is not just renewal of the physical cosmos to its functional state as in the time of Noah. What is required is for Yahweh to completely alter the human heart's disposition from evil to good; thereby putting to an end a cycle of human rebellion with its negative

---

Old Testament, 2–3; Koch, *The Prophets*, vol. 2, 111; Cody, *Ezekiel*, 173; Weinfeld, "Jeremiah and Spiritual Metamorphosis," 17–56.

cosmic effect. The first human couple due to their inclination toward evil brought a curse to the cosmos that affected the conditions under which the cosmos was to continue to function, whereas their descendants, the subsequent generations – the Adamic generation, the Noahic generation, and the Abrahamic generation, continually corrupted the cosmos. For these prophets, the re-creation of the cosmos without a reconstruction of the human heart only places creation at risk of corruption all over again. Thus, humankind's actions could affect creation, both pre-fall and post-fall, for the better or for the worse – transformation or reversal.

Conclusion

In this chapter, I have shown that creation in its original state is a paradigm for both eschatological uncreation and re-creation. Creation in its nonfunctional state became a symbol of judgment, whereas creation in its functional state became a symbol of hope, a hope for something better. The eschatological new creation as envisioned by the prophets is one that qualitatively supersedes the first creation in its original state of goodness. The first creation is now regarded as the "old thing" not simply temporally, but even more so qualitatively when contrasted with the new. The "very good" of Genesis 1:31 does not imply incapable of being improved upon; rather, creation is "very good" because it functionally looks forward to its improvement. The verse "The heavens and the earth were finished and all the host of them" (Gen 2:1, RSV) indicates that the operational system was in place for creation to reach its intended goal.

CHAPTER 7

Conclusion

In my dialogic-canonical reading of Genesis 1–3, I engaged and challenged the traditional progressive reading, which regards it as a story of the good creation followed by the fall. In traditional progressive reading the goodness of creation is often interpreted as denoting "perfect," that is, unmarred, undistorted, spotless, without sin. Genesis 3, the fall narrative, is regarded as narrating events subsequent to the good creation as a distortion thereof. However, in this book I argued that Genesis 1–3 be viewed as a story of a creation that is functionally "very good" despite the inherent bad and the fall that characterize it. This alternative understanding of Genesis 1–3 particularly takes into consideration the tensions and awkwardness in the relationship between Genesis 1, Genesis 2, and Genesis 3, and between Genesis 1–3 and other Old Testament voices on the subject of creation.

I have demonstrated that the formula of approval in Genesis 1 was no idealization of the first creation or a declaration of perfection over creation; rather, it was God's satisfaction with the functionality of the cosmos. Creation at the end of the sixth day was fallen, yet functionally "very good" because it looked forward to its redemptive and transformative goal.

The canonical dialogic approach, which I utilised, proved beneficial in two ways: First, it allowed me to investigate the internal dialogue inherent in Genesis 1–3. I was able to explore some of the rhetorical plays within this text, especially focusing on the dialogic opposition of the terms *bad* and *good*. I was also able to orchestrate dialogue between two creation narratives that make up this text – Genesis 1:1–2:4a and Genesis 2:4b–3:24. Second, this approach allowed me to widen the dialogue to encompass the entire Old Testament.

Reading Genesis 1–3 in dialogue with other canonical voices significantly enriched this text in new and unexpected ways.

I have shown that the tendency to idealize the first creation in its original state of goodness by regarding that state of creation as perfect is questionable on the basis of Genesis 1–3 and the rest of the canonical metanarrative; rather, creation in its state of goodness has an eschatological focus.

I argued that the "goodness" of creation does not have the overtone of perfection. Instead, there are a number of factors that suggest that creation in its original state of goodness was not ideal: First, in the rhetorical plays within Genesis 1:1–2:4a, the deep and the darkness of the first day of creation are not pronounced good, and the second day, the day in which the *rāqîaʿ* was set up as a separator between the waters above and the waters below, is not pronounced good. The deep and the darkness, I argued, are not pronounced good because they made the earthly realm in its initial state a *tohû wābohû*, that is, an unproductive and uninhabitable place, dead or lifeless, so to speak. The second day is not pronounced good, I argued, because the *rāqîaʿ*, a separator, was set between the heavenly realm, God's dwelling, and the earthly realm, which became man's dwelling. This in turn implied that God's presence was not fully manifested in the earthly realm; rather, it was limited to a secluded spot on earth, the garden of Eden, the first earthly sanctuary.

Second, in Genesis 2:4b–3:24, particularly in what may be regarded as the pre-fall narrative, that is, up to Genesis 3:5, there are a number of factors that do indicate that conditions are not ideal: (a) humanity is dust from the ground, which implies that humanity is a frail, earthly creature who is characterized by mortality from the beginning. (b) The tree of the knowledge of good and bad, to which is attached the curse of death, stood alongside the tree of life in paradise. (c) human beings in their original state had potential to do good by obeying God's command not to eat from the tree of the knowledge of good and bad or to do bad by disobeying God's command by eating from the tree of the knowledge of good and bad. (d) The creation of a woman was a correction of a situation that was not good in paradise – the man had been alone. (e) God's presence in paradise was not unlimited: paradise was a sacred spot where humankind and God had special communion. However, paradise did not overcome the absence of God, the dualism of creation that had heaven as God's dwelling and the earth as humankind's dwelling; rather, God's dwelling was still in heaven. (f) The presence of a rebellious serpent in paradise suggests that paradise was disrupted – the sacred space was violated by the serpent, who is presented as God's antagonist.

Third, I argued that Genesis 3, the fall narrative, should be regarded as falling within the seven-day framework as a resumption of the activities that took place within the sixth day of creation just as much as Genesis 2:4b–25 did. Genesis 3, I argued, establishes the immediacy of the fall. On the day that humankind was created and placed in paradise, humans sinned and were expelled from paradise. This implies that creation in its original state was pronounced "very good" even with the fall within the creation process. This does not imply that humanity's rebellion did not corrupt God's creation, because it did. I suggested that considering the textual evidence, it is highly plausible that God could have made such a positive assessment of his creation even with the fall of man having occurred within the creation process.

In order to substantiate this, I argued that the story of Genesis 1–3 is parallel to the story of Israel's erection of the tabernacle as narrated in Exodus 24:15–40:38. Both narratives follow a sevenfold pattern of creation, and both narratives establish the immediacy of the fall. The incident of the golden calf is portrayed in Exodus as an interruption of the building of the tabernacle; however, the rebellion of Israel did not frustrate God's plan to build a tabernacle within Israel. The work of building the tabernacle continued and still received a positive evaluation. In the same way, I argued that God's purpose and plan for creation were not frustrated by humankind's disobedience; rather, he still brought his work to its proper conclusion and gave it a positive evaluation.

I also suggested that God's creation week should be viewed as a vertical week, whereas humankind's first week, which continues on a horizontal plane, begins within God's creation week. God's creation week, unlike humankind's week, which was on its first day, is a week that finds culmination on the seventh day. This day, I argued, transcends the good creation; it is a holy and blessed day. God's Sabbath day is a sacred space and sacred time that is to be identified with God's heavenly dwelling, God's holy of holies. The seventh day of creation is a day without evening and morning that continues on the horizontal axis parallel to world history, or the earthly realm. The seventh day of creation gave a sense of purpose and hope for creation, which is still on its sixth day, moving toward its goal.

Considering the arguments above, it is reasonable to conclude that the language of "good" was not a pronouncement of perfection on creation; rather, it was an aesthetic judgment on the part of God on the functional cosmos. God had moved creation from its initial state, in which it was unproductive and uninhabited, to a state in which it was productive and inhabited, and it was "very good." Although humankind's rebellion endangered the project by bringing curses upon the earth, creation was "very good" because the redemptive program aimed not just at rectifying the sin of humankind but also at bringing to realization the transformative goal of creation, which was already set in motion but which the first human couple failed to fulfill.

The good creation, that is, the finished heavens and earth at the end of the sixth day of creation, was not an end; rather, it still looks forward to the seventh day of creation. The seventh day of creation is the day that transcends the good creation – it is קדש, holy or set apart. Thus, creation in its original state of goodness is sub-eschatological, a non-ideal beginning still awaiting its Sabbath day, the day of holiness.

I expanded the dialogue to include other Old Testament voices that further enhance the idea that creation in its original state is non-ideal. In chapter 5, I illustrated that three rebellions took place within the creation process:

The first rebellion was at sea by the sea serpent. This rebellion is not hinted at in Genesis 1–3; however, other Old Testament voices do suggest that there was such a rebellion by the sea serpent at creation (Job 26:11–12; Pss 74:13–14; 89:10–14). The rebellious sea serpent, variously called the dragon, Leviathan, and Rahab, was crushed by God at creation; but we are not told why this creature rebelled or why God found it necessary to crush this creature. I also argued at this point against Gunkel's view that the sea serpent is to be identified with the *tĕhôm*, which he regarded as a primordial opponent of Yahweh. The Old Testament, I argued, does not posit creation through conflict, that is, God's conflict with the anti-creation forces that resulted in the coming into being of the cosmos, as Gunkel and his followers suggest; rather, the Old Testament posits the idea of conflicts arising within the creation process, the first of which was probably with the sea serpent, whom God crushed at sea.

The second and third rebellions were on land by the land serpent and by humankind. This rebellion is spelled out in Genesis 3, which, as I have already noted, should be regarded as falling with the sixth day of creation. Just as with the sea serpent, the land serpent is presented as an antagonist of Yahweh; however, just as in the case of the sea serpent, we are not told why this creature rebelled against God and why he found it necessary to lure humankind to rebel against God. Humankind, on the other hand, rebelled by succumbing to the serpent's deception and ate from the tree of the knowledge of good and bad that God commanded them not to eat from. I also suggested that the serpentine language used for the rebellious sea creature and the rebellious land beast metaphorically represent Yahweh's antagonist, whom humankind failed to counter at creation. The Old Testament, however, does not seem to elevate the sea serpent and land serpent to the status of gods; instead, they are rebellious creatures of God just like humankind. These multiple rebellions within the creation process all speak of the non-ideal nature of creation in its original state of goodness.

In chapter 6, I argued that creation in its state of goodness is presented as a paradigm of eschatological uncreation and re-creation. Creation in its state of goodness is presented as always in danger of reverting to its initial state of *tohû wābohû*, in which it was flooded and darkened due to humankind's sin and wickedness. There are two points in the history of creation at which creation is presented as receiving a negative evaluation from God and as reverting to its initial state.

The first is the Noahic flood. During the time of Noah, creation had become corrupted by sin (Gen 6:5; cf. 6:11–12). As a result, God reversed creation to its initial state by undoing all the boundaries set at creation; however, uncreation was only the penultimate answer to the problem of human wickedness, as God created again by reestablishing the boundaries that were set at creation and by the survival of Noah and his family and the creatures with him.

The second was Israel's exile. Israel's story, I argued, is presented as an extended replay of the Genesis 1–11 narrative, the story of creation, uncreation, and re-creation. Israel's story, like the story of the Adamic generation, also involves a tragic climax, with the twelve tribes exiled and dissolved and the surviving two tribes almost having the same tragic end. The exile of Israel and Judah is presented by the prophets as a reversal of creation (Jer 4:23–28; Hosea 4:1–3; Amos 5:18–27; 8:9–14; Zeph 1:2–3); however, uncreation again was only the penultimate answer to the problem of Israel's wickedness. The prophets also envision an eschatological re-creation of Israel (Isa 40–55) that requires heart surgery to guarantee covenantal loyalty (Jer 31:31–34; Ezek 11:19–20; 36:26–27), and that ultimately leads to the cosmic new heavens and new earth (Isa 55–66). Thus, the goal of creation, as envisioned by the prophets, lies not in the non-ideal beginning but rather in the eschatological ideal of new heavens and new earth.

This book is not the final word on Genesis 1–3; the "semantic treasures" and the intentional potentiality of this text cannot be exhausted. However, this study does raise issues that do deserve further consideration. First, it is necessary to revisit the common systematic conceptualization of the biblical plot as creation-fall-redemption-consummation. If my reading of Genesis 1–3 is at all correct, the fall happened on the sixth day of the creation week, and yet creation was pronounced "very good" at the end of the sixth day. Therefore, it is worth exploring what impact this might have on the doctrine of creation. Second, in the same vein as the first, the contrast between pre-fall creation as good and post-fall creation as bad, which does have some validity on the basis of the text, needs to be differentiated more carefully from God's aesthetic judgment of creation as good, because creation in its state of goodness is already fallen. Third, the period prior to the fall of humanity is sometimes referred to as a "preredemptive" stage, implying that the redemptive program was initiated pursuant to the fall of humankind. Genesis 3, I suggest, may just as well be viewed from a redemptive perspective, to be more specific, as a "failed redemptive program."

Bibliography

Abasciano, Brian J. *Paul's Use of the Old Testament in Romans 9:1–9: An Intertextual Theological Exegesis*. London: T&T Clark, 2005.

Aichele, George, Fred W. Burnett, Elizabeth A. Castelli, Robert M. Fowler, David Jobling, Stephen D. Moore, Gary A. Phillips, Tina Pippin, Regina M. Schwartz, and Wilhelm Wuellner. *The Postmodern Bible: The Bible and Culture Collective*. New Haven: Yale University Press, 1995.

Albright, William F. "The Refrain 'And God Saw Ki Tob' in Genesis 1." In *Mélanges bibliques redigés en honneur de André Robert*, 22–26. Travaux de l'Institut Catholique de Paris 4, Paris: Bloud and Gay, 1995.

Alexander, T. Desmond. *From Eden to the New Jerusalem: An Introduction to Biblical Theology*. Grand Rapids: Kregel, 2008.

Allen, Graham. *Intertextuality*. London: Routledge, 2000.

Alter, Robert. *The Art of Biblical Narrative*. New York: Basic Books, 1985.

———. "A Literary Approach to the Bible." *Commentary* 60 (1975): 70–77.

Alter, R., and F. Kenmode, eds. *The Literary Guide to the Bible*. London: Fontana, 1989.

Anderson, Bernhard W. *Creation versus Chaos: The Reinterpretation of Mythical Symbolism in the Bible*. Philadelphia: Fortress, 1987.

———. "From Analysis to Synthesis: The Interpretation of Genesis 1–11." *Journal of Biblical Literature* 97 (1978): 23–39.

———. *From Creation to New Creation: Old Testament Perspectives*. Minneapolis: Fortress, 1994.

———. "A Stylistic Study of the Priestly Creation Story." In *Canon and Authority: Essays in Old Testament Religion and Theology*, edited by G. W. Coats and B. O. Long, 148–62. Philadelphia: Fortress, 1977.

Anderson, Francis I. "What Biblical Scholars Might Learn from Emily Dickinson." In *Words Remembered, Texts Renewed: Essays in Honour of J. F. A Sawyer*, 52–74. Journal for the Study of the Old Testament Supplement 156. Sheffield: Sheffield Academic Press, 1995.

Anderson, Gary A. The Genesis of Perfection: Adam and Eve in Jewish and Christian Imagination. Louisville: Westminster John Knox, 2001.

Atkinson, David. *The Message of Genesis 1–11*. Downers Grove: InterVarsity, 1990.

Bailey, Albert Edward, and Charles Foster Kent. *History of the Hebrew Commonwealth*. New York: Charles Scribner's Sons, 1935.

Baines, John. "Ancient Egyptian Kingship; Official Forms, Rhetoric, Context." In *King and Messiah in Israel and the Ancient Near East*, edited by John Day, 16–53. Journal for the Study of the Old Testament Supplement 270. Sheffield: Sheffield Academic Press, 1998.

Baker, David L. Two Testaments, One Bible: A Study of the Relationship between the Old and New Testaments. Leicester: InterVarsity, 1991.

Baker, David W. "Diversity and Unity in the Literary Structure of Genesis." In *Essays on the Patriarchal Narratives*, edited by Alan R. Millard and D. J. Wiseman, 189–205. Leicester: InterVarsity, 1980.

Bakhtin, Mikhail M. *The Dialogic Imagination: Four Essays*. Edited by M. Holquist. Translated by C. Emerson and M. Holquist. Austin: University of Texas, 1981.

———. *Problems of Dostoevsky's Poetics*. Translated and Edited by C. Emerson, Minneapolis: University of Minnesota Press, 1984.

———. *Speech Genres and Other Late Essays*. Edited by C. Emerson and M. Holquist. Translated by V. W. McGee. Austin: University of Texas Press, 1986.

Bakhtin, M. M., and P. N. Medvedev. *Formal Method in Literary Scholarship: A Critical Introduction to Sociological Poetics*. Translated by Albert J. Wehrle. Baltimore: John Hopkins University Press, 1978.

Bakhtin, M. M., and V. N. Volosinov. *Freudianism: A Critical Sketch*. Edited by I. R. Titunik and N. H. Buss. Translated by I. R. Titunik. Indianapolis: Indiana University Press, 1987.

———. *Marxism and the Philosophy of Language*. Translated by L. Matejka and I. R. Titunik. Cambridge: Harvard University Press, 1986.

Bal, Miecke. "Sexuality, Sin, and Sorrow: The Emergence of Female Character: A Reading of Genesis 1–3." In *The Female Body in Western Culture*, edited by S. R. Suleiman, 317–38. Cambridge: Harvard University Press, 1986.

Baltzer, Klaus. *Deutero-Isaiah: A Commentary on Isaiah 40–55*. Hermeneia – A Critical and Historical Commentary on the Bible. Minneapolis: Fortress, 2001.

Barr, James. "Is God a Liar?" *The Journal of Theological Studies* 57, no. 1 (2006): 1–22.

———. The Garden of Eden and the Hope of Immortality. Minneapolis: Fortress, 1993.

———. "The Meaning of 'Mythology' in Relation to the Old Testament." *Vetus Testamentum* 9 (1959): 1–10.

———. "Was Everything That God Created Really Good?" In *God in the Fray: A Tribute to Walter Brueggemann*, edited by Tod Linafelt and Timothy K. Beal, 55–65. Minneapolis: Augsburg Fortress, 1998.

Barton, John. *Reading the Old Testament: Method in Biblical Study*. 2nd ed. Louisville: Westminster, 1996.

———. "Unity and Diversity in the Biblical Canon." In Die Einheit der Schrift und die Vielfalt des Kanons/ The Unity of Scripture and the Diversity of the Canon, 11–26. Berlin: de Gruyter, 2003.

Batto, Bernard F. "The Covenant of Peace: A Neglected Ancient Near Eastern Motif." *Catholic Biblical Quarterly* 49 (1987): 197–201.

———. Slaying the Dragon: Mythmaking in the Biblical Tradition. Louisville: Westmister John Knox, 1992.

Bavinck, Herman. *In the Beginning: Foundation of Creation Theology*. Edited by John Bolt. Translated by John Vriend. Grand Rapids: Baker, 1999.

———. *Reformed Dogmatics: Sin and Salvation in Christ*, vol 3. Edited by John Bolt. Translated by John Vriend. Grand Rapids: Baker, 2006.

Baxter, Leslie A. "Dialogues of Relating." In *Dialogue: Theorizing Difference in Communication Studies*, edited by Rob Anderson, Leslie A. Baxter, and Kenneth N. Cissna, 107–24. London: SAGE, 2004.

Beale, Gregory K. "Eden, the Temple, and the Church's Mission in the New Creation." *Journal of Evangelical Theological Society* 48, no. 1 (2005): 5–31.

———. "The Final Vision of the Apocalypse and Its Implications for a Biblical Theology of the Temple." In *Heaven on Earth: The Temple in Biblical Theology*, edited by T. D. Alexander and S. Gathercole, 191–209. Carlisle: Paternoster, 2004.

———. The Temple and the Church's Mission: A Biblical Theology of the Dwelling of God. New Studies in Biblical Theology 17. Downers Grove: InterVarsity, 2004.

Bechtel, L. M. "Rethinking the Interpretation of Genesis 2–3." In *A Feminist Companion to Genesis*, edited by A. Brenner, 77–117. Feminist Companion to the Bible 2. Sheffield: Sheffield Academic Press, 1993.

Berkhof, Louis. *Systematic Theology*. Grand Rapids: Eerdmans, 1938. Reprint. Grand Rapids: Baker, 1996.

Birch, Bruce C., Walter Brueggemann, Terence E. Fretheim, and David L. Petersen. *A Theological Introduction to the Old Testament*. Nashville: Abingdon, 1999.

Bird, Phyllis A. "Genesis 3 in der gegenwärtigen biblischen Forschung." *Jahrbuch für Biblische Theologie* 9 (1994): 3–24.

Blenkinsopp, Joseph. *Isaiah 1–39*. Anchor Bible 19A. New York: Doubleday, 2000.

———. The Pentateuch: An Introduction to the First Five Books of the Bible. New York: Doubleday, 1992.

———. *Prophecy and Canon*. University of Notre Dame Center for the Study of Judaism and Christianity in Antiquity 3. Notre Dame: University of Notre Dame, 1977.

Boice, James Montgomery. *Genesis: An Expository Commentary*. Vol. 1. Grand Rapids: Zondervan, 1982.

Bonhoeffer, Dietrich. *Creation and Fall: A Theological Interpretation of Genesis 1–3*. Translated by John C. Fletcher. New York: Macmillan, 1959.

Boomershine, T. E. "Structure and Narrative Rhetoric in Genesis 2–3." In *Society of Biblical Literature Seminar Papers*, edited by P. J. Achtemeier, 31–49. Vol. 1. Missoula: Scholars, 1978.

Boyd, Gregory A. *God at War: The Bible and Spiritual Conflict*. Downers Grove: InterVarsity, 1997.

Bremmer, Jan N. "Paradise: From Persia, via Greece, into the Septuagint." In *Paradise Interpreted: Representations of Biblical Paradise in Judaism and Christianity*, edited by Gerard P. Luttikhuizen, 1–20. Leiden: Brill, 1999.

Brenner, Athalya, ed. *A Feminist Companion to Genesis*. Feminist Companion to the Bible 2. Sheffield: Sheffield Academic Press, 1993.

Brongers, Hendrik A. *De Scheppingstradities bÿ de Profeten*. Amsterdam: J. J. Paris, 1945.

Bronner, Leah. *Biblical Personalities and Archaeology*. Jerusalem: Keter, 1974.

Brown, Robert F. "On the Necessary Imperfection of Creation: Irenaeus' Adversus Haereses IV, 38." *Scottish Journal of Theology* 28 (1975): 17–25.

Brueggemann, Walter. "From Dust to Kingship (I Kings 16:2; Genesis 3:19)." *Zeitschrift für alttestamentliche Wissenschaft* 84 (1972): 1–18.

———. *Genesis*. Interpretation – A Biblical Commentary for Teaching and Preaching. Atlanta: John Knox, 1982.

———. "Jeremiah: Creatio in Extremis." In *God Who Creates: Essays in Honor of W. Sibley Towner*, edited by William P. Brown and S. Dean McBride, Jr., 152–70. Grand Rapids: Eerdmans, 2000.

———. *Prophetic Imagination*. 2nd ed. Minneapolis: Fortress, 2001.

———. "Remember, You Are Dust." *Journal for Preachers* 14, no. 2 (1991): 3–10.

———. "A Shape for Old Testament Theology, I: Structure Legitimation." *Catholic Biblical Quarterly* 47 (1985): 28–46.

———. Theology of the Old Testament: Testimony, Dispute, Advocacy. Minneapolis: Fortress, 1997.

Budde, Karl. Die biblische Urgeschichte (Gen. 1–12.5). Anhang: Die alteste Gestalt der biblischen Urgeschichte, versuchsweise wiederhergestellt, hebraischer text un uebersetzung. Giessen: J. Ricker, 1883.

Cage, Warren Austin. The Gospel of Genesis: Studies in Protology and Eschatology. Winona Lake: Carpenter Books, 1984.

Calvin, John. *Commentaries on the First Book of Moses Called Genesis.* Vol. 1. Translated by John King. Grand Rapids: Baker, 1979.

Candlish, Robert S. *Commentary on Genesis.* Grand Rapids: Zondervan, 1998.

Carr, David M. "Politics of Textual Subversion: A Diachronic Perspective on the Garden of Eden Story." *Journal of Biblical Literature* 112/4 (1993): 577–95.

———. Reading the Fractures of Genesis: Historical and Literary Approaches. Louisville: Westminster John Knox, 1996.

Carroll, Robert P. *Jeremiah: A Commentary.* Old Testament Library. Philadelphia: Westminster, 1986.

Cassuto, Umberto. A Commentary on the Book of Genesis. Part One: From Adam to Noah. Jerusalem: Magnes, 1961.

———. A Commentary on the Book of Genesis. Part Two: From Noah to Abraham. Jerusalem: Magnes, 1961.

Chaine, Joseph. *Le livre de Genèse.* Lection Divina 3. Paris: Cerf, 1948.

Childs, Brevard S. *Biblical Theology in Crisis.* Philadelphia: Westminster, 1970.

———. Biblical Theology of the Old and New Testament: Theological Reflection on the Christian Bible. Minneapolis: Fortress, 1992.

———. The Book of Exodus: A Critical, Theological Commentary. Louisville: Westminster, 1974.

———. "The Enemy from the North and the Chaos Tradition." *Journal of Biblical Literature* 78 (1959): 187–98.

———. Introduction to the Old Testament as Scripture. London: SCM, 1979.

———. *Isaiah.* Louisville: Westminster John Knox, 2001.

———. *Myth and Reality in the Old Testament.* Studies in Biblical Theology 1/27. London: SCM, 1960.

———. "The Nature of the Christian Bible: One Book, Two Testament." In *The Rule of Faith: Scripture, Canon and Creed in a Critical Age*, edited by Ephraim Radner and George Sumner, 115–25. Harrisburg: Morehouse, 1998.

———. *The Old Testament Theology in a Canonical Context.* Old Testament Library. Philadelphia: Fortress, 1986.

———. "Psalm 8 in the Context of the Christian Canon." *Interpretation* 23, no. 1 (1969): 20–31.

Chisholm, Robert B., Jr. "'The Everlasting Covenant' and the 'City of Chaos': Intentional Ambiguity and Irony in Isaiah 24." *Criswell Theological Review* 6 (1993): 237–53.

Claassens, L. Juliana M. "Biblical Theology as Dialogue: Continuing the Conversation on Mikhail Bakhtin and Biblical Theology." *Journal of Biblical Literature* 122, no. 1 (2003): 127–44.

Clements, R. E. *Isaiah 1–39.* Grand Rapids: Eerdmans, 1980.

Clifford, Richard J. "Cosmogonies in the Ugaritic Texts and in the Bible." *Orientalia* 53 (1984): 183–201.

———. *Creation Accounts in the Ancient Near East and in the Bible*. Catholic Biblical Quarterly Monograph Series 26. Washington, D. C.: Catholic University Press, 1994.

———. "Creation in the Psalms." In *Creation in Biblical Traditions*, edited by Richard J. Clifford and John J. Collins, 57–69. Catholic Biblical Quarterly Monograph Series. Washington, D. C.: Catholic Biblical Association of America, 1992.

———. "The Hebrew Scriptures and the Theology of Creation." *Theological Studies* 46 (1985): 507–23.

———. "Psalm 89: A Lament over the Davidic Ruler's Continued Failure." *Harvard Theological Review* 73 (1980): 35–47.

———. "The Temple and the Holy Mountain." In *Temple in Antiquity: Ancient Records and Modern Perspectives*, edited by Truman G. Madsen, 107–24. The Religious Studies Monograph Series 9. Provo: BYU Religious Studies Center, 1984.

Clines, David J. A. "The Image of God in Man." *Tyndale Bulletin* 19 (1968): 53–103. Reprinted as "Humanity as Image of God." In *On the Way to the Postmodern: Old Testament Essays, 1967–1998*, by D. J. A. Clines, 447–97. Vol. 2. Journal for the Study of the Old Testament Supplement 293. Sheffield: Sheffield Academic Press, 1998.

———. "Theme in Genesis 1–11." *Catholic Biblical Quarterly* 38, no. 4 (1976): 483–507.

———. *The Theme of the Pentateuch*. Journal for the Study of the Old Testament Supplement 10. Sheffield: Sheffield Academic Press, 1997.

———. "Theology of the Flood Narrative." *Folia Theologica* 100 (1972–73): 128–42.

———. "What Does Eve Do to Help? And Other Irredeemably Androcentric Orientations in Genesis 1–3." In *What Does Eve Do to Help? And Other Readerly Questions to the Old Testament*, 25–48. Journal for the Study of the Old Testament Supplement 94. Sheffield: JSOT, 1990.

———. *What Does Eve Do to Help? And Other Readerly Questions to the Old Testament*. Journal for the Study of the Old Testament 94. Sheffield: JSOT Press, 1990.

Cody, Aelred. *Ezekiel: With an Excursus on Old Testament Priesthood*. Old Testament Message 11. Wilmington: Michael Glazier, 1984.

Coleridge, Mark. "Life in the Crypt or Why Bother with Biblical Studies?" *Biblical Interpretation* 2 (1994): 139–51.

Collins, C. John. *Genesis 1–4: A Linguistic, Literary, and Theological Commentary*. Phillipsburg: Presbyterian & Reformed, 2006.

Cothenet, E. "Paradis." In *Dictionnaire de la Bible*, edited by L. Pirot, A. Robert, and Henri Cazelles, 1177–220. Vol. 6. Paris: Letouzey, 1960.

Craigie, Peter C., Page H. Kelly, and Joel F. Drinkard Jr. *Jeremiah 1-25*. Word Biblical Commentary 26. Dallas: Word, 1991.

Culley, Robert C. "Action Sequences in Genesis 2-3." In *Society of Biblical Literature Seminar Papers*, edited by P. J. Achtemeier, 51-60. Vol. 1. Missoula: Scholars, 1978.

Curtis, Edward Mason. "Image of God (OT)." In *The Anchor Bible Dictionary*, edited by David Noel Freedman, 389-91. Vol. 3. New York: Doubleday, 1992.

———. *Man as the Image of God in Genesis in the Light of Ancient Near Eastern Parallels*. PhD diss., University of Pennsylvania, 1984.

Dahood, Mitchell J. *Psalms II, 51-100*. Anchor Bible 17. Garden City: Doubleday, 1968.

Davidson, Richard M. "Biblical Evidence for the Universality of the Genesis Flood." In *Creation, Catastrophe, and Calvary: Why a Global Flood Is Vital to the Doctrine of Atonement*, edited by John Templeton Baldwin, 69-92. Washington, D.C.: Review and Herald Pub. Assoc, 2000.

Day, John. *God's Conflict with the Dragon and the Sea: Echoes of a Canaanite Myth in the Old Testament*. University of Cambridge Oriental Publications 35. Cambridge: Cambridge University Press, 1985.

———. *Yahweh and the Gods and Goddesses of Canaan*. Journal for the Study of the Old Testament Supplement 265. Sheffield: Sheffield Academic Press, 2000.

Delitzsch, Friedrich. *Wo lag das Paradies? Eine biblisch-assyrioligische Studie.* Leipzig: J. C. Hinrinsch'sche Buchhandlung, 1881.

Deimel, A. "Die biblische Paradieserzahlung und ihre babylonische Parallelen (Schluss)." *Orientalia* 16 (1925): 90-100.

Deroche, Michael. "The Reversal of Creation in Hosea." *Vetus Testamentum* 31 (1981): 400-409.

———. "Zephaniah 1:2-3: The 'Sweeping' of Creation." *Vetus Testamentum* 30 (1980): 104-8.

Dohmen, Christoph. Schöpfung und Tod: Die Entfaltung theologischer und anthropologischer Konzeptionen in Gen 2/3. Stuttgarter biblische Beiträge 35. Stuttgart: Katholisches Bibelwerk, 1996.

Doukhan, J. "Allusions à la création dans le livre de Daniel." In *The Book of Daniel in Light of New Findings*, edited by A. S. van der Woude, 285-92. Leuven-Louvain: Leuven University Press, 1993.

Driver, Samuel D. An Introduction to the Literature of the Old Testament. New York: Meridian, 1967.

Driver, Samuel R. *The Book of Genesis*. London: Methuen, 1948 (1904).

Dumbrell, William J. *Covenant and Creation*. Nashville: Thomas Nelson, 1984.

Dus, Jan. "Zwei Schichten der biblischen Paradiesgeschichte." *Zeitschrift für die alttestamentliche Wissenschaft* 71 (1959): 162-72.

Eichrodt, Walther. *Theology of the Old Testament*. 2 vols. Philadelphia: Westminster, 1960/67.

Emerton, John A. "'Spring and Torrent' in Psalm lxxiv 14." In *Volume du Congres: Geneve 1965*, 122–33. Supplement to Vetus Testamentum 15. Leiden: Brill, 1966.

Engell, I. "'Knowledge' and 'Life' in the Creation Story." *Vetus Testamentum* 3 (1955): 103–19.

Eppstein, Victor. "The Day of Yahweh in Jeremiah 4:23–26." *Journal of Biblical Literature* 87 (1968): 93–97.

Farrow, Douglas. "St. Irenaeus of Lyons: The Church and the World." *Pro Ecclesia* 4 (1995): 333–55.

Feldmann, Joseph. Paradies und Sündefall. Der Sinn der biblischen Erzählung nach der Exegese und unter Beruksichtigung der ausserbiblischen Uberlieferungen. Alttesamentliche Abhhandlungen 4. Münster: Aschendorffsche Verlagsbuchhandlung, 1913.

Fewell, D. N. "Reading the Bible Ideologically: Feminist Criticism." In *To Each Its Own Meaning: An Introduction to Biblical Interpretation and Their Applications*, edited by S. L. McKenzie and S. R. Haynes, 237–51. Louisville: Westminster John Knox, 1993.

Fewell, D. N., and D. M. Gunn. "Genesis 2–3: Women, Men and God." In *Narrative in the Hebrew Bible*, edited by David M. Gunn and Danna N. Fewell, 194–205. Oxford: Oxford University Press, 1993.

Fishbane, Michael. "Jeremiah IV 23–26 and Job III 3–13: A Recovered Use of the Creation Pattern." *Vetus Testamentum* 21 (1971): 151–67.

Fisher, Loren R. "Creation at Ugarit and in the Old Testament." *Vetus Testamentum* 15 (1965): 313–24.

Foerster, Werner. "Ktizo." In *Theologisches Wörterbuch zum Neuen Testament*, edited by Gerhard Kittel and Gerhard Friedrich, 999–1015. Abkürzungs-Verzeichnis. Stuttgart: W. Kohlhammer, 1960.

Fokkelman, Jan P. *Reading Biblical Narrative: An Introductory Guide*. Louisville: Westminster John Knox, 1999.

Foster, Benjamin. "Epic of Creation" (*Enuma Elish*). In *Context of Scripture: Canonical Compositions from the Biblical World*, edited by William W. Hallo and K. Lawson Younger Jr., 390–403. Vol. 1. Leiden: Brill, 1997.

Fox, Everett. "Can Genesis Be Read as a Book?" *Semeia* 46 (1989): 31–40.

Fretheim, Terence E. *Creation, Fall, and Flood: Studies in Genesis 1–11*. Minneapolis: Augsburg Publishing House, 1969.

———. *Exodus*. Interpretation: A Bible Commentary for Teaching and Preaching. Louisville: John Knox, 1991.

———. *God and World in the Old Testament: A Relational Theology of Creation*. Nashville: Abingdon, 2005.

———. "Is Genesis 3 a Fall Story?" *Word & World* 14, no. 2 (1994): 144–53.

———. *The Suffering of God: An Old Testament Perspective*. Philadelphia: Fortress, 1984.

Friedman, Richard E. *The Exile and Biblical Narrative: The Formation of the Deuteronomistic and Priestly Works*. Harvard Semitic Monographs 22. Chico: Scholars, 1981.

Fuller, Daniel P. *The Unity of the Bible: Unfolding of God's Plan for Humanity*. Grand Rapids: Zondervan, 1992.

Gaffin, Richard B. *Calvin and the Sabbath: The Controversy of Applying the Fourth Commandment*. Fearn, Ross-Shire: Mentor, 2008.

Gibson, John C. L. *Genesis*. Philadelphia: Westminster, 1981.

———. "The Kingship of Yahweh against Its Canaanite Background." In *Ugarit and The Bible: Proceedings of the International Symposium on Ugarit and the Bible Manchester, September 1992*, edited by George J. Brooke, Adrian H. W. Curtis, and John F. Healey, 101–12. Ugaritisch-Biblische Literatur 11. Münster: Ugarit-Verlag, 1994.

Gilkey, Langdon. *Maker of Heaven and Earth: The Doctrine of Creation in Light of Modern Knowledge*. New York: Doubleday, 1959.

Gleason, Kathryn. "Gardens in Preclassical Times." In *Oxford Encyclopedia of Archaeology in the Near East*, edited by E. Meyers, 383–85. Vol 2. New York: Oxford University Press, 1997.

Goldingay, John. "How Far Do Readers Make Sense? Interpreting Biblical Narrative." *Themelios* 18, no. 2 (1993): 5–10.

———. "Postmodernizing Eve and Adam: Can I Have My Apricot as Well as Eating It?" In *The World of Genesis: Persons, Places, Perspectives*, edited by Philip R. Davies and David J. A. Clines, 50–59. Sheffield: Sheffield Academic Press, 1998.

———. *Psalms*. Vol. 2. Baker Commentary on the Old Testament. Grand Rapids: Baker, 2006.

Gordon, Robert P. "טוב." In *The New International Dictionary of the Old Testament Theology & Exegesis*, edited by Willem A. VanGemeren, 353–57. Vol. 2. Grand Rapids: Zondervan, 1997.

Gowan, Donald E. *Eschatology in the Old Testament*. Philadelphia: Fortress, 1986.

Green, Alberto R. W. *The Storm-God in the Ancient Near East*. Biblical and Judaic Studies 8. Winona Lake: Eisenbrauns, 2003.

Gressmann, H. "Mythische Reste in der Paradieserzählung." *Archiv für Religionswissenschaft* 10 (1907): 345–67.

Grønback, J. H. "Baal's Battle with Yam: A Canaanite Creation Fight." *Journal for the Study of the Old Testament* 33 (1985): 27–44.

Grudem, Wayne. *Systematic Theology*. Grand Rapids: Zondervan, 1994.

Gunkel, Herman. *Genesis*. Translated by M. E. Briddle. Mercer Library of Biblical Studies. Macon: Mercer University Press, 1997.

———. "The Influence of Babylonian Mythology upon the Biblical Creation Story." In *Creation in the Old Testament*, edited by Bernhard W. Anderson, 25–52. Issues in Religion and Theology 6. Philadelphia: Fortress, 1984.

———. *Schöpfung und Chaos in Urzeit und Endzeit: Eine religionsgeschichtliche Untersuchung über Gen 1 und Ap Joh 12*. Göttingen: Vandenhoeck & Ruprecht, 1895. (English Translation). *Creation and Chaos in the Primeval Era and the Eschaton: A Religio-historical Study of Genesis 1 and Revelation 12*. Edited by Heinrich Zimmern. Translated by K. William Whitney, Jr. Grand Rapids: Eerdmans, 2006.

Gunneweg, Antonius H. J. *Understanding the Old Testament*. Old Testament Library. London: SCM, 1978.

Haag, Herbert. "Die Komposition der Sündenfall-Erzählung: Gen 2:4b–3:24." *Theologische Quartalschrift* 146 (1966): 1–7.

———. *Der Mensch am Anfang. Die alttestamentliche Paradiesvorstellung nach Gn 2–3*. Trierer Theologische Studien 24. Trier: Paulinus, 1970.

Hafemann, Scott J. *Paul, Moses, and the History of Israel: The Letter/Spirit Contrast and the Argument from Scripture in 2 Corinthians 3*. Peabody: Hendrickson, 1995.

Hagopian, David, ed. *The Genesis Debate: Three Views on the Days of Creation*. Mission Viejo: Crux Press, 2001.

Hallo, William W. "Texts, Statues and the Cult of the Divine King." In *Congress Volume: Jerusalem*, 54–66. Supplement to Vetus Testamentum. Leiden: Brill, 1988.

Hamilton, Victor P. *The Book of Genesis: Chapters 1–17*. New International Commentary on the Old Testament Series. Grand Rapids: Eerdmans, 1990.

Harland, P. J. *The Value of Human Life: A Study of the Story of the Flood (Genesis 6–9)*. Supplement of Vetus Testamentum LXIV. Leiden: Brill, 1996.

Harner, Philip B. "Creation Faith in Deutero-Isaiah." *Vetus Testamentum* 17 (1967): 298–306.

Hart, Ian. "Genesis 1:1–2:3 as a Prologue to the Book of Genesis." *Tyndale Bulletin* 46, no. 2 (1995): 315–36.

Hartman, Louis F. "Sin in Paradise." *Catholic Biblical Quarterly* 20 (1958): 26–40.

Hasel, Gerhard. "Recent Translations of Genesis 1:1." *The Bible Translator* 22, no. 4 (1971): 156–67.

Hauser, Alan Jon. "Genesis 2–3: Theme of Intimacy and Alienation." In *Art and Meaning: Rhetoric in Biblical Literature*, edited by D. J. A. Clines, D. M. Gunn, and A. J. Hauser, 20–36. Journal for the Study of the Old Testament Supplement 19. Sheffield: JSOT Press, 1982.

Heinisch, Paul. *Probleme der biblishcen Urgeschichte*. Luzern: Räber & Cie, 1947.

Herdner, Andreé. *Corpus des tablettes en cunéiforms alphabétiques.* Vol. 3. Mission de Ras Shamra X. Paris: Imprimerie Nationale, 1963.
Heward, P. W. "And the Earth Was without Form and Void." *Journal of the Transaction of the Victoria Institute* 78 (1946): 13–37.
Hick, John. *Evil and the God of Love.* New York: Harper & Row, 1966.
Hodge, Charles. *Systematic Theology.* Vol. 1. New York: Scribner, 1889. Reprint, Grand Rapids: Eerdmans, 1991.
Hoeksema, Herman. *Reformed Dogmatics.* 2nd ed. Grandville: Reformed Free Publishing Association, 2004.
Hoffman, Yair. "The First Creation Story: Canonical and Diachronical Aspects." In *Creation in Jewish and Christian Tradition*, edited by Henning Graf Reventlow and Yair Hoffman, 32–53. Journal for the Study of the Old Testament Supplement 319. Sheffield: Sheffield Academic Press, 2002.
Hofius, Otfried. *Der Vorhang or dem Thron Gottes: Eine exegetisch-religiongeschichteeliche Untersuchung zu Hebräer 6:19f. und 10:19f. Wissenschaftliche Untersuchngen zum Neuen Testmanent 14.* Tübingen: Mohr Siebeck, 1972.
Holzinger, Heinrich. *Einleitung in den Hexateuch.* Freiburg: Mohr Siebeck, 1893.
———. *Genesis, II. Das Paradies und der Sündenfall.* Freiburg: Mohr Siebeck, 1898.
Houtman, Cornelis. *Exodus.* 3 vols. Historical Commentary on the Old Testament. Leuven: Peeters, 2000.
Hvidberg, Flemming. "The Canaanite Background of Gen I–III." *Vetus Testamentum* 10 (1960): 285–94.
Jacobsen, Thorkild. "Mesopotamian Gods and Pantheons." In *Toward the Image of Tammuz*, edited by W. Moran, 16–38. Cambridge: Harvard University Press, 1970.
Jenni, E. "Die theologische Begründung des Sabbathgebots im Alten Testament." *Theologische Stüdein* 46 (1956): 3–40.
Jenson, Philip P. *Graded Holiness: A Key to the Priestly Conception of the World.* Journal for the Study of the Old Testament Supplement 106. Sheffield: JSOT Press, 1992.
Jobling, David. "Myth and Its Limits in Genesis 2:4b–3:24." In *The Sense of Biblical Narrative, II. Structural Analysis of the Hebrew Bible*, edited by D. Jobling, 17–43. Journal of the Study of the Old Testament Supplement 39. Sheffield: JSOT Press, 1986.
———. "A Structural Analysis of Genesis 2:4b–3:24." In *Society of Biblical Literature Seminar Papers*, edited by P. J. Achtemeier, 61–69. Vol. 1. Missoula: Scholars, 1978.

Johnson, Dan G. *From Chaos to Restoration: An Integrative Reading of Isaiah 24–27*. Journal for the Study of the Old Testament Supplement 61. Sheffield: JSOT Press, 1988.

Joines, Karen R. "The Serpent in Gen. 3." *Zeitschrift für di alttestamentliche Wissenschaft* 87 (1975): 1–11.

———. *Serpent Symbolism in the Old Testament*. Haddonfield: Haddonfield House, 1974.

Kaiser, Otto. *Isaiah 13–39: A Commentary*. London: SCM, 1974.

———. *Die mythische Bedeutung des Meeres in Ägypten, Ugarit und Israel*. Beihefte zur Zeitschrift für die alttestamentliche Wissenschaft 78. Berlin: Verlag Alfred Topelmann, 1962.

Karlberg, Mark W. "The Original State of Adam: Tensions in Reformed Theology." *The Evangelical Quarterly* 59 (1987): 291–309.

Kaufmann, Yehezkel. *The Religion of Israel: From Its Beginning to the Babylonian Exile*. Translated by M. Greenberg. Chicago: Chicago University Press, 1960.

Kearney, Peter J. "Creation and Liturgy: The P Redaction of Ex 25–40." *Zeitschrift für die alttestamentliche Wissenschaft* 89 (1977): 375–87.

Kikawada Isaac M., and Arthur Quinn. *Before Abraham Was: The Unity of Genesis 1–11*. Nashville: Abingdon, 1985.

Kimmelman, Reuven. "The Seduction of Eve and the Exegetical Politics of Gender." *Biblical Interpretation* 4, no. 1 (1996): 1–39.

Kissane, E. J. *The Book of Isaiah: Translated from a Critically Revised Hebrew Text with Commentary*. Rev. ed. Dublin: Browne & Nolan, 1961.

Kline, Meredith G. "Creation in the Image of the Glory-Spirit." *Westminster Theological Journal* 39, no. 2 (1977): 250–72.

———. *Kingdom Prologue*. South Hamilton: Gordon-Conwell Theological Seminary, 1989.

Kloos, C. *Yhwh's Combat with the Sea: A Canaanite Tradition in the Religion of Ancient Israel*. Leiden: Brill, 1986.

Knierim, Rolf P. *The Task of Old Testament Theology: Substance, Method, and Cases*. Grand Rapids: Eerdmans, 1995.

Knight, George A. F. *Theology in Pictures: A Commentary on Genesis Chapters One to Eleven*. Edinburgh: Handsel Press, 1981.

Koch, Klaus. *The Prophets*. Vol. 2. London: SCM, 1980.

Kovacs, Brian W. "Structure and Narrative Rhetoric in Genesis 2–3: Reflections on the Problem of Non-Convergent Structuralist Exegetical Methodologies." *Semeia* 18 (1980): 139–47.

Kraus, Hans-Joachim. *Psalms: A Commentary*. Vol. 2. Minneapolis: Augsburg, 1989.

Kselman, John S. "The Recovery of Poetic Fragments from the Pentateuchal Priestly Source." *Journal of Biblical Literature* 97 (1978):161–73.

LaCocque, André. "Allusions to Creation in Daniel 7." In *The Book of Daniel: Composition and Reception*, edited by John J. Collins and Peter W. Flint, 114–31. Leiden: Brill, 2001.

———. "Cracks in the Wall." In *Thinking Biblically: Exegetical and Hermeneutical Studies* by A. LaCocque and P. Ricoeur, 3–29. Chicago: University of Chicago Press, 1998.

Lambert, M. "A Study of the First Chapter of Genesis." *Hebrew Union College Annual* 1 (1924): 3–12.

Landersdorfer, P. Simon. *Die sumerischen Parallelen zur biblischen urgeschichte.* Alttestamentliche Abhandlungen VII/5. Münster: Aschendorffsche Verlagsbuchhandlung, 1917.

Landy. Francis. *Paradoxes of Paradise: Identity and Difference in the Song of Songs.* Bible and Literature Series 7. Sheffield: Almond, 1983.

LaRondelle, Hans Karl. Perfection and Perfectionism: A Dogmatic-Ethical Study of Biblical Perfection and Phenomenal Perfectionism. Kampen: Vrije Universiteit Amsterdam, 1971.

Leach, Edmund. *Genesis as Myth and Other Essays.* London: Jonathan Cape, 1969.

Leene, Hendrik. "Ezekiel and Jeremiah: Promises of Inner Renewal in Diachronic Perspective." In *Past, Present, Future: The Deuteronomistic History and the Prophets*, edited by Johannes C. de Moor and H. F. van Rooy, 150–72. Oudtestamentische Studiën. Leiden: Brill, 2000.

Lefèvre, A. "Bulletin d'exégèse de l'AT." *Rercherches de science religieuse* 36 (1949): 455–80.

Leupold, Herbert C. *Exposition of Genesis.* Columbus: Wartburg, 1942.

Levenson, Jon D. Creation and Persistence of Evil: The Jewish Drama of Divine Omnipotence. Princeton: Princeton University Press, 1988.

———. "The Temple and the World." *Journal of Religion* 64 (1984): 275–98.

Levin, Christoph. "The Yahwist: The Earliest Editor of the Pentateuch." *Journal of Biblical Literature* 126 (2007): 209–30.

———. *Der Jahwist.* Göttingen: Vandenhoeck & Ruprecht, 1993.

Loete, Joseph. "A Premature Hymn of Praise: The Meaning and Function of Isaiah 24.14–16c in Its Present Context." In *Studies in Isaiah 24–27*, edited by Hendrik Jan Bosman, Harm van Grol, and Jesaja Werkplaats, 226–38. Leiden: Brill, 2000.

Lohfink, Nobert. *Das Siegeslied am Schilfmeer.* Frankfurt am Main: Josef Knecht, 1965.

Loretz, O. "Wortbericht-Vorlage and Tatbericht-Interpretation im Schöpfungsbericht Gn 1, 1–2, 4a." *Ugarit-Forschungen* 11 (1977): 279–87.

Ludwig, Otto. Die Stadt in der Jesaja-Apokalypse: zur Datierung von Jes. 24–27. Cologne: Kleikamp, 1961.

Lundquist, John M. "The Common Temple Ideology of the Ancient Near East." In *Temple in Antiquity: Ancient Records and Modern Perspectives*, edited by T. G. Madsen, 54–76. The Religious Studies Monograph Series 9. Provo: BYU Religious Studies Center, 1984.

Luther, Martin. *Luther's Commentary on Genesis*. Vol. 1. Translated by J. Theodore Mueller. Grand Rapids: Zondervan, 1958.

MacIntosh, Charles H. *Genesis to Deuteronomy: Notes on the Pentateuch*. 1880. Reprint, Neptune: Liozeaux Brothers, 1974.

Mann, Thomas W. "Stars, Sprouts, and Streams: The Creative Redeemer in Second Isaiah." In *God Who Creates: Essays in Honor of W. Sibley Towner*, edited by William P. Brown and S. Dean Mcbride Jr., 135–51. Grand Rapids: Eerdmans, 2000.

Mason, Steven D. "Another Flood? Genesis 9 and Isaiah's Broken Eternal Covenant." *Journal for the Study of the Old Testament* 32, no. 2 (2007): 177–98.

Mayes, Andrew David H. *Deuteronomy*. New Century Bible. Grand Rapids: Eerdmans, 1981.

Mays, James Luther. *Psalms*. Intepretation: A Biblical Commentary for Teaching and Preaching. Louisville: John Knox, 1994.

McKenzie, John L. "The Literary Characteristics of Genesis 2–3." *Theological Studies* 15 (1954): 541–72.

———. *The Two-Edged Sword*. New York: Image, 1966.

Mettinger, Tryggve N. D. *The Eden Narrative*. Winona Lake: Eisenbrauns, 2007.

———. "Fighting the Powers of Chaos and Hell – Towards the Biblical Portrait of God." *Studia Theologica* 39 (1985): 21–38.

Meyers, Carol L. *The Tabernacle Menorah: A Synthetic Study of a Symbol from the Biblical Cult*. Missoula: Scholars, 1976.

Middleton, J. Richard. *The Liberating Image: The Imago Dei in Genesis 1*. Grand Rapids: Branzos Press, 2005.

Milgrom, Jacob. *Leviticus 1–16*. Garden City: Doubleday, 1991.

Millard, A. R. "The Etymology of Eden." *Vetus Testamentum* 34 (1984): 103–6.

Milne, P. J. "The Patriarchal Stamp of Scripture: The Implications of Structural Analyses for Feminist Hermeneutics." *Journal of Feminist Studies in Religion* 5 (1989): 17–34. Reprint with an Afterword, in *A Feminist Companion to Genesis*, edited by A. Brenner, 146–72. Feminist Companion to the Bible 2. Sheffield: Sheffield Academic Press, 1993.

Miscall, Peter D. "Isaiah: New Heavens, New Earth, New Book." In *Reading between Texts: Intertextuality and the Hebrew Bible*. Literary Currents in Biblical Interpretation, edited by Danna Nolan Fewell, 41–56. Louisville: Westminster John Knox, 1992.

———. "Jacques Derrida in the Garden of Eden." *Union Seminary Quarterly Review* 44 (1990): 1–9.

Moberly, R. Walter L. *At the Mountain of God: Story and Theology of Exodus 32–34*. Journal for the Study of the Old Testament Supplement 22. Sheffield: University of Sheffield, 1983.

———. "Did the Serpent Get It Right?" *Journal of Theological Studies* 39 (1988): 1–27.

Morgenstern, Julian. "The Sources of the Creation Story." *American Journal of Semitic Languages and Literature* 36 (1919/20): 169–212.

———. "The Sources of the Paradise Story." *Journal of Jewish Lore and Philosophy* 1 (1910): 105–23.

Morris, Henry. *The Genesis Record*. San Diego: Creation-Life, 1976.

Morris, P. "A Walk in the Garden: Images of Eden." In *A Walk in the Garden: Biblical, Iconographical and Literary Images of Eden*, edited by P. Morris and D. Sawyer, 21–38. Journal for the Study of the Old Testament Supplement 136. Sheffield: Sheffield Academic Press, 1992.

Morson, Gary Saul, and Caryl Emerson. *Mikhail Bakhtin: Creation of Prosaics*. Stanford: Stanford University Press, 1990.

Motyer, J. Alec. *The Prophecy of Isaiah*. Leicester: InterVarsity, 1993.

Motyer, Steve. "Two Testaments, One Biblical Theology." In *Between Two Horizons: Spanning New Testament Studies and Systematic Theology*, edited by Joel B. Green and Max Turner, 143–64. Grand Rapids: Eerdmans, 2000.

Mulder, M. J. "Baal." In *Theological Dictionary of the Old Testament*, edited by G. Johannes Botterweck and Helmer Ringgren, 181–200. Vol. 2. Translated by John T. Willis. Grand Rapids: Eerdmans, 1975.

Muilenburg, James A. "Form Criticism and Beyond." *Journal of Biblical Literature* 88 (1969): 1–18.

Newsom, Carol A. "Bakhtin, the Bible, and Dialogic Truth." *Journal of Religion* 76 (1996): 290–306.

Nicholson, Ernest. "The Interpretation of Exod 24:10." *Vetus Testamentum* 24 (1974): 77–97.

———. *The Pentateuch in the Twentieth Century: The Legacy of Wellhausen*. Oxford: Clarendon, 1998.

Niditch, Susan. *Chaos to Cosmos: Studies in Biblical Patterns of Creation*. Scholars Press in the Humanities 6. Chico: Scholars, 1985.

Nielsen, Eduard. *The Ten Commandments in Recent Perspectives*. Translated by David J. Bourke. Naperville: A. R. Allenson, 1968.

Noort, Ed. "The Creation of Light in Genesis 1:1–5." In The Creation of Heaven and Earth: Re-interpretations of Genesis 1 in the Context of Judaism, Ancient Philosophy, Christianity, and Modern Physics, edited by George H. van Kooten, 3–20. Themes in Biblical Narrative 8. Leiden: Brill, 2005.

Olson, Dennis T. "Biblical Theology as Provisional Monologization: A Dialogue with Childs, Brueggemann, and Bakhtin." *Biblical Interpretation* 6 (1998): 162–80.

———. "Jeremiah 4:5–31 and Apocalyptic Myth. *Journal for the Study of the Old Testament* 73 (1997): 81–107.

Oswalt, J. N. *The Book of Isaiah: Chapters 1–39*. New International Commentary of the Old Testament. Grand Rapids: Eerdmans, 1986.

Otto, Eckart. "Die Paradieserzählung Genesis 2–3: Eine nachpriesteliche Lehrerzahlung in ihrem religionhistorischen Kontext." In *"Jedes Ding hat seine Zeit . . ." Studien zur israelitische und altorientalischen Weisheit. Diethelm Michel zum 65. Geburtstag*, edited by Anja A. Diesel, Reinhard G. Lehmann, Eckart Otto, and Andreas Wagner, 167–92. Beihefte zur Zeitschrift für die alttestamentliche Wissenschaft 241. Berlin: de Gruyter, 1996.

———. Review of John van Seters, The Edited Bible: The Curious History of the "Editor" in Biblical Criticism. Review of Biblical Literature. No page numbers. Cited 18 April 2008. http://www.bookreviews.org/.

Pannenberg, Wolfhart. *Jesus, God and Man*. Translated by Lewis L. Wilkins and Duane A. Priebe. Philadelphia: Westminster, 1977.

———. *Systematic Theology*. Vol. 2. Translated by Geoffrey W. Bromiley. Grand Rapids: Eerdmans, 1994.

Pardee, Dennis. "The Baʻlu Myth." In *The Context of Scripture: Canonical Compositions from the Biblical World*, edited by William W. Hallo and K. Lawson Younger, Jr., 241–74. Vol.1. Leiden: Brill, 2003.

Pardes, Ilana. *Countertraditions in the Bible: A Feminist Approach*. Cambridge: Harvard University Press, 1992.

Patrick, Dale, and Allen Scult. *Rhetoric and Biblical Interpretation*. Journal for the Study of the Old Testament Supplement 82. Sheffield: Almond, 1990.

Pedersen, Johannes. "The Fall of Man." In *Interpretationes ad VT pertinentes Sigmundo Mowinckel septuagenario*, edited by N. A. Dahl and A. S. Kapelrud, 167–72. Norks Teologisk Tidsskrift 56. Oslo: Forlaget Land og Kirke, 1955.

Plumley, J. Martin. "The Cosmology of Ancient Egypt." In *Ancient Cosmologies*, edited by C. Blacker and M. Loewe, 17–41. London: George Allen & Unwin, 1975.

Pohl, A. "Der Schopfungshymnus der Bible." *Stimmen der Zeit* 162 (1958): 252–66.

Polak, Frank H. "Poetic Style and Parallelism in the Creation Account (Genesis 1.1–2.3)." In *Creation in Jewish and Christian Tradition*, edited by Henning Graf Reventlow and Yair Hoffman, 2–31. Journal for the Study of the Old Testament Supplement 319. London: Sheffield Academic Press, 2002.

Polaski, Donald. "Reflections on a Mosaic Covenant: The Eternal Covenant (Isaiah 24.5) and Intertextuality." *Journal for the Study of the Old Testament* 77 (1998): 55–73.

Poythress, Vern S. *God-Centered Biblical Interpretation*. Phillipsburg: Presbyterian and Reformed Publishing, 1999.

———. "Science and Hermeneutics: Implications of Scientific Method for Biblical Interpretation." In *Foundations of Contemporary Interpretation*, edited by Moises Silva, 431–531. Grand Rapids: Zondervan, 1996.

———. *Symphonic Theology: A Validity of Multiple Perspectives in Theology*. Grand Rapids: Zondervan, 1987. Reprint, Phillipsburg: Presbyterian & Reformed, 2001.

———. "What Does God Say through Human Authors?" In *Inerrancy and Hermeneutic*, edited by Harvie Conn, 81–99. Grand Rapids: Baker, 1988.

Pritchard, James B. "Man's Predicament in Eden." *Review of Religion* 13 (1948): 5–23.

Ramantswana, Hulisani. "Conflicts at Creation: Genesis 1–3 in Dialogue with the Psalter," *Old Testament Essays* 27, no. 2 (2014): 553–578.

Ramantswana, Hulisani. "Day Two of Creation: Why Is the *Rāqîaʽ* (Firmament) Not Pronounced Good?" *Journal for Semitics* 22, no. 1 (2013): 101–23.

———. "From Bad to Good: A Dialogic Reading of Genesis 1." *Journal for Semitics* 21, no. 2 (2012): 237–68.

———. "Humanity Not Pronounced Good: Humanity's Death within the Scope of God's Very Good Creation in Light of Genesis 2–3." *Old Testament Essays* 26, no.3 (2013): 804–18.

———. "Humanity Not Pronounced Good: A Re-reading of Genesis 1:26–31 in Dialogue with Genesis 2–3." *Old Testament Essays* 26, no. 2 (2013): 425–44.

Rashkow, Ilona N. *The Phallacy of Genesis: A Feminist-Psychoanalytical Approach*. Louisville: Westminster John Knox Press, 1993.

Ray, William. *Literary Meaning: From Phenomenology to Deconstruction*. Oxford: Blackwell, 1984.

Reed, Walter. Dialogue of the Word: The Bible as Literature according to Bakhtin. New York: Oxford University Press, 1993.

Rendsburg, Gary A. *The Redaction of Genesis*. Winona Lake: Eisenbrauns, 1986.

Rendtorff, Rolf. "Some Reflections on Creation as a Topic of Old Testament Theology." In *Priests, Prophets and Scribes: Essays on the Formation and Heritage of Second Temple Judaism in Honour of Joseph Blenkinsopp*, edited by Eugene Ulrich, John W. Wright, Robert P. Carroll, and Philip R. Davies, 205–12. Journal for the Study of the Old Testament Supplement Series 149. Sheffield: JSOT Press, 1992.

———. "Die theologische Stellung des Schopfungsgluabens bei Deuterojesaja." *Zeitschrift für Theologie und Kirche* 51 (1954): 3–13.

Reumann, John. *Creation and New Creation: The Past, Present and Future of God's Creative Activity*. Minneapolis: Augsburg, 1973.

Reymond, Robert L. *A New Systematic Theology of the Christian Faith*. Nashville: Thomas Nelson, 1998.

Richter, Sandra L. *Epic of Eden: A Christian Entry into the Old Testament*. Downers Grove: InterVarsity, 2008.

Robinson, Gnaba. *The Origin and Development of the Old Testament Sabbath: A Comprehensive Exegetical Approach*. Bangalore: United Theological College, 1998.

Robinson, R. B. "Literary Functions of the Genealogies in Genesis." *Catholic Biblical Quarterly* 48 (1986): 595–608.

Rosenberg, J. W. "The Garden Story Forward and Backward: The Non-narrative Dimension of Gen 2–3." *Prooftexts* 1 (1981): 1–27.

Ross, Allen P. *Creation and Blessing*. Grand Rapids: Baker, 1988.

Rudman, Dominic. "Midrash in the Isaiah Apocalypse." *Zeitschrift für die alttestamentliche Wissenschaft* 112 (2000): 404–8.

Russell, D. M. *The "New Heavens and New Earth": Hope for the Creation in Jewish Apocalyptic and the New Testament*. Studies in Biblical Apocalyptic Literature 1. Philadelphia: Visionary Press, 1996.

Ryken, Leland, James C. Wilhoit, and Tremper Longman III. *Dictionary of Biblical Imagery: An Encylopedic Exploration of the Images, Symbols, Motifs, Metaphors, Figures of Speech and Literary Patterns of the Bible*. Downers Grove: InterVarsity, 1998.

Saggs, H. W. F. *The Encounter with the Divine in Mesopotamia and Israel*. London: Athlone, 1978.

Sailhamer, John. "Exegetical Notes: Genesis 1:1–2:4a." *Trinity Journal* 5 (1984): 73–82.

———. *Genesis*. In *The Expositor's Bible Commentary: Genesis, Exodus, Leviticus, Numbers*, edited by Frank E. Gæbelein, 1–284. Vol. 2. Grand Rapids: Zondervan, 1990.

———. *Genesis Unbound: A Provocative New Look at the Creation Account*. Sisters: Multnomah, 1996.

Sanders, James. *Canon and Authority: A Guide to Canonical Criticism*. Philadelphia: Fortress, 1984.

———. "Canonical Context and Canonical Criticism." *Horizons in Biblical Theology* 2, no. 1 (1980): 173–97.

———. *From Sacred Story to Sacred Text*. Philadelphia: Fortress, 1987.

———. "Hermeneutics in True and False Prophecy." In *Canon and Authority*, edited by George W. Coats and Burke O. Long, 21–41. Philadelphia: Fortress, 1977.

———. *Torah and Canon*. 2nd ed. Philadelphia: Fortress, 1974.

Sarna, Nahum M. *Genesis: The JPS Torah Commentary*. Philadelphia: The Jewish Publication Society, 1989.

———. "The Psalm for the Sabbath Day (Ps. 92)." *Journal of Biblical Literature* 81 (1962): 155–68.

———. *Understanding Genesis*. New York: Schocken, 1978.

Schmidt, W. H. *Einführung in das Alte Testament*. Berlin: de Gruyter, 1979.

———. "Die Geschichte von Paradies und Sündenfall." *Sammlung gemeinverständlicher Vorträge und Schriften* 154 (1931).

———. *Die Schöpfungshymnus in Gen 1*. Wissenschafliche Monographien zum Alten und Neun Testament 17. Neukirchen-Vluyn: Neukirchener, 1974.

———. *Die Schöpfungsgeschichte der Priesterschrift von Gen 1,1–2,4a und 2,4b–3,24*. Wissenschaftliche Monographien zum Alten und Neuen Testament 17. 2nd ed. Neukirchen-Vluyn: Neukirchener, 1964.

Schultz, H. Alttestamentliche Theologie: Die Offenbarugnsreligion auf ihrer vorschristlichen Entwicklunsstufe. 1869. 5th Revised Edition, Frankfurt: 1896. English Translation of the 4th edition: Old Testament Theology: The Religion of Revelation in its Pre-Christian Stage of Development. 2 vols. Edinburgh: T&T Clark 1892.

Scullion, John. *Genesis: A Commentary for Students, Teachers, and Preachers*. Collegeville: Michael Glazier, 1992.

Seely, Paul H. "Firmament and the Water Above. Part I: The Meaning of raqia' in Gen 1:6–8." *Westminster Theological Journal* 53, no. 2 (1991): 227–40.

———. "The Firmament and the Water Above, Part II: The Meaning of 'The Water above the Firmament' in Gen 1:6–8." *Westminster Theological Journal* 54, no. 1 (1992): 31–46.

Seitz, Christopher R. *Isaiah 1–39*. Louisville: John Knox, 1993.

Sellers, Susan. Myth and Fairy Tale in Contemporary Women's Fiction. New York: Palgrave, 2002.

Seybold, Klaus. *Die Psalmen*. Tübingen: Mohr Siebeck, 1996.

Shea, William H. "Literary Structural Parallels between Genesis 1 and 2." *Origins* 16, no. 2 (1989): 49–68.

Shepherd, David. "Bakhtin and the Reader." In *Bakhtin and Cultural Theory*, edited by Ken Hirschkop and David Shepherd, 91–108. Manchester: Manchester University Press, 2002.

Simkins, Ronald A. Creator and Creation: Nature in the Worldview of Ancient Israel. Peabody: Hendrickson, 1994.

Ska, Jean-Louis. "A Plea on Behalf of the Biblical Redactors." *Studia Theologica* 59 (2005): 4–18.

Skinner, John A. *A Critical and Exegetical Commentary on Genesis*. 2nd ed. Edinburgh: T&T Clark, 1930.

Slivniak, Dmitri M. "The Garden of Double Messages: Deconstructing Hierarchical Oppositions in the Garden Story." *Journal for the Study of the Old Testament* 27, no. 4 (2003): 439–60.

Smend, Rudolf. *Die Entstehung des Alten Testaments*. Theologische Wissenschaft 1. Stuttgart: Kohlhammer, 1978.

———. *Die Erzählung des Hexateuch auf ihre Quellen untersucht*. Berlin: Reimer, 1912.

Smick, Elmer B. "Mythopoetic Language in the Psalms." *Westminster Theological Journal* 44 (1982): 88–98.

Smith, George. *The Chaldean Account of Genesis. Containing the Description of the Creation, the Fall of Man, the Deluge, the Tower of Babel, the Time of the Patriarchs and Nimrod*. London: Sampson Low, Marston, Searle & Rivington, 1876.

Smith, Gary V. "Structure and Purpose in Genesis 1–11." *Journal of Evangelical Theological Society* 20 (1977): 307–19.

Smith, Mark S. "Light in Genesis 1:3–Created or Uncreated: A Question of Priestly Mysticism?" In *Birkat Shalom: Studies in the Bible, Ancient Near Eastern Literature, and Postbiblical Judaism Presented to Shalom M. Paul on the Occasion of His Seventieth Birthday*, edited by Chaim Cohen, V. A. Hurowitz, A. M. Hurvitz, Y. Muffs, B. J. Schwartz, and J. H. Tigay, 125–34. Winona Lake: Eisenbrauns, 2008.

———. *The Memoirs of God: History, Memory, and the Experience of the Divine in Ancient Israel*. Minneapolis: Fortress, 2004.

———. *The Origins of Biblical Monotheism: Israel's Polytheistic Background and the Ugaritic Texts*. New York: Oxford University Press, 2001.

———. *The Ugaritic Baal Cycle: Introduction with Text, Translation and Commentary of KTU 1.1–1.2*, vol. 1. Supplements to Vetus Testamentum 55. Leiden: Brill, 1994.

Sommer, Benjamin D. *A Prophet Reads the Scriptures: Allusion in Isaiah 40–66*. Stanford: Stanford University Press, 1998.

Sponheim, Paul R. "Sin and Evil." In *Christian Dogmatics*, edited by Carl E. Braaten and Robert W. Jenson, 363–463. Vol. 1. Philadelphia: Fortress, 1984.

Spykman, Gordon J. Reformational Theology: A New Paradigm for Doing Dogmatics. Grand Rapids: Eerdmans, 1992.

Stade, Bernhard. "Der Mythus von Paradies Gn 2.3 und die Zeit seiner Einwanderung in Israel." *Zeitschrift für di altestamenlich Wissenschaft* 23 (1903): 172–79.

Stamm, J. J., and M. E. Andrew. *The Ten Commandments in Recent Research*. Translated by M. E. Andrew. Naperville: A. R. Allenson, 1968.

Stanton, R. Todd. "Asking Question of the Divine Announcement in the Flood Stories from Ancient Mesopotamia and Israel." In *Gilgameš and the World of Assyria: The Proceedings of the Conference Held at Mandelbaum House, The University of Sydney, 21–23 July 2004*, edited by Joseph Azize and Noel Weeks, 147–72. Ancient Near Eastern Studies Supplement 21. Leuven: Peeters, 2007.

Steck, Odil H. "Der neue Himmel und die neue Erde. Beobachtunge zur Rezeption von Gen 1–3 in Jes 65,16b–25." In *Studies in the Book of Isaiah*, edited by J. van Ruiten and M. Vervenne, 350–65. Bibliotheca ephemeridum theologicarum lovaniensium 32. Leuven: University Press and Peeters, 1997.

———. Der Schöpfungsbericht der Priesterschrift: Studien zür literarkritischen überlieferungsgeschichtlen Problematik von Genesis 1,1–2,4a. Forschungen zur Religion und Literatur des Alten und Neuen Testaments 115. Göttingen: Vandenhoeck & Ruprecht, 1975.

Steinberg, Naomi. "The Genealogical Framework of the Family Stories in Genesis." *Semeia* 46 (1989): 41–50.

Sternberg, Meir. "Double Cave, Double Talk: The Indirections of Biblical Dialogue." In *"Not in Heaven": Coherence and Complexity in Biblical Narrative*, edited by Jason P. Rosenblatt and Joseph C. Sitterson Jr., 28–57. Bloomington: Indiana University Press, 1991.

———. *The Poetics of Biblical Narrative: Ideological Literature and the Drama of Reading*. Indiana Studies in Biblical Literature. Bloomington: Indiana University Press, 1985.

Stigers, Harold G. *A Commentary on Genesis*. Grand Rapids: Zondervan, 1979.

Stolz, F. "Sabbath, Schöpfungswoche und Herbstfest." *Wort und Dienst* 11 (1971): 159–79.

Stordalen, Terje. *Echoes of Eden: Genesis 2–3 and Symbolism of the Eden Garden in Biblical Hebrew Literature*. Biblical Exegesis and Theology 25. Leuven: Peeters, 2000.

Stuhlmueller, Carroll. *Creative Redemption in Deutero-Isaiah*. Analecta Biblica 43. Rome: Biblical Institute, 1970.

Sweeney, Marvin E. *Form and Intertextuality in Prophetic and Apocalyptic Literature*. Forschungen zum Alten Testament 45. Tübingen: Mohr Siebeck, 2005.

Tate, Marvin E. *Psalms 51–100*. Word Biblical Commentary 20. Dallas: Word, 1990.

The Scofield Reference Bible. New York: Oxford University Press, 1909.

Thiselton, Anthony C. *The Hermeneutics of Doctrine*. Grand Rapids: Eerdmans, 2007.

Timmer, Daniel C. *Creation, Tabernacle, and Sabbath: The Sabbath Frame of Exodus 31:12 –17; 35:1 –3 in Exegetical and Theological Perspective*. Forschungen zur Religion und Literatur des Alten und Neuen Testaments 227. Göttingen: Vandenhoeck & Ruprecht, 2009.

Todorov, Tzvetan. *Mikhail Bakhtin: The Dialogical Principle*. Theory and History of Literature 13. Translated by Wlad Godzich. Minneapolis: University of Minnesota Press, 1984.

Townsend, P. Wayne. "Eve's Answer to the Serpent: An Alternative Paradigm for Sin and Some Implications in Theology." *Calvin Theological Journal* 33 (1998): 399–420.

Trible, Phyllis. "Depatriarchalizing in Biblical Interpretation." *Journal of American Academy of Religion* 41 (1973): 30–48.

———. "Feminist Hermeneutics and Biblical Studies: Emerging Trends in Biblical Thought; 4th in a Series." *Church Century* 99 (1982): 116–18.

———. *God and the Rhetoric of Sexuality*. Overtures to Biblical Theology 2. Philadelphia: Fortress, 1978.

Tsumura, David T. Creation and Destruction: A Reappraisal of the Chaoskampf Theory in the Old Testament. Winona Lake: Eisenbrauns, 2005.

———. *The Earth and the Waters in Genesis 1 and 2: A Linguistic Investigation*. Sheffield: Sheffield Academic Press, 1989.

Turner, L. A. *Announcements of Plot in Genesis*. Journal for the Study of the Old Testament 96. Sheffield: JSOT Press, 1990.

Vanhoozer, Kevin. *The Drama of Doctrine: A Canonical Linguistic Approach to Christian Theology*. Louisville: Westminster John Knox, 2005.

———. "Pilgrim's Digress: Christian Thinking on and about the Post/Modern Way." In *Christianity and the Postmodern Turn: Six Views*, edited by Myron B. Penner, 71–103. Grand Rapids: Brazos, 2005.

Van Ruiten, Jacques T. A. G. M. "Back to Chaos: The Relationship between Jeremiah 4:23–26 and Genesis 1." In *The Creation of Heaven and Earth: Re-interpretations of Genesis 1 in the Context of Judaism, Ancient Philosophy, Christianity, and Modern Physics*, edited by George H. van Kooten, 21–30. Themes in Biblical Narrative: Jewish and Christians 8. Leiden: Brill, 2005.

———. "Eve's Pain in Childbearing? Interpretations of Gen 3:16a in Biblical and Early Jewish Texts." In *Eve's Children: The Biblical Stories Retold and Interpreted in Jewish and Christian Traditions*, edited by Gerard P. Luttikhuizen, 3–26. Biblical Narrative 5. Leiden: Brill, 2003.

———. "The Intertextual Relationship between Isaiah 65,25 and Isaiah 11,6–9." In *The Scriptures and the Scrolls*, edited by F. Garcia Martinez, A. Hilhorst, and C.J. Labuschagne, 31–42. Supplement to Vetus Testamentum 49. Leiden: Brill, 1992.

Van Seters, John. "Author or Redactor?" *Journal of Hebrew Scriptures* 7 (2007): 1–22. Article no. 9. No pages. Cited 18 April 2008. Online: http://www.jhsonline.org.

———. *The Edited Bible: The Curious History of the "Editor" in Biblical Criticism*. Winona Lake: Eisenbrauns, 2006.

———. "An Ironic Circle: Wellhausen and the Rise of Redactional Criticism." *Zeitschrift für di altestamentliche Wissenschaft* 115 (2003): 487–500.

———. *Prologue to History: The Yahwist as Historian in Genesis*. Louisville: Westminster John Knox, 1992.

———. "The Redactor in Biblical Studies: A Nineteenth Century Anachronism." *Journal of Northwest Semitic Languages* 29, no. 1 (2003): 1–19.

Van Wolde, Ellen. "Intertextuality: Ruth in Dialogue with Tamar." In *A Feminist Companion to Reading the Bible: Approaches, Methods, and Strategies*, edited by Athalya Brenner and Carole Fontaine, 426–51. Sheffield: Sheffield Academic Press, 1997.

———. A Semiotic Analysis of Genesis 2–3: A Semiotic Theory and Method of Analysis Applied to the Story of Garden of Eden. Studia semitica neerlandica 25. Assen: van Gorcum, 1989.

———. Words Become Worlds: Semantic Studies of Genesis 1–11. Leiden: Brill, 1994.

Vawter, Bruce. *On Genesis: A New Reading*. New York: Doubleday, 1977.

Vervenne, Marc. "Genesis 1:1–2:4: The Compositional Texture of the Priestly Overture to the Pentateuch." In *Studies in the Book of Genesis: Literature, Redaction and History*, 35–79. Bibliotheca Ephemeridum Theologicarum Lovaniensium CLV. Leuven: Leuven University Press, 2001.

Von Rad, Gerhard. "The Form Critical Problem of the Hexateuch." In *From Genesis to Chronicles: Explorations in Old Testament Theology* by G. von Rad, 1–58. Edited by K. C. Hanson. Fortress Classics in Biblical Studies Series. Minneapolis: Fortress, 2005.

———. *Genesis. A Commentary*. Translated by J. H. Marks. Old Testament Library. Rev. ed. Philadelphia: Westminster, 1972.

———. *Old Testament Theology*. 2 vols. Translated by D. M. G. Stalker. Peabody: Prince Press, 2005.

———. "Das theologische Problem des alttestamentlichen Schöfungsglauben." Beihefte zur Zeitschrift fur die alttestameliche Wissenschaft 66. Berlin: de Gruyter, 1936. English Translation of this edition: "The Theological Problem of the Old Testament Doctrine of Creation." In *The Problem of the Hexateuch and Other Essays* by Gerhard von Rad, 131–43. New York: McGraw-Hill, 1966.

Vos, Geerharus. "The Idea of Biblical Theology as a Science and as a Theological Discipline." Inauguration Address at Princeton Theological Seminary. 8 May 1894.

Vos, Howard. *Genesis*. Chicago: Moody Press, 1982.

Vriezen, Theodor C. Onderzoek naar de paradijsvoorstelling bij de oude semietische volken. Wageningen: H. Veenman & zonen, 1937.

Wakeman, Mary K. God's Battle with the Monster: A Study in Biblical Imagery. PhD diss., Brandeis University, 1969.

Wallace, Howard N. *The Eden Narrative*. Harvard Semitic Monographs 32. Atlanta: Scholars, 1985.

Walsh, Jerome T. "Genesis 2:4b–3:24: A Synchronic Approach." *Journal of Biblical Literature* 96 (1977): 167–77.

Waltke, Bruce K. *Creation and Chaos*. Portland: Western Conservative Baptist Seminary, 1974.

———. "The Literary Genre of Genesis, Chapter One." *Crux* 27, no. 4 (1991): 2–10.

Walton, John H. *Ancient Near Eastern Thought and the Old Testament: Introducing the Conceptual World of the Hebrew Bible*. Grand Rapids: Baker Academic, 2006.

———. *Genesis*. The New International Version Application Commentary. Grand Rapids: Zondervan, 2001.

———. *The Lost World of Genesis One*. Downers Grove: InterVarsity, Academic, 2009.

Watson, Rebecca S. *Chaos Uncreated: A Reassessment of the Theme of "Chaos" in the Hebrew Bible*. Berlin: de Gruyter, 2005.

Weinfeld, Moshe. "God the Creator in Gen. 1 and in the Prophecy of Second Isaiah." *Tarbiz* 37 (1968): 105–32.

———. "Jeremiah and the Spiritual Metamorphosis of Israel." *Zeitschrift für die alttestamentliche Wissenschaft* 88 (1976): 17–56.

———. "Sabbath, Temple Building, and the Enthronement of the Lord – The Problem of the Sitz im Leben in Genesis 1:1–2:3." In *Melanges biblique et orientaux en l'honneur de M. Henri Cazelles*, edited by A. Caquot and M. Delcor, 501–12. Alter Orient und Altes Testament 212. Kevalaer: Butzon and Bercker; Neukirchen-Vluyn: Neukirchener, 1981.

Weippert, Helga. *Schöpfer des Himmels und der Erde: Ein Beitrag zur Theologie des Jerremiabuches*. Stuttgart Bibelstudien 102. Stuttgart: Katholisches Bibelwerk, 1981.

Wellhausen, Julius. "Die Composition des Hexateuchs und der historischen Bücher des Alten Testaments." *Jahrbuch für deutsche Theologie* 21 (1876): 392–450. *Die Composition des Hexateuchs und der historischen Bücher des Alten Testaments*. 4th ed. Reprint, Berlin: de Gruyter, 1963.

———. *Geschichte Israels: Erster Band – Prolegomena zur Geschichte Israel*. Berlin: G. Reimer, 1883. English Translation. *Prolegomena to the History of Ancient Israel*. Translated by J. S. Black and A. Menzies. New York: Meridian, 1957.

Wenham, Gordon J. *Genesis 1–15*. Word Biblical Commentary 1. Waco: Word, 1987.

———. "Sanctuary Symbolism in the Garden of Eden Story." In *Proceedings of the Ninth World Congress of Jewish Studies*, 19–25. Jerusalem: World Union of Jewish Studies, 1986.

Westermann, Claus. *Creation*. Philadelphia: Fortress, 1974.

———. *Genesis 1–11*. Translated by John J. Scullion. Continental Commentaries. Minneapolis: Fortress, 1994.

White, Hugh C. *Narration and Discourse in the Book of Genesis*. Cambridge: Cambridge University Press, 1991.

Whybray, R. N. *The Making of the Pentateuch*. Journal for the Study of the Old Testament Supplement 53. Sheffield: Sheffield Academic Press, 1989.

Wildberger, Hans. "Das Abbild Gottes: Gen. 1:26-30." *Theologische Zeitschrift* 21 (1965): 245-59.

Willey, Patricia Tull. *Remember the Former Things: The Recollection of Previous Texts in Second Isaiah*. Atlanta: Scholars, 1997.

———. "The Rhetoric of Recollection." In *Congress Volume Oslo 1998*, edited by André Lemaire and Magne Sæbø, 71-78. Supplement for Vetus Testamentum 80. Leiden: Brill, 2000.

Williams, A. J. "The Relationship of Genesis 3:20 to the Serpent." *Zeitschrift für die alttestamentliche Wissenschaft* 89 (1977): 357-74.

Williams, Robert R. "Sin and Evil." In *Christian Theology: An Introduction to Its Traditions and Tasks*, edited by Peter Crafts Hodgson and Robert Harlen King, 194-221. Minneapolis: Fortress, 1994.

Wilson, Robert R. "Creation and New Creation: The Role of Creation Imagery in the Book of Daniel." In *God Who Creates: Essays in Honor of W. Sibley Towner*, edited by William P. Brown and S. Dean McBride Jr., 103-203. Grand Rapids: Eerdmans, 2000.

Wiseman, D. J., ed. Ancient Records and the Structure of Genesis. A Case for Literary Unity. Nashville: Thomas Nelson, 1985.

Wolff, Hans Walter. *Hosea: A Commentary on the Book of the Prophet Hosea*. Hermenia - A Critical and Historical Commentary on the Bible. Philadelphia: Fortress, 1974.

———. Joel and Amos: A Commentary on the Books of the Prophets Joel and Amos. Philadelphia: Fortress, 1977.

Wolters, Albert M. *Creation Regained: Biblical Basics for Reformational Worldview*. Grand Rapids: Eerdmans, 2005.

Woudstra, Martin H. "The Everlasting Covenant in Ezekiel 16:59-63." *Calvin Theological Journal* 6 (1971): 22-48.

Wyatt, Nicolas. "The Darkness of Genesis 1:2." *Vetus Testamentum* 43, no. 4 (1993): 543-54.

———. *Myths of Power: A Study of Royal Myth and Ideology in Ugaritic and Biblical Tradition*. Ugaritisch-Biblische Literatur 13. Münster: Ugarit-Verlag, 1996.

Young, Edward J. The Book of Isaiah: A Commentary. II. Chapters 19-39. Grand Rapids: Eerdmans, 1996.

———. *Studies in Genesis One*. Philadelphia: Presbyterian & Reformed, 1964.

Zimmerli, W. *I. Mose 1-11: Die Urgeschichte*. Zürcher Bibelkommentare. 2nd ed. Zurich: Zwingli, 1957.

Langham Literature, with its publishing work, is a ministry of Langham Partnership.

Langham Partnership is a global fellowship working in pursuit of the vision God entrusted to its founder John Stott –

> *to facilitate the growth of the church in maturity and Christ-likeness through raising the standards of biblical preaching and teaching.*

Our vision is to see churches in the Majority World equipped for mission and growing to maturity in Christ through the ministry of pastors and leaders who believe, teach and live by the word of God.

Our mission is to strengthen the ministry of the word of God through:
- nurturing national movements for biblical preaching
- fostering the creation and distribution of evangelical literature
- enhancing evangelical theological education

especially in countries where churches are under-resourced.

Our ministry

Langham Preaching partners with national leaders to nurture indigenous biblical preaching movements for pastors and lay preachers all around the world. With the support of a team of trainers from many countries, a multi-level programme of seminars provides practical training, and is followed by a programme for training local facilitators. Local preachers' groups and national and regional networks ensure continuity and ongoing development, seeking to build vigorous movements committed to Bible exposition.

Langham Literature provides Majority World preachers, scholars and seminary libraries with evangelical books and electronic resources through publishing and distribution, grants and discounts. The programme also fosters the creation of indigenous evangelical books in many languages, through writer's grants, strengthening local evangelical publishing houses, and investment in major regional literature projects, such as one volume Bible commentaries like the *Africa Bible Commentary* and the *South Asia Bible Commentary*.

Langham Scholars provides financial support for evangelical doctoral students from the Majority World so that, when they return home, they may train pastors and other Christian leaders with sound, biblical and theological teaching. This programme equips those who equip others. Langham Scholars also works in partnership with Majority World seminaries in strengthening evangelical theological education. A growing number of Langham Scholars study in high quality doctoral programmes in the Majority World itself. As well as teaching the next generation of pastors, graduated Langham Scholars exercise significant influence through their writing and leadership.

To learn more about Langham Partnership and the work we do visit **langham.org**

www.ingramcontent.com/pod-product-compliance
Lightning Source LLC
Chambersburg PA
CBHW070804230426
43665CB00017B/2487